Nava Alpana

New Decorative Designs of India

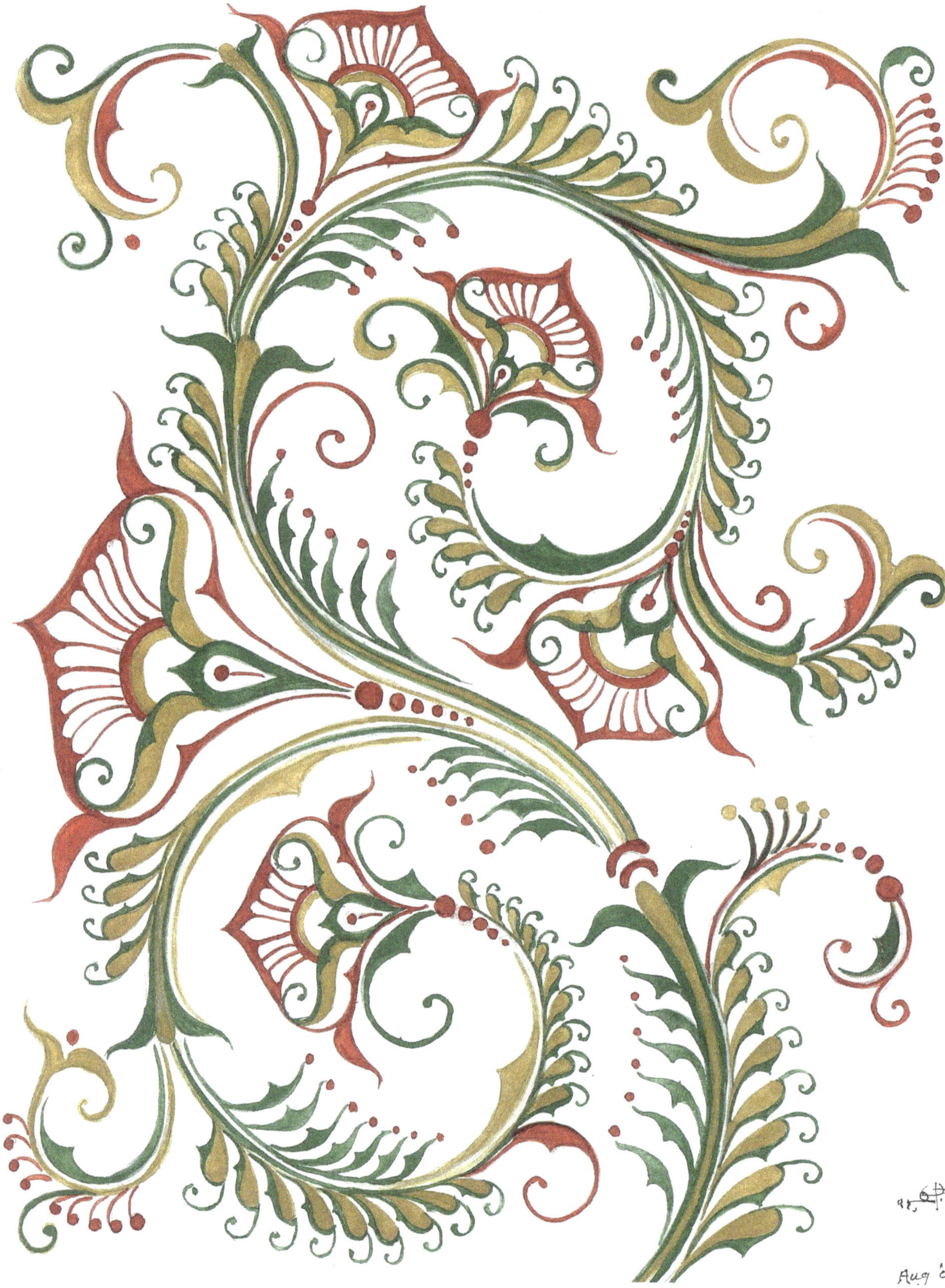

Aug '04

Nava Alpana
New Decorative Designs of India

Kajal Dass Beck

Introduction by Guy L. Beck

Blazing Sapphire Press
715 E. McPherson
Kirksville, Missouri 63501
2016

ISBN 978-1-936135-21-9 (1-936135-21-3)

Library of Congress Control Number: 2016935909

Published by:
Blazing Sapphire Press
715 E. McPherson
Kirksville, Missouri 63501

Available at:
Nitai's Bookstore
715 E. McPherson
Kirksville, Missouri, 63501
Phone: (660) 665-0273
http://www.nitaisbookstore.com
http://www.blazing-sapphire-press.com
Email: neal@blazing-sapphire-press.com

To my parents,

Sri Sisir Kumar Dass and Smt. Arati Dass

Goddess Sarasvatī Mantra - Hindu

sarasvati mahābhāge
vidye kamala-locane|
viśvarūpe viśālākṣi
vidyāṃ dehi namas tu te ||

Sarasvatī, Goddess of Wisdom, Music, and Art. You are the lotus-eyed reservoir of knowledge. Please bless me with your eternal wisdom. Your wide lotus eyes take the form of the entire universe.

Pavamāna Mantra – Brahmo Samaj
(from *Bṛhadāraṇyaka Upaniṣad*, 1.3.28)

asato mā sad gamaya
tamaso mā jyotir gamaya
mṛtyor māmṛtaṃ gamaya

From the unreal lead me to the real,
from darkness lead me to light,
and from death lead me to immortality.

Contents

Preface by Kajal Dass Beck

This book is the result of many years of observation and training in the art of *alpana*, beginning in my childhood and extending through adult life. As in most forms of domestic folk art, the true credit begins with family members who carefully cultivated and preserved this art and passed it along to the younger generations. In my case, exposure to *alpana* came from two different streams of tradition in eastern India—Hinduism and Brahmo Samaj. While the Hindu religion is thousands of years old, the Brahmo Samaj is a modern reform movement founded in Calcutta by Raja Ram Mohan Roy in 1828, and later associated with the famous Tagore family. My paternal household in Howrah, West Bengal, was thoroughly Hindu. My father, Sisir Kumar Dass, as the eldest son of prominent industrialist Sri Alamohan Dass, grew up with all the features and customs associated with the Hindu religion. My first exposure to *alpana* in the Hindu sense, at about age of five or six, was under the guidance of my paternal grandmother, Srimati Capaladevi, who during numerous domestic ceremonies and weddings directed all the details according to Hindu custom. Various deities were worshipped and many sacred rituals were performed. A principal aspect of these events was the proper decoration of *alpana* in order to please the Goddess Lakshmi and ensure an auspicious outcome. In the Hindu context, there is certainly a strong spiritual element in most forms of art. In fact, the Hindu way of life is full of sacred designs and motifs at every turn.

On the maternal side of the family, the influence of the Brahmo Samaj was prevalent, and differed to some extent from the Hindu approach to *alpana*. The Brahmo Samaj does not recognize specific Hindu deities like Lakshmi, and prefers to worship the invisible Brahman as described in the Upanishads. This has an effect on the meaning of *alpana*, which for them is less ritualistic and more artful or decorative. Though married at an early age, my mother Srimati Arati Das quickly adjusted to the customs of her new Hindu environment. This transition did not inhibit her to flourish in many directions, as she had a very strong spirit. My maternal grandmother, Srimati Kamaladevi, as a member of the Brahmo Samaj, was very artistic and had been raised in a cultured family. She was a great influence upon my mother who was also very involved with handicrafts and dedicated to social work. As both grandmother and mother made *alpana* designs, I also followed them and gradually made the designs myself according to tradition. Unlike Hindu practice, the Brahmo Samaj utilizes modest decorative motifs and *alpana* designs only on special occasions, especially during weddings. These designs are purely decorative and provide delightful ornamentation to the floor space or other surfaces without reference to spiritual or sacred energies.

Since childhood, I have thus been surrounded by multiple varieties of *alpana* patterns and motifs to the extent that they are all part of my artistic vocabulary. As I began to elaborate on the basic *alpana* designs that I made as a youth, I soon developed my own creative style and interpretation as represented in the designs in this book. And as I gained more formal training in art and design, first in school and later at the Government College of Art and Craft in Calcutta, I was greatly inspired by the writings and philosophy of Rabindranath Tagore, and in turn nurtured by the styles of design established by his brother Abanindranath Tagore and the Bengal School of Art at Visvabharati University at Santiniketan in West Bengal. In several ways, I represent the successful integration of these two approaches, enlarging upon the ritualistic Hindu patterns in combination with the creative and free-flowing spirit of the Brahmo Samaj to bring *alpana* to a new depth and higher level of expression.

About the Artist

Kajal Dass Beck was born in Kolkata, West Bengal, to the prominent Dass family, and has been studying and teaching art in the United States for over twenty-five years. From the age of six she has been involved with *alpana*, having participated in religious gatherings and weddings. Raised in a large, prominent, joint family, she observed and learned *alpana* from her mother and grandmothers. Displaying a natural talent for art and design in her school life, she went on to complete a degree in Fine Art/Batik from the Government College of Art and Craft in Calcutta (1973); she has exhibited at the Academy of Fine Arts in Calcutta (1976) and also managed her own art school, Suranjana School of Art and Craft, in India for more than six years. Coming to America in 1980, she continued with specialization in watercolor and other mediums with instruction from Syracuse University and Loyola University, New Orleans. Beside *alpana* designs, her creative blend of eastern and western styles in modern format has been highly appreciated at exhibitions at University of South Florida (1981), Southern University (1990), Rice University (1994), Loyola University (1997), World Trade Center in New Orleans (1998), Medical University of South Carolina (1999), Louisiana State Archives in Baton Rouge (2000), University of Victoria, British Columbia (2001), LSU Union Gallery (2005), University of Central Missouri Art Gallery (2009), and the New Orleans Museum of Art (2011). She has taught art and design at the University of South Florida in Tampa and, since 2004, courses in Decorative Designs of India and Tie-Dye at Louisiana State University in Baton Rouge, Louisiana.

Introduction by Guy L. Beck, Ph.D.

During visits to India in the 1970s, my principal focus was on religious literature, language, and music. As a scholar of Hinduism and a student of Indian vocal music, I surrounded myself with books in Sanskrit, Hindi, and Bengali, and zealously sought out classical music teachers, enrolled in music lessons, and collected various recordings. I also regularly attended Hindu temple services, music concerts, as well as lectures and seminars on various topics in religion and philosophy. However, as I now confess, though occasionally taking notice of visual art and folk culture while roaming about on foot or in a conveyance, I was stubbornly ignorant as to the depth and sophistication of what one of my teachers had called "little traditions," namely handicrafts, floral painting, *alpana*, *batik*, and textile designs. Yet as I continued attending music lessons at various institutions, I noticed that, alongside music, classes in various arts and crafts were offered to droves of students eager to learn all methods of artistic and cultural expression. Reflecting on this experience, I soon came to realize that to properly understand Indian music one must also appreciate the beauty and depth of the Indian imagination as represented in color and design. It was in 1977 that I met my future wife, Kajal Dass, who was teaching art and handicrafts at her school, Suranjana School of Art and Craft, in South Calcutta (Kolkata). On occasion, I would drop in unannounced for tea and to practice my favorite Brahms on her piano. Once, after she played a Tagore song, Kajal revealed to me her beautiful paintings, *batiks*, and handicrafts, including those of her students. I was amazed, and quickly modified my exclusive veneration of the so-called "great traditions," and came to truly appreciate how the creative spirit is present in every artistic expression of Bengal and India.

This book is a presentation of new decorative designs by artist Kajal Dass Beck. Displaying her unique sense of creativity and imagination, they are nonetheless based upon and inspired by the traditional folk art of Bengal known as *alpana* (alpona in Bengali pronunciation). Thus she has chosen the title, Nava Alpana ("New Alpana"). *Alpana* belongs to the larger category of what is known as Indian '*rangoli*,' in which patterns are created on floors of temples, courtyards, living spaces, or other surfaces utilizing rice flour, water, and other materials for religious and domestic ceremonies. In various parts of India these practices carry different names. The ubiquitous presence of *alpana* in Bengal is mainly due to its use in religious ceremonies and home decoration, where it is believed to bring good luck and prevent misfortune. Specific designs are unique to each area of India, but it is only in Bengal that this folk art has reached high degrees of creativity and aesthetic appeal. *Alpana* is traditionally done by women, and forms a necessary part of religious festivals, auspicious observances, weddings, *vrata* (vows), and other occasions. This book by an accomplished Bengali woman artist is the first authentic expression of a vibrant 'folk' tradition that has been largely ignored in the international world of art appreciation.

Beginning with easy step by step instructions and illustrations, the book takes one on an exciting journey through the creative art of *alpana* under the guidance of a distinguished artist and teacher. With extensive training in drawing and painting, Kajal Dass Beck is an artist native to the Bengal area who has learned from many qualified art teachers of the Indian traditions. She was formally trained at the Government College of Art and Craft, one of the oldest art colleges in India founded in 1854. Abanindranath Tagore, brother of Rabindranath Tagore of the renowned Tagore family, served as its principal in the early twentieth-century and developed what became known as the Bengal School of Art. Notable alumni include artists of national renown like Nandalal Bose and Jaimini Roy. Throughout an artistic career that spans several decades, Kajal Beck has exhibited her work at many prominent venues in the United States and India, and has broadened the scope of the traditional style, greatly enhancing the genre of *alpana* to include a wide spectrum of designs and motifs drawn from wildlife and nature. After this Introduction, the book presents some basic patterns and motifs of *alpana*, followed by creatively original *alpana* designs reflecting various sacred symbols as well as categorical items of the natural world, including fruits, vegetables, birds, animals, reptiles, amphibians, and even insects.

In terms of readership, the desire is to attract people involved in the art professions, whether as creative artists, art educators, commercial artists, art and design students, architects, or interior designers, as well as lay persons who want to expand their skills and understanding of non-Western art and culture. The designs of *alpana* are not strictly limited to floral patterns or painting, but can be readily applied to various other media, such as print-making, clothing and fabric design, wood-carving, stone-carving, furniture upholstery, wallpaper, and even floor tile. Thus, this book also fills a growing need for more content in the area of design motifs and patterns of an authentic nature that will also inspire others to develop their own creativity in novel ways.

This book also seeks to fill a vacuum in the area of Indian folk art. According to Stephen P. Huyler (1994: 10), "Indian women's decorative art has received almost no recognition. No specific books and very few articles have been written about it." In fact, the only work in English specifically on the art of *alpana*, first published in 1948, is the out-of-print book, *Alpona: Ritual Decoration in Bengal*, by Tapan Mohan Chatterji, with notes by Tarak Chandra Das (Calcutta: Orient Longmans Ltd., 1948, 1965) and illustrations taken from the collection of Abanindranath Tagore. Like other works in the field of *rangoli*, this small book includes 'traditional' patterns and designs that represent a living tradition in and around Santiniketan, the university established by Rabindranath Tagore in rural Bengal in the early twentieth century. But unlike this work prepared by mostly non-artist male writers who have published illustrations by 'anonymous' folk artists that remain within more traditional formats, the current book reveals how this genre of women's folk art has been greatly enlarged by a woman artist, and placed within the realms of sophisticated artistic expression and aesthetic innovation. In short, as there is no current book available on *alpana* designs published by an individual artist working creatively in this tradition, this book by Kajal Dass Beck is the first attempt by a traditional Bengali female artist to publish original works in this field of artistic endeavor.

Since the time of Chatterji's book, several popular-style art books covering the theme of *rangoli* designs and other Indian art motifs have appeared. Most of these are short, designed for children, and without much discussion of the patterns or original context. *Rangoli: Discovering the Art of Indian Decoration*, by Anuradha Ananth and Shailja Jain (Frances Lincoln Children's Books, 2007), is essentially a kind of storybook for children who are beginners in art. *Rangoli Patterns*, by C. R. Patel (Create Space Independent Publishing, 2008), contains a very elementary introduction, with no historical or regional information. Marty Noble's two books, *Designs and Motifs from India* (Dover, 2006) and *Traditional Designs from India* (Dover, 2006) contain only black and white illustrations and are geared toward eight to twelve year old children. For purely geometric patterns presented on a dot grid, there is *Rangoli: An India Art Activity Book*, by Suma O'Farrell (Mazaa, 2012), for children age nine and up. In *1000 Decorative Designs from India*, by Devi Thapa, Kiran Chaudhri, and V.S. Navalkar (Dover, 2007), the images are small and the graphics of mixed quality.

For introductory descriptions of *rangoli* and *alpana*, one may consult *Handicrafts of India* by Kamaladevi Chattopadhyay (1975, Rev. 1985), section, "Folk Painting," pp. 130-139, yet this work contains no visual illustrations or examples. *Painted Prayers: Women's Art in Village India*, by Stephen P. Huyler (1994), is an excellent study of various forms of women's wall and floor painting according to region of India except for Bengal. With 170 beautiful photographs, Huyler combines colorful images with words of the painters to create an authentic representation.

What is the real nature and purpose of *alpana*, and how does such a creative folk medium function within normal Hindu religious practice? More broadly, how might creativity be valued so highly in what some view as a rigid traditional heritage of religious observance that must be performed "by the book," so to speak? Answers to these and other questions can be rendered by approaching the subject of Hindu religion and aesthetics as well as the cultural influence of the life and work of Rabindranath Tagore. In ancient India, the religious world was centered on Vedic fire sacrifices to gods who were worshipped for their role in sustaining the universe, a universe that was also conceived to be a divine unity known as Brahman. The gods were creative and often displayed their handiwork by intervening in human affairs, which allowed for humans to admire and eventually imitate them by fashioning images and composing poetry. At some point in remote antiquity, the Vedic society that relied on fire sacrifices was totally transformed into one that was to worship deities like Brahma, Vishnu, Shiva, Sarasvati, and Lakshmi as represented in sculpture and painting. Religious art was born. Whether as symbols or statues, the objects of Hindu worship were believed to be inhabited by a spiritual presence that was made accessible to the larger population due to material representation. Heather Elgood, in *Hinduism and the Religious Arts* (1999: 1), explains how the literary descriptions of the gods in the Vedic literature were cast into material form as art that nonetheless functioned religiously: "It became necessary to convey abstract concepts about the gods in a form that changed words into images that were recognizable to the whole community. These images became known and acknowledged across wide areas. Religious art was created, not as 'art for art's sake,' but rather to meet the burgeoning spiritual needs of the community. It was believed that these images provided protection from the fickle, invisible spirit world." In her essay, "The Spiritual Dimension of Indian Art" (*Hindu Spirituality: Postclassical and Modern*, 1997: 460), Bettina Baumer cites the ancient art treatises known as the *silpa-sastras* which describe how the human artist is believed to imitate the gods. According to these texts, "the artist is called the architect of the universe (Visvakarman) or his earthly representative because one can create a work of art worth the name only if one partakes in the divine creative power." Since the universe itself is divine, anything the artist fashions reflects the spirituality of the cosmos as well as that of the self (460): "The metaphor of the artist befits the creator because the artist remains himself in his own creation."

However, many religions hold a dualistic interpretation which views the sensual world of art as inferior to transcendence. How can art be spiritual? The Hindu view is more complicated such that while the universe is ultimately inter-connected, and one should avoid attachments to material realities, aspects of this world including material nature can be spiritually transformed through a process called sacralization. This notion is clearly articulated in the Tantric philosophy which permeates a significant part of Hinduism (Baumer 1997: 461): "The senses themselves are the means of experiencing the Divine, provided that they are purified of egoistic attachment. The Tantric yogi can enjoy song and other artistic expressions which lead directly to divine bliss." Jessica Frazier, in "Hinduism—Visual Art and Architecture" (*The Oxford Handbook of Religion and the Arts*, 2014: 350-351), applies the method of 'visual hermeneutics' in order to interpret the complexity of the relation between the divine and the human as mediated through art: "the visual arts have their own unique mode of expressing Hindu theology—one that relies on the unique character of visual art." With the example from the profusion of popular art used in religious practice, she describes how the material world becomes spiritual (351): "Many statues and posters of deities are not merely figurative representations—they make the divine materially present in the world, turning artistic creation into a form of in-carnation or embodiment. Tantric abstract images are not mere symbols—they transform the very fabric of reality." Furthermore, Elgood (1999: 3) explains that, "these images are representations of or actually become vessels for the numinous presence of the divine." And among the varieties of Hindu worship and ritual, the private or family deities and images are significantly important in this regard (1999: 11): "Domestic details of family life mirror the grander dimension of the individual's relationship with the divine."

Looking more closely at the domestic art of *alpana* we find that *alpana* is a regional variation of a pan-Indian folk practice referred to as simply *rangoli*, which is also the term used in Maharashtra. Here I will use *rangoli* to speak generally about this form of Indian folk art, and *alpana* when speaking about the Bengal form. The word *alpana* derives from the Sanskrit *alepana*, which means something like designing by smearing or pasting. Elgood (1999: 208) describes the variations in terminology according to region or state of India: "It is called *alepan* (wall) or *aripan* (floor) in Bihar, *alpona* in Bengal, *chowka purna* and *sona rakhna* in Uttar Pradesh, *mehndi mandana* in Rajasthan, *sathiya* in Gujerat, and *rangoli* in Maharashtra, *kolam* (and *muggu*) in South India, and *chita* in Orissa. In West and South India the patterns are strictly geometrical while richer symbolic shapes are used in Bengal, Bihar, and elsewhere in North India."

As a ritual practice within the tradition of Hinduism, *rangoli* is done mainly for purification purposes, to ritually "cleanse" the worship area and to ward off inauspicious elements that might defile the ritual space or ceremonial occasion. The *rangoli* designs essentially create a sacred space as a kind of enclosure of auspiciousness, over against outside or inauspicious elements. The Hindu occasion, whether a *puja* (deity worship), *vrata* (vow), wedding, initiation ceremony, tonsure, grand opening of a business, laying the cornerstone of a building, birth of a child, etc., must be circumscribed with specific geometrical or symbolic images, often in combination with astrological guidelines, in order to ensure that the area remain ritually pure and devoid of all impurities. As guarantees of success and prosperity, these directions are outlined in Hindu scriptures and ritual manuals and originally instructed by Brahmins or priests within the tradition. These are in turn handed down within families as part of their cultural inheritance. Kamaladevi Chattopadhyay, in *Handicrafts of India* (1975: 130), has listed the basic *rangoli* designs that are commonly found in Hindu ritual practice throughout India: "The designs are symbolic and basically common to the whole country, like geometrical patterns, with lines, dots, squares, circles, triangles; then the swastikas, the lotus, trident fish, conch shell, footprints, supposed to be of the Goddess Lakshmi, creepers, leaves, trees, flowers, animals and anthropomorphic figures." Whichever pattern is used, and despite the free-flowing impression of these designs, there is a strict separation between "inside" the diagram which is believed to be a sacred space, and "outside" which is profane space that is understood in terms of auspicious versus inauspicious elements: "The entire graph must be an unbroken line, no gaps to be left anywhere in the line for an evil spirit to enter." The precise process of applying the rice powder is described by Elgood (1999: 209-210): "Floor designs are usually drawn freehand by women trickling rice paste or powder down their middle fingers on to the ground or they may be daubed or sprayed. Some of these are drawn freehand but most are created by connecting or drawing around a series of dots laid out in rows according to the required pattern. These patterns are achieved by the delineation from the centre outwards. In most cases dots or dashes are aligned in the various sacred directions to form auspicious configurations."

The precise origin of *rangoli* or *alpana* will most probably remain elusive and lost to us. However, oral tradition in rural India suggests its origin in the Hindu tales of the gods, especially the *avatar* or incarnation of Vishnu popularly known as Rama. In the epic *Ramayana*, the mythic narrative of Rama's divine birth and pastimes on earth in which he defeats the demon Ravana, there is a scene where Rama must attend to a sighting of a golden deer by his wife Sita, who is also believed to be a form of the Goddess Lakshmi. As conveyed by Stephen P. Huyler (1994: 19), "When asked about the origin of wall and floor decorations, women say that in the ancient Hindu epic, the *Ramayana*, the goddess Sita painted her forest home with sacred designs when her husband, the god Rama, left her to hunt the magic deer. It is possible that this tradition of ornamentation has been passed down from mother to daughter for thousands of years." As Rama's wife, Sita came to symbolize the "ideal Hindu wife" who dutifully obeys and honors her husband, making her presence in the home very auspicious.

As conveyed by informants from various parts of India, the designs have been made for centuries as an invitation to Lakshmi, the most important goddess of the Indian household, ensuring fertility, successful motherhood, prosperity, and protection from outside dangers. Lakshmi, unlike other Hindu deities which sometimes have multiple arms or heads, appears as a normal woman in human form holding a pot in her left hand as a symbol of wealth and prosperity. The nocturnal owl is her vehicle which serves as a kind of protective guardian. Her worship is done with vegetarian offerings on a daily basis with special offerings on the full moon day. The annual Hindu festival known as Diwali (Festival of Lights) in the autumn season (October-November) is held in her honor. This celebration involves *rangoli* designs, but especially the lighting of lamps (*diyas*) to invite Lakshmi to the home. Alok Dutta, in the journal *Prabuddha Bharata* or *Awakened India* (2015), has described her role as one which pervades all social classes, from the elite to the peasantry: "Mother Lakshmi can indeed be worshipped in the homes of kings, rulers, and other wealthy people. They too need a happy family life. But she is needed more in the new palm-leaf roof of a dilapidated thatched roof hut, in the new mud coat on a cracked wall, in the cow-dung coating on a mud floor, and above in the artistic decorations made from rice paste and in the practice of the rural art of wall painting." In *Painted Prayers: Women's Art in Village India* (1994: 16), Stephen P. Huyler, who has travelled in India for many years researching women's folk art, describes further the connection between Lakshmi, home protection, and painting: "Lakshmi is the pan-Indian goddess of abundance, fertility, and prosperity, and is usually considered to be the deity that protects the home. Although there are exceptions, most of the household painting and the decoration of walls and floors by Indian women are dedicated to her. They are visual forms of prayer beseeching her aid to ensure the health and prosperity of the family." Many homes are decorated with peacocks, elephants and other symbols that are believed to please Lakshmi. As expressed firsthand by an Indian woman artist (16): "We believe that if the painting is pleasing to her, then she will want to bless our home and our family will prosper." Yet the designs also ward off evil spirits and real impending threats, reminiscent of American traditions (16): "Although many rituals are intended to beautify the home and honor the gods, others are created to ward off danger and evil. Wall and floor decorations are often magical diagrams to prevent the intrusion of harm into the home, similar in purpose to hex signs on Pennsylvania Dutch barns." The Indian view of danger is carefully noted and monitored, such that the home is treated like a serene oasis that can only be sustained by the mercy of the goddess and the feminine spirit (15): "A household in balance is believed to be in spiritual harmony and must be cared for and protected. Danger lurks outside the home, in the form of diseases, natural calamities, accidents, violence, and the greed, manipulation, and malevolence of others. The collective household spirit is most often viewed as feminine and is worshipped as a manifestation of the goddess."

The *rangoli* diagrams must be made or "written" correctly to have full effect, as explained by Elgood (1999: 210-211): "With the correct performance this sacred drawing is believed to have the potential to hold force and protect the threshold from the inner and outer world and to encourage the auspicious entry of Lakshmi." The sense of auspiciousness is further enhanced by the fact that the rice powder also feeds insects and ants, a duty prescribed in the Dharma Sastras or Hindu lawbooks. The presence of the Goddess or deity, once invoked, is actually contained within the diagram and is referenced in relation to power. Art historian Stella Kramrisch, in *Exploring India's Sacred Art, Selected Writings* (1983: 106), explains how, "It is believed that within confines, within the more or less intricate geometrical lines of the diagram an invoked presence finds its allotted place. Its power is confined and thereby held in its place and for the purpose of which the diagram was drawn. The magic diagram makes it possible for power to be present, and it brings this presence into the power of the person who has made the diagram."

Alpana, in common with the general features of *rangoli* in India, is enacted during many of the life-cycle rituals of Bengali society, but has also served as a springboard for creativity. Partha Mitter, in *Indian Art, Oxford History of Art* (2001: 159), discusses *rangoli* and *alpana*, and highlights their important role in Hindu social life: "The domestic art of floral paintings, with variant forms in different regions, such as *alpana* in West Bengal, *rangoli* in Maharashtra, and *kolam* in South India, is associated with ceremonies marking rites of passage, such as birth, puberty, marriage, and death." He stresses that these rituals overshadow the importance of brahmanical priestly ceremonies in the daily life of communities: "Female rituals involving art have played a more significant role in Hindu social life than the ministrations of Brahmin priests. The prevalence of goddess worship in Bengal is reflected in the great importance given to women, women's wish-fulfillment, and the principle of Sakti or female energy: "It is also no accident that the Great Goddess is the central figure in this ritual matriarchy, for this is an activity, albeit temporary, that releases women from the subordinate status in society. Women teach *alpana* to girls to enable them to perform wish-fulfillment rituals (*brata*), such as obtaining suitable husbands." *Alpana* is thus performed only by women. A significant difference between the floral painting in Bengal and elsewhere is the provision of individual creativity and expression of talent: "Although governed by convention, *alpana* demands imagination and skill, thus giving scope for individual talent."

Tapan Mohan Chatterji, in *Alpona: Ritual Decoration in Bengal* (1948), was the first native Bengali to describe *alpana* and its applications in rural Bengal. He writes (1948: 32), "Generally Alpona is executed with rice-paste mixed with water. A quantity of sunned rice (*atap chaul*) is kept immersed for an hour or two in water and then ground into a paste. It is next mixed with water in a small cup. The girl-artist holds a little piece of cloth (about 10 to 12 square inches) with the tips of the first four fingers of her right hand and dips it in the mixture of rice-paste already prepared. The piece of cloth soaks a little of this mixture. She then draws the different designs of the Alpona with the middle finger of her right hand which slightly protrudes beyond the other fingers holding the piece of cloth and which is fed with the mixture from the cloth. The design is never traced on the ground before the mixture is applied. The artist always starts her work from the centre of the Alpona and goes on building it up, step by step, with different decorative designs, viz., ceremonial and decorative." While the artist must follow certain conventions, she always has the option to express her creativity and imagination in terms of decorative design (32): "The artist is required to put the ceremonial designs in their proper shape and place and has no option regarding these factors. But she is free to give play to her imagination in respect of the decorative designs." But while Chatterji has stated this point very correctly, and was able to document many of the traditional forms and diagrams of alpana in village Bengal, he could not have anticipated how the imagination of Bengali women, specifically of artist Kajal Dass Beck, would take flight and bear fruit in the twenty-first century in the form of the new *alpana* designs contained in this book.

In order to fully appreciate the new decorative designs in this book, we now turn to one of India's greatest intellectual giants, Rabindranath Tagore, whose principal outlook on Indian life and art has permeated large segments of India and the world. The iconic presence in Bengal of the person and work of Rabindranath Tagore (1861-1941) cannot be overestimated. Not only a master of poetry and literature and winner of the Nobel Prize in Literature in 1913, he was also a philosopher, composer of songs, and a painter. His philosophy of life and art drew upon his original Hindu roots yet, as member of the Tagore family, was also deeply affected by the free spirit of the Brahmo Samaj, a reform movement founded by Raja Ram Mohan Roy in 1828. In an essay by Sitansu Sekhar Chakravarti, "The Spirituality of Rabindranath Tagore: The Religion of an Artist" (1997: 270), Tagore's philosophy of art is contrasted with the traditional Hindu school of Advaita Vedanta which tended to downplay the natural world as *maya* or illusory: "Spiritual pursuit implies a change in one's attitude to the world, which frees one from the dimension of pleasure and suffering, which are rooted in one's egotistic learnings, to that of *ananda* or unconditional joy. The change for Tagore was not in ignoring nature as a nullity to the extent that the world is looked upon as false, as in the tradition of the Advaita Vedanta, but in finding oneness with nature, through the creativity of the artist, poet, or singer, wherein the meaning of life lies." The human life is in fact incomplete without art, which is required to experience the true joy of life in its fullest form: "The human being needs to discover the beauty, the spontaneity, and the rhythm in nature in all its vitality, and in the mood of an artist become a part of the total creation and partake of the joy that is all around." Tagore's religion was not that of the monk who seeks the divine on mountain tops or in caves, but of the creative artist who revels in the joys of everyday life. He believed in Almighty God as Jivan Devata, "Lord of Life," who could be fully realized through creativity in the arts. Tagore exemplified this philosophy by his abundant proliferation of poems, songs, and paintings. By creating art one can realize one's full potential as a creator in the image of the divine, as Brahma. Art for Tagore was not the simple expression of feeling, but an ongoing attempt to personalize nature by bringing it closer to the human soul and making it one's own. Art serves to animate the objects of material existence and give them life and spirit for our present time on earth. Whatever initially seems alien or unfriendly in an impersonal world, art brings it up close and personal. For Tagore, art is thus a bridge across the chasm which normally separates the individual from the world around him.

While Tagore is celebrated most for his poetry, plays, songs, and novels, among his English non-fiction works are two short essays on art, "The Artist," in his book, *The Religion of Man* (1931), and "The Religion of an Artist," part of the collection, *Boundless Sky* (1964), which reveal his thoughts on art as a way of life. These thoughts provide some insight into the underlying inspiration behind the Nava Alpana designs. In the latter essay, Tagore confesses (1964: 211) to a profound kinship with the natural world: "I had a deep sense almost from infancy of the beauty of Nature, an intimate feeling of companionship with the trees and the clouds, and felt in tune with the musical touch of the seasons in the air. At the same time, I had a peculiar susceptibility to human kindness. All these craved expression." Each of the natural elements "spoke to him." For Tagore, all human life is blessed with a surplus of feeling and energy that must be channeled into artistic productivity which is an end in itself and outside of the ordinary needs of life (217): "Of all living creatures in the world, man has his vital and mental energy vastly in excess of his need, which urges him to work in various lines of creation for its own sake. Like Brahma himself, he takes joy in productions that are unnecessary to him, and therefore representing his extravagance and not his hand-to-mouth penury. The voice that is just enough can speak and cry to the extent needed for everyday use, but that which is abundant sings, and in it we find our joy. Art reveals man's wealth of life, which seeks its freedom in forms of perfection which are an end in themselves ... . Life is perpetually creative because it contains in itself that surplus which ever overflows the boundaries of the immediate time and space, restlessly pursuing its adventure of expression in the varied forms of self-realization." To live a life without art or creative expression is to be inert and inanimate. The very substance of art, its lines and curves, words and phrases, notes and beats, point one to divine truths (218): "What in common language we call beauty, which is in harmony of lines, colours, sounds, or in grouping of words or thoughts, delights us only because we cannot help admitting the truth in it that it is ultimate." Art for Tagore is characterized as a magic force or wand that spiritualizes everything in its wake (222): "That is art. It has the magic wand which gives undying reality to all things it touches, and relates them to the personal being in us. We stand before its productions and say: I know you as I know myself, you are real."

The life of an artist for Tagore affords everyone the opportunity to find philosophical and spiritual unity in all creation (1931: 82-83): "According to the stages of our consciousness we have more or less been able to identify ourselves with this world, if not as a whole, at least in fragments; and our enjoyment dwells in that wherein we feel ourselves united. In art we express the delight of this unity by which this world is realized as humanly significant to us." Tagore ultimately held that the human being is by nature an artist due to an active imagination that cannot or should not be suppressed (83): "For man by nature is an artist; he never receives passively and accurately in his mind a physical representation of things around him. There goes on a continual adaptation, a transformation of facts into human imagery, through constant touches of his sentiments and imagination." In the end Tagore provides us with the most cogent answer to one of life's most important questions (87): "What is art? It is the response of man's creative soul to the call of the Real." We hope that you will also find unity and depth in these Nava Alpana designs by Kajal Dass Beck.

Bibliography

Ayyub, Abu Sayeed. "The Aesthetic Philosophy of Tagore." In *Quest: A Quarterly of Inquiry, Criticism and Ideas. Special Issue: Tagore and His Land.* Bombay: Indian Committee for Cultural Freedom, May 1961, 27-34.

Baumer, Bettina. "The Spiritual Dimension of Indian Art." In *Hindu Spirituality: Postclassical and Modern.* Edited by K.R. Sundararajan and Bithika Mukerji, 459-475. New York: Crossroad Publishing, 1997.

Chakravarti, Sitansu Sekhar. "The Spirituality of Rabindranath Tagore: The Religion of an Artist." In *Hindu Spirituality: Postclassical and Modern.* Edited by K.R. Sundararajan and Bithika Mukerji, 268-282. New York: Crossroad Publishing, 1997.

Chatterji, Tapan Mohan. *Alpona: Ritual Decoration in Bengal.* With notes by Tarak Chandra Das. Calcutta: Orient Longmans Ltd., 1965 (1948). Illustrations taken from the collection of Abanindranath Tagore.

Chattopadhyay, Kamaladevi. *Handicrafts of India.* New Delhi: Indian Council for Cultural Relations, 1975. Rev. 1985. "Folk Painting" pp. 130-139.

Dutta, Alok. "Lakshmi." *Prabuddha Bharata* or *Awakened India: A Monthly Journal of the Ramakrishna Order started by Swami Vivekananda in 1896.* Vol. 120, No. 5 (May 2015): 361-363.

Elgood, Heather. *Hinduism and the Religious Arts.* London and New York: Cassell, 1999.

Frazier, Jessica. "Hinduism—Visual Art and Architecture." In *The Oxford Handbook of Religion and the Arts.* Edited by Frank Burch Brown, 350-357. New York: Oxford University Press, 2014.

Huyler, Stephen P. *Painted Prayers: Women's Art in Village India.* New York: Rizzoli, 1994.

Kramrisch, Stella. *Exploring India's Sacred Art, Selected Writings.* Edited by Barbara Stoler Miller. Philadelphia: University of Pennsylvania Press, 1983.

Mitter, Partha. *Indian Art (Oxford History of Art).* New York: Oxford University Press, 2001.

Tagore, Rabindranath. *Boundless Sky.* Calcutta: Visvabharati, 1964. "The Religion of an Artist," pp. 205-230.

Tagore, Rabindranath. *The Religion of Man.* London: George Allen & Unwin, 1931, 1961. "The Artist," pp. 80-88.

Nava Alpana

New Decorative Designs of India

Part I

Black & White Art

Leaf

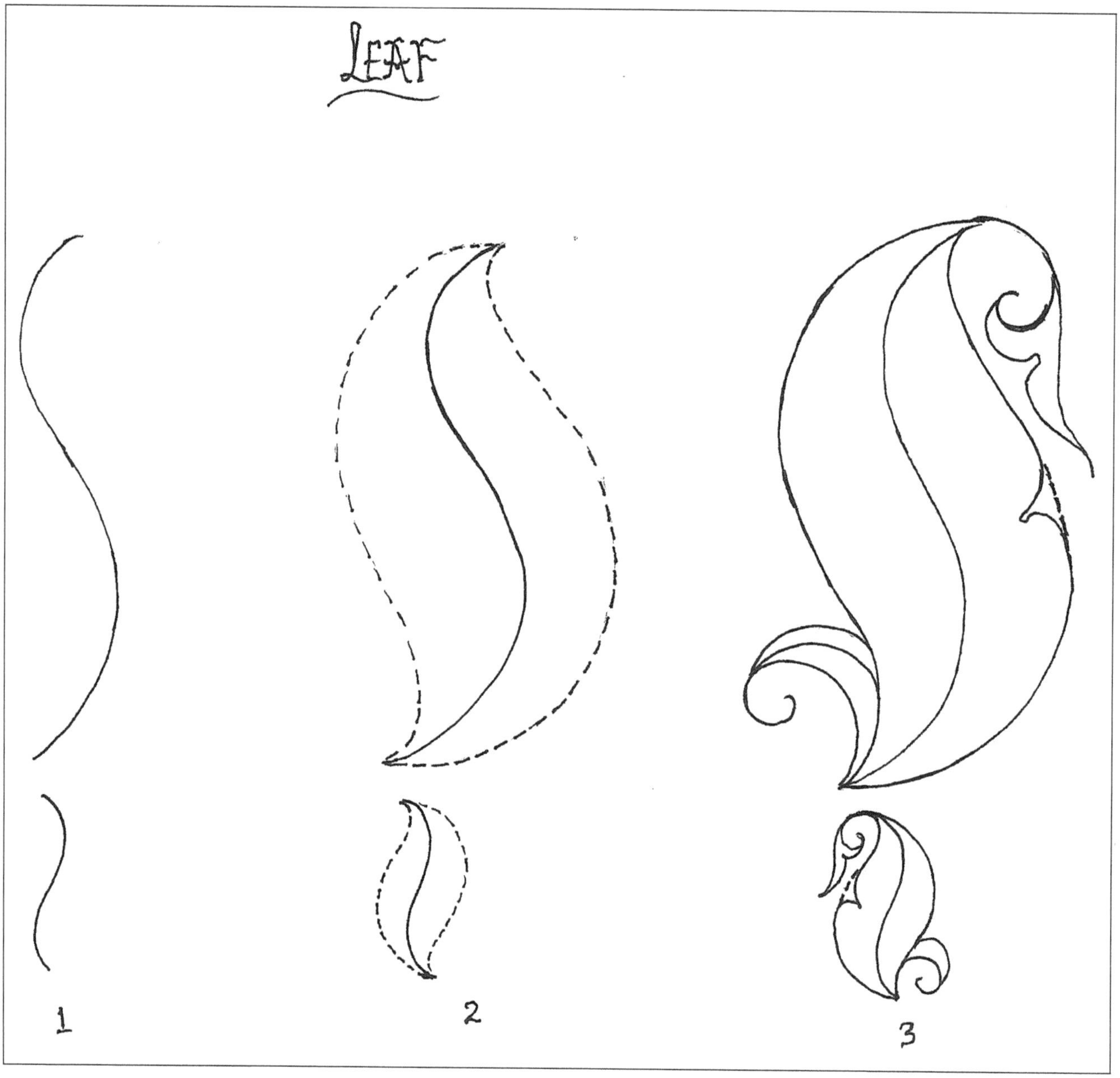
LEAF
1
2
3

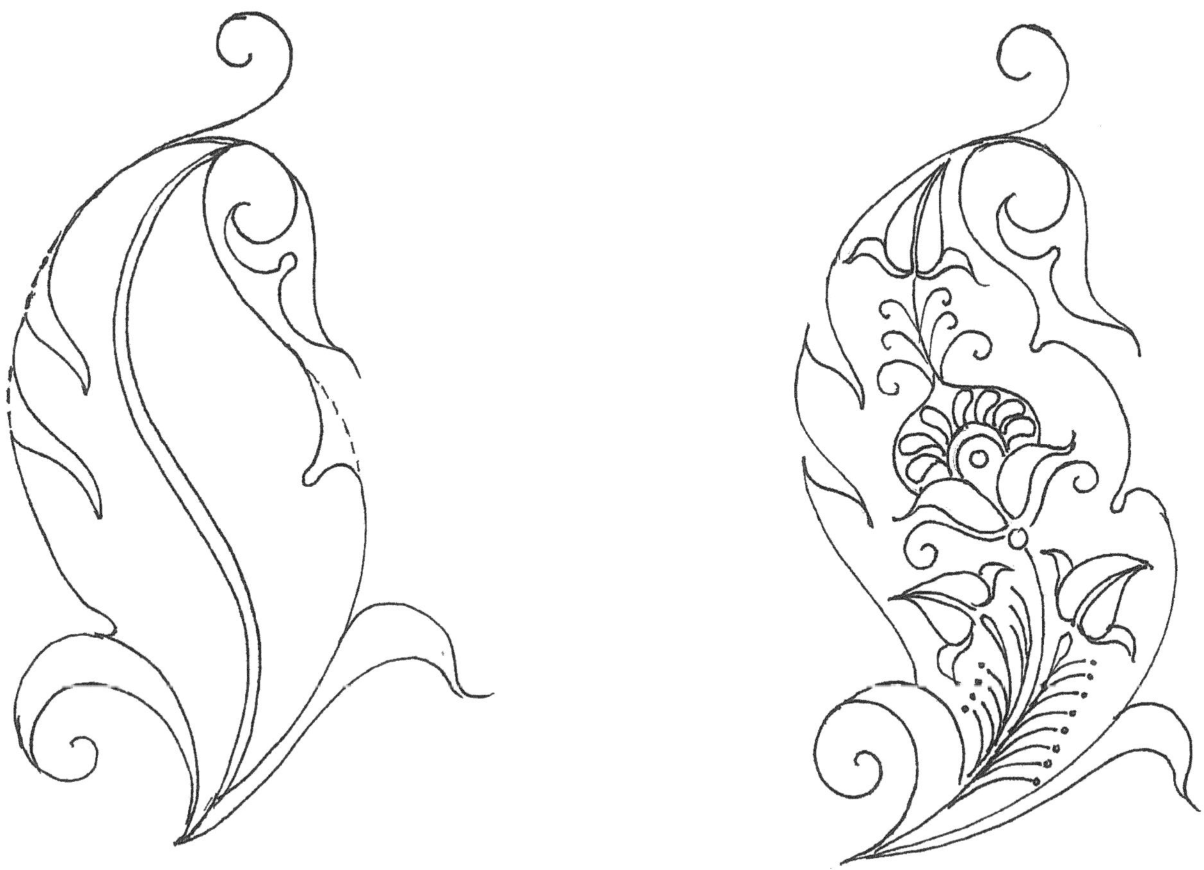

4 5

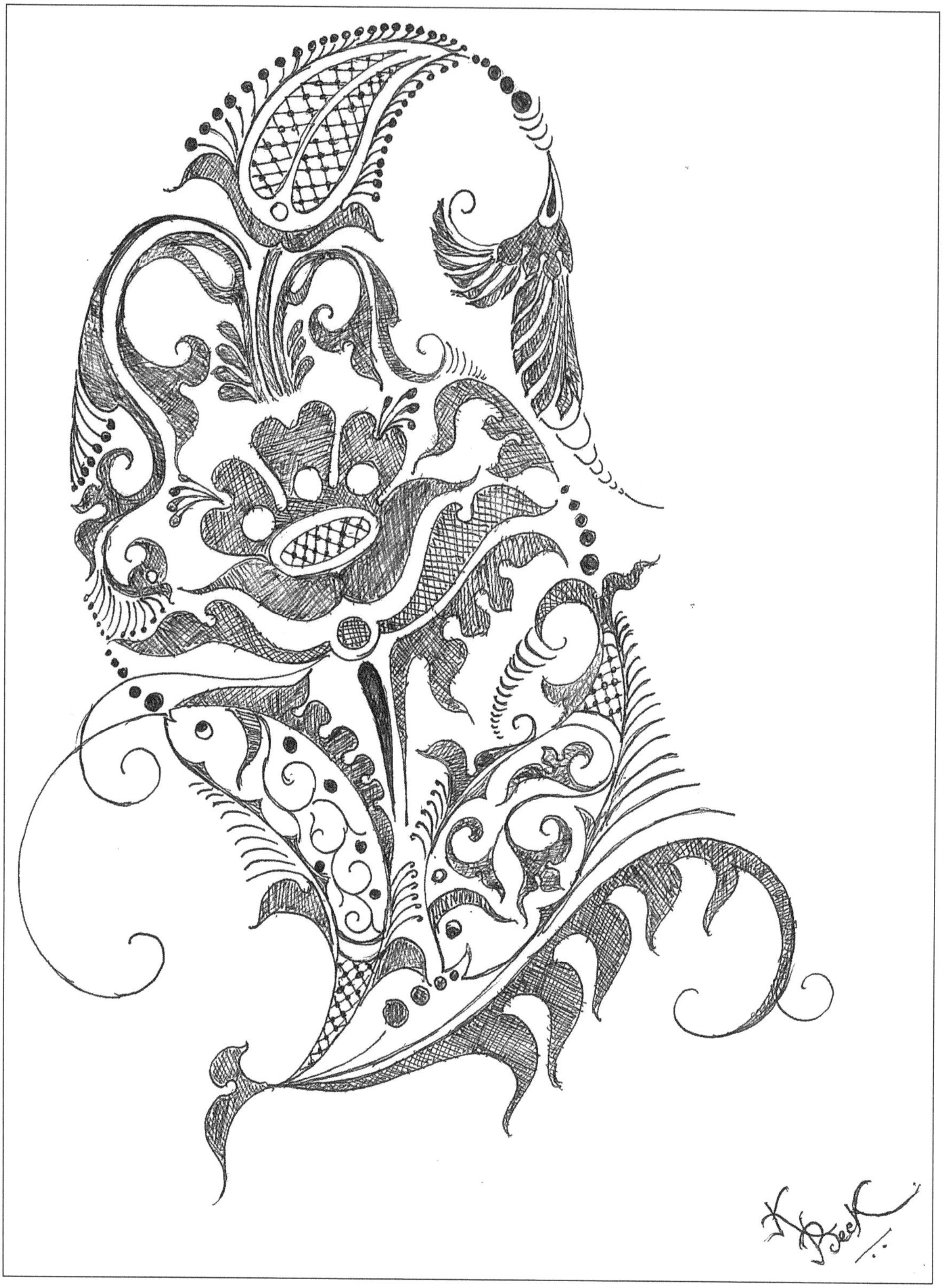

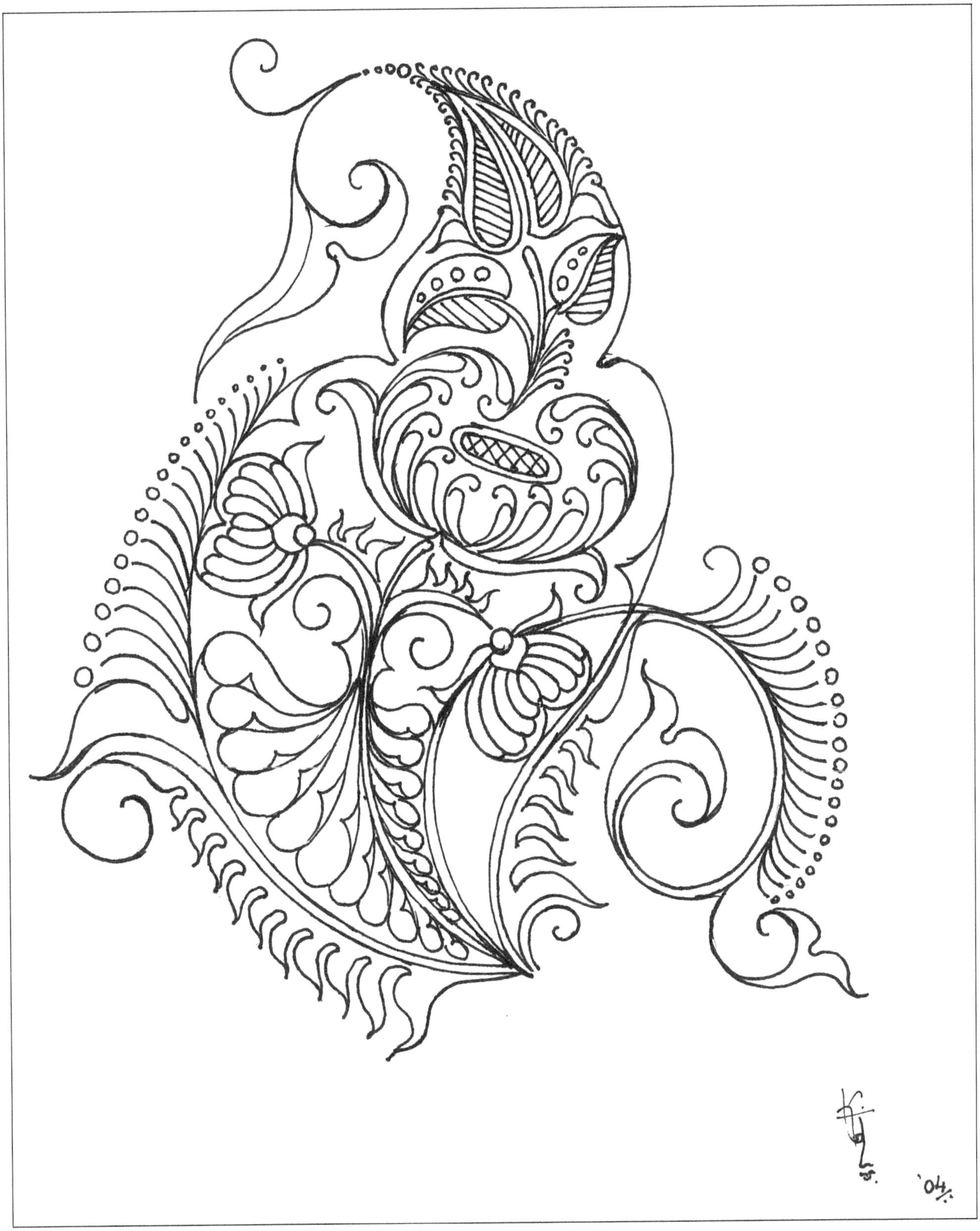

Branch

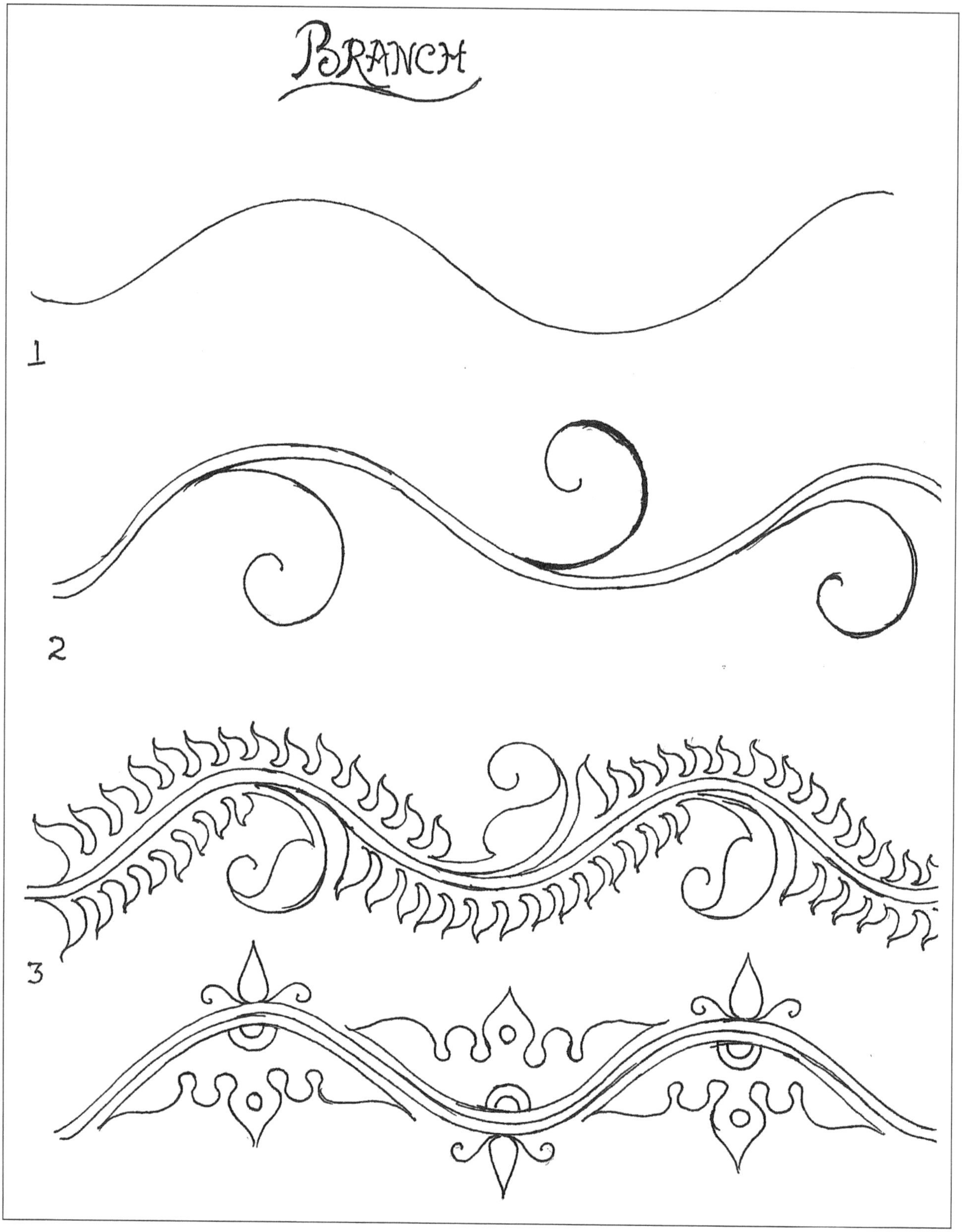
BRANCH
1
2
3

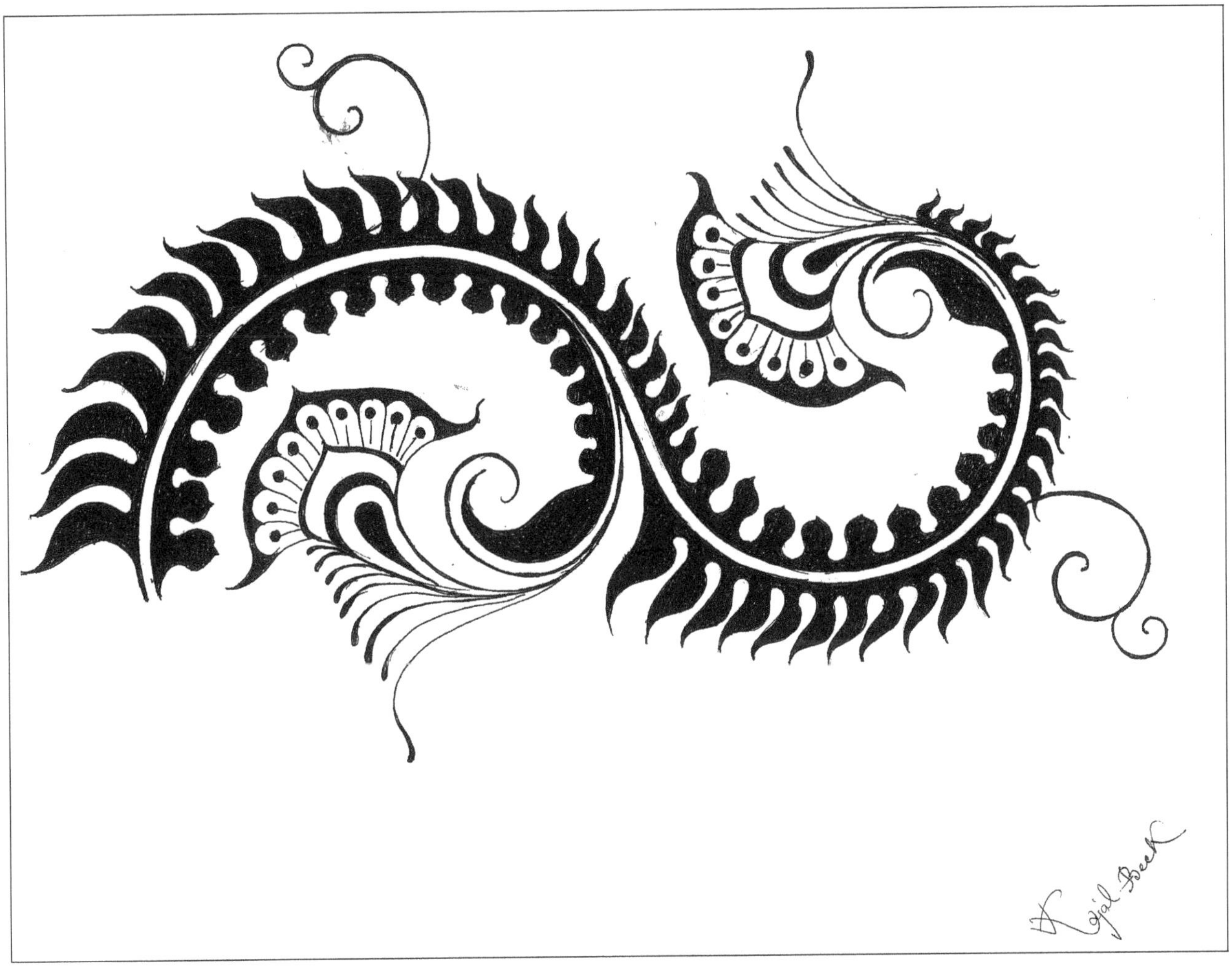

Circle

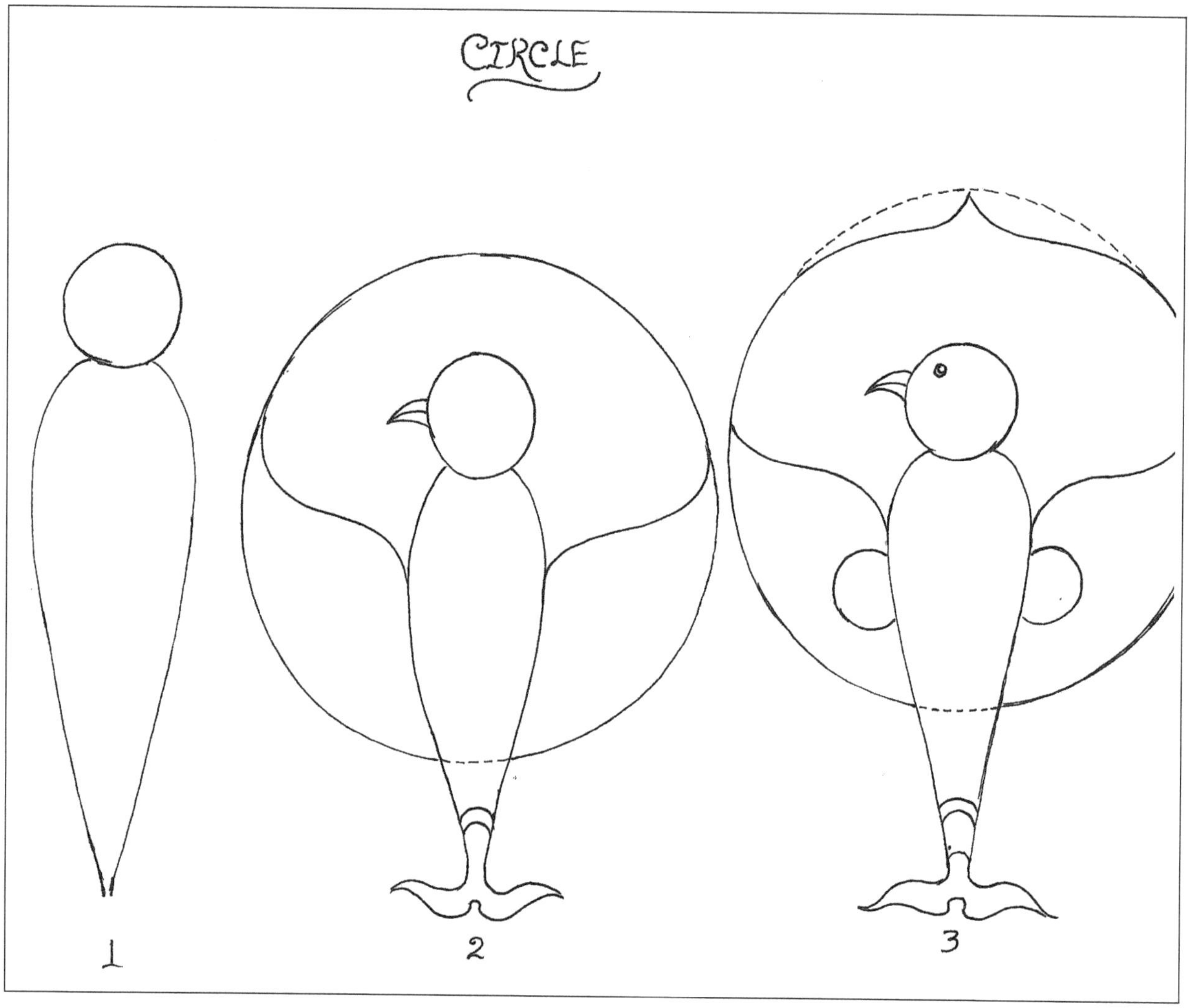
CIRCLE
1
2
3

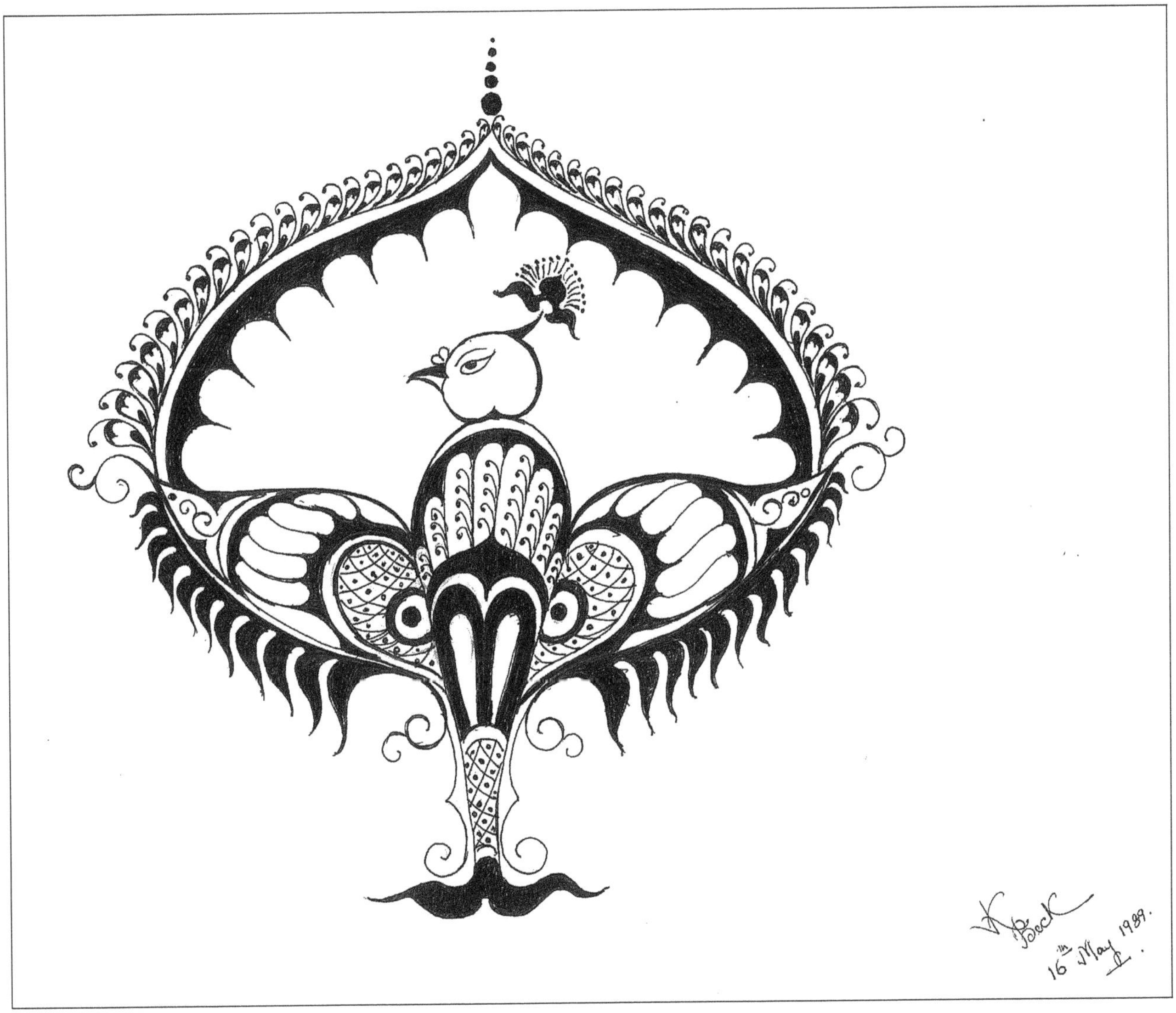
16th May 1989.

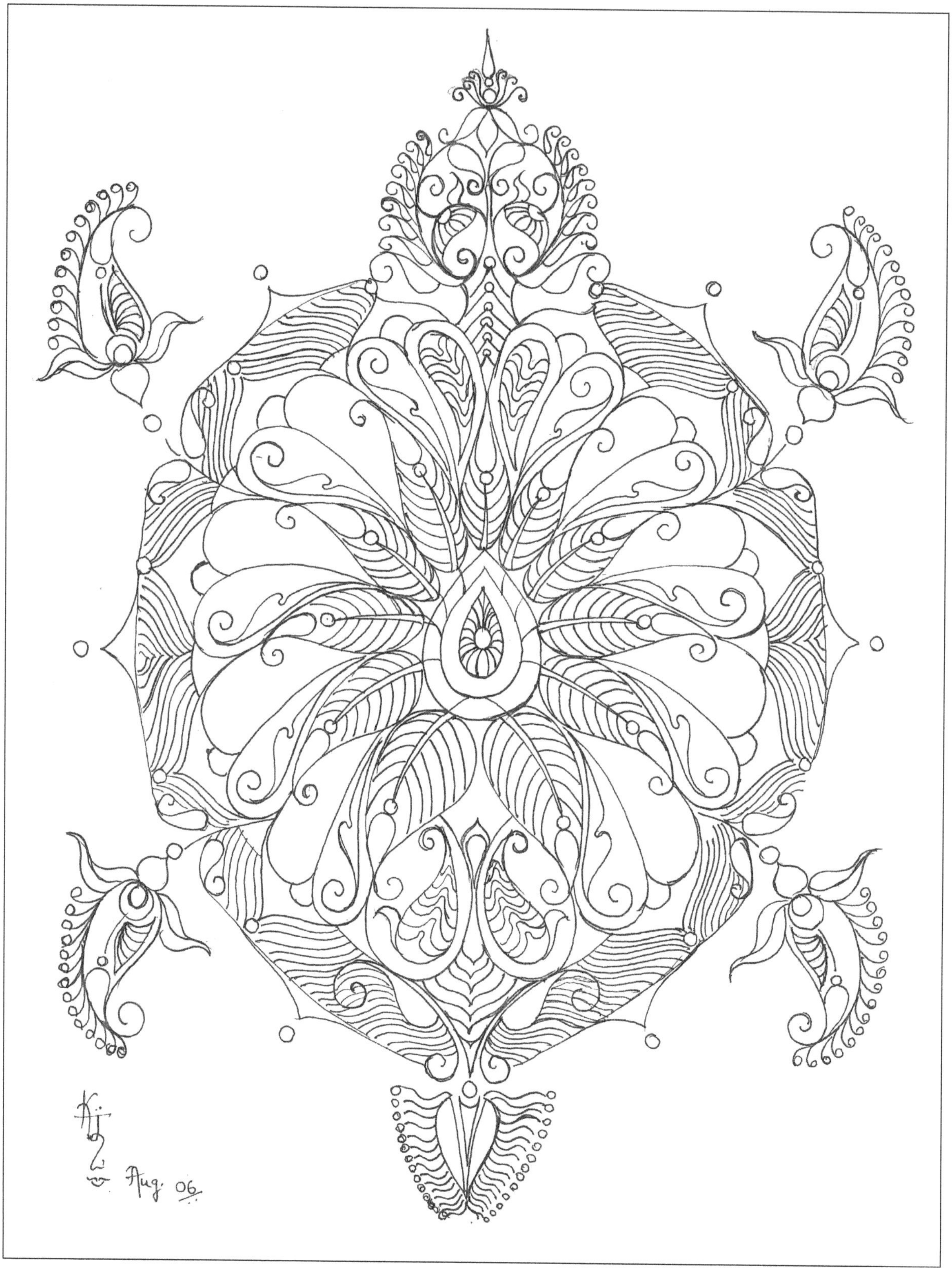
Aug. 06

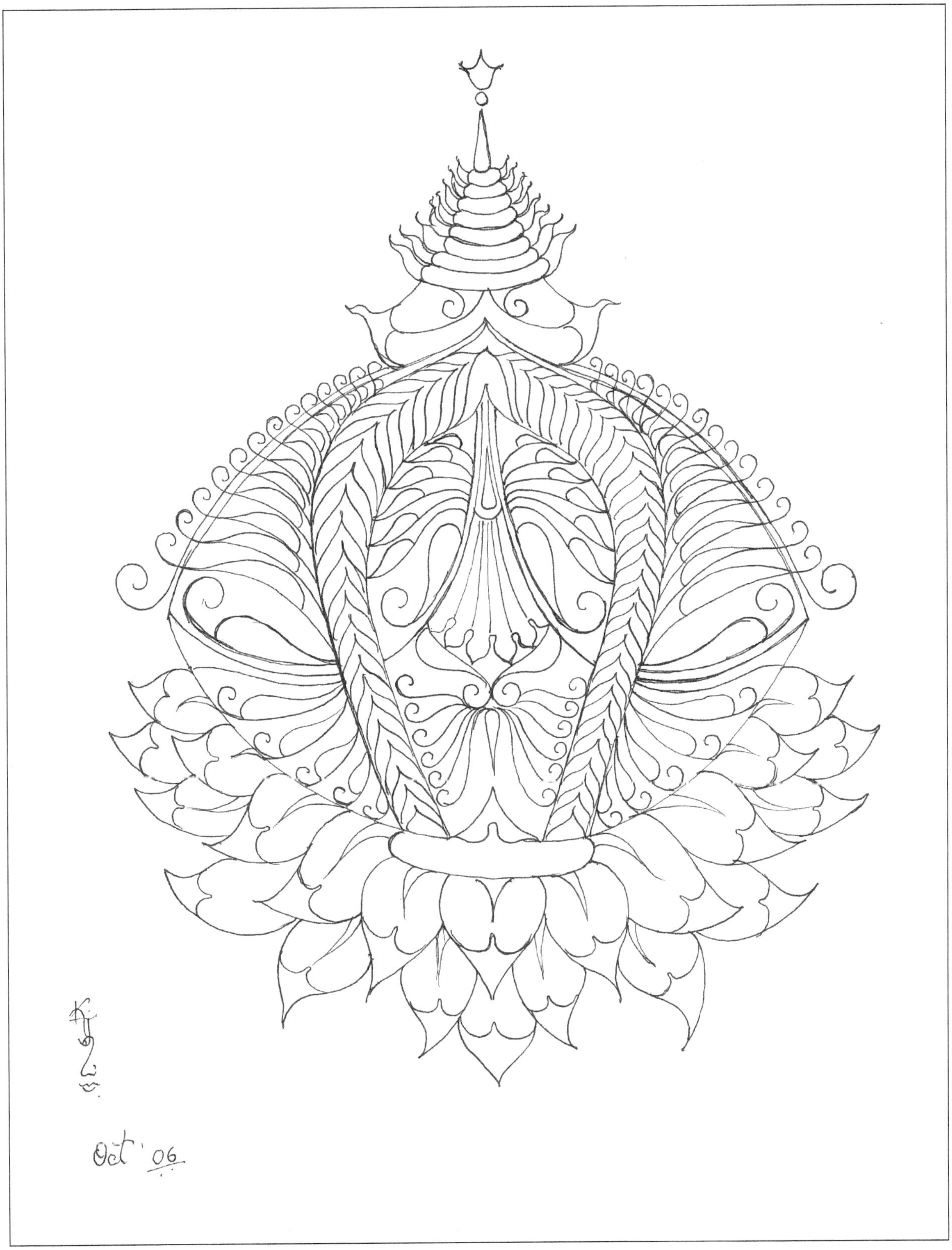
Oct '06

Square

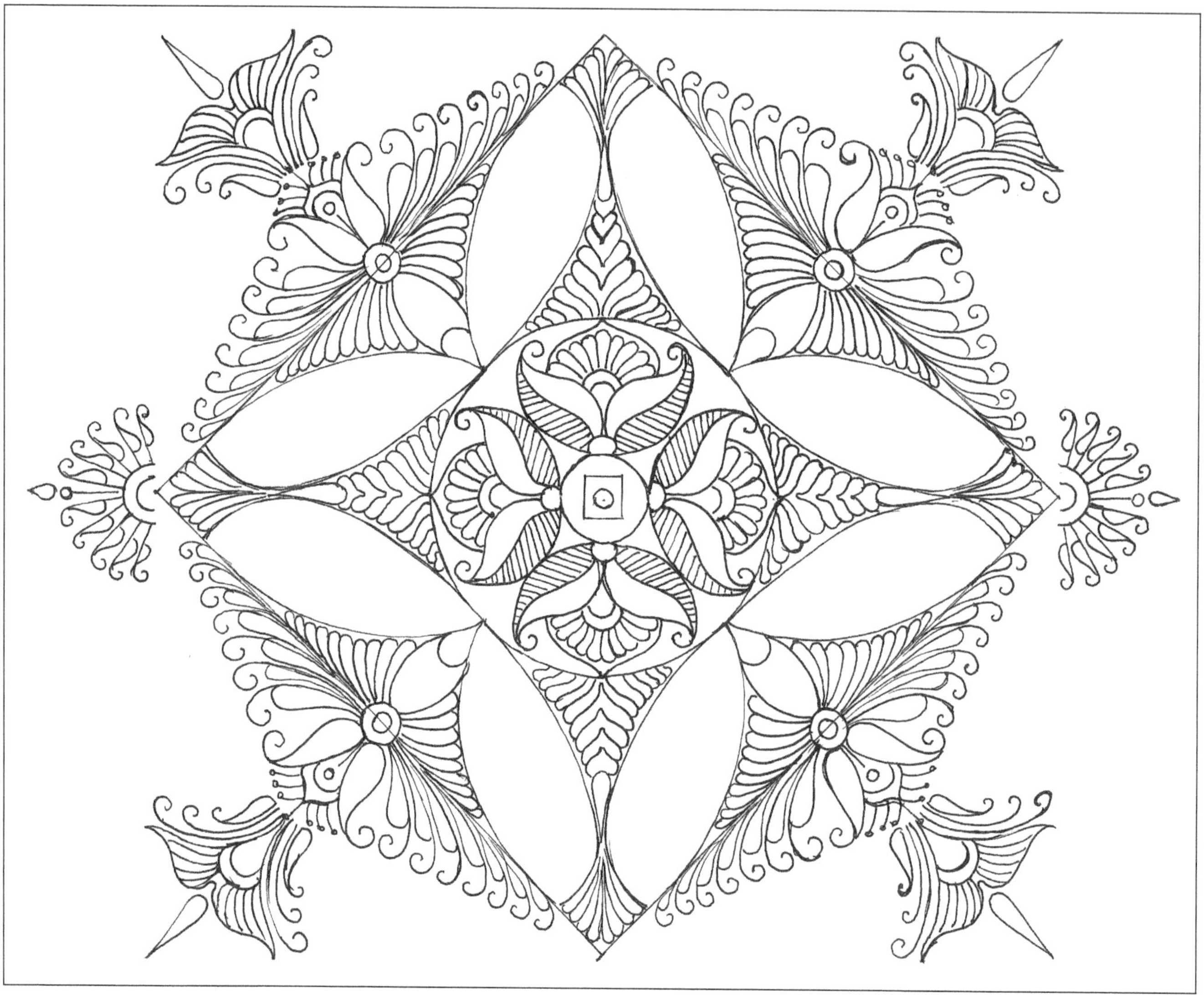

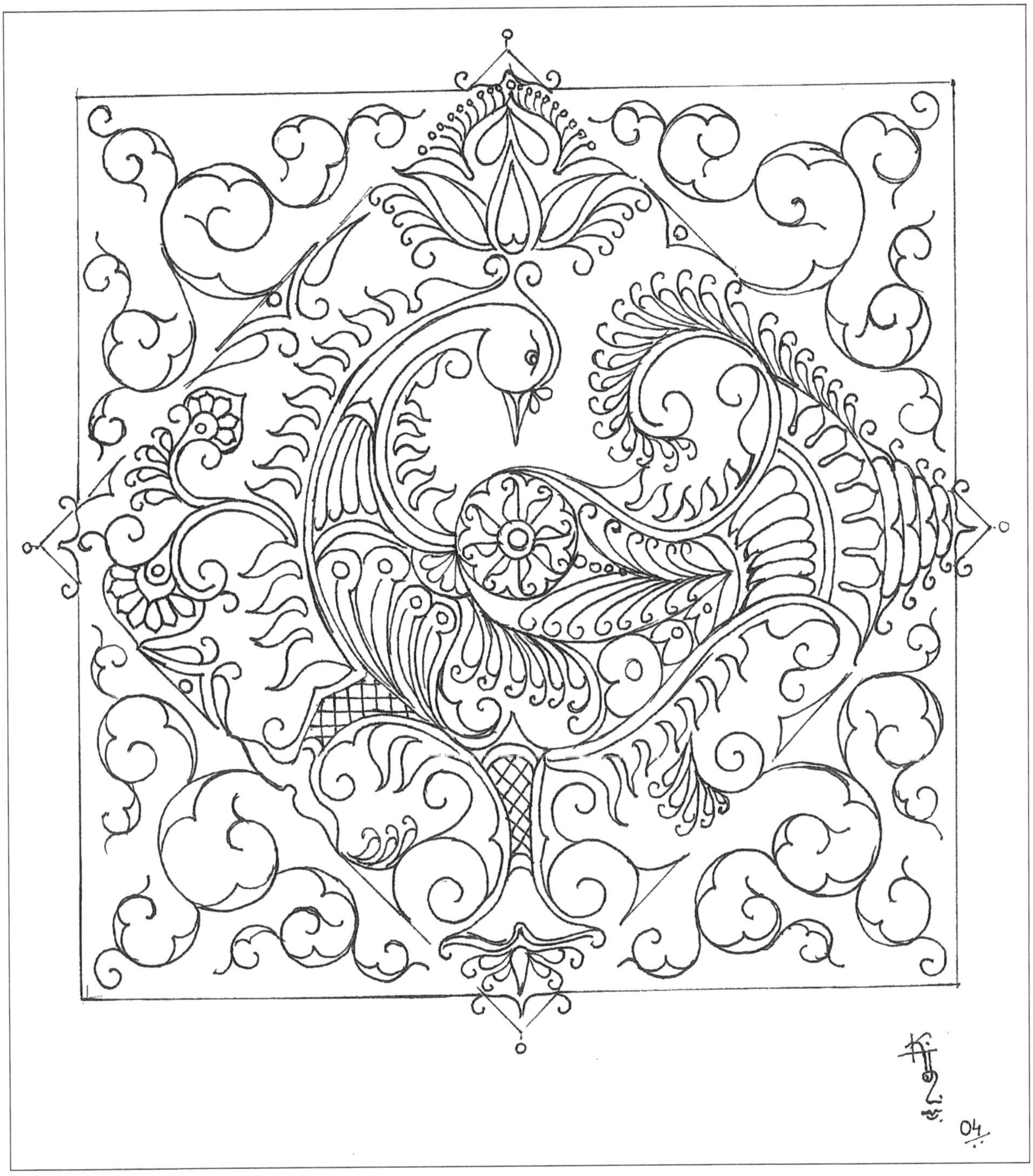

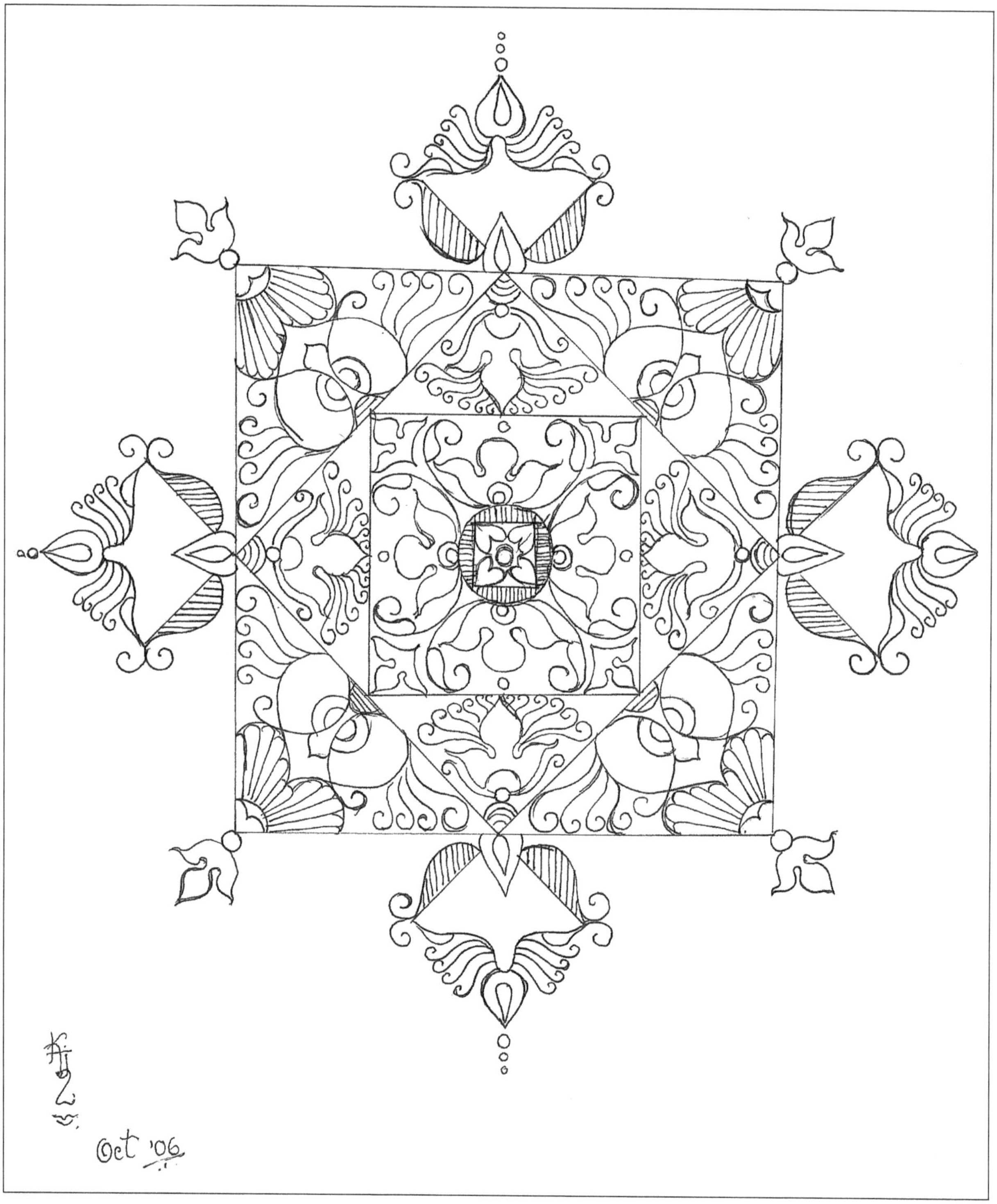
Oct '06

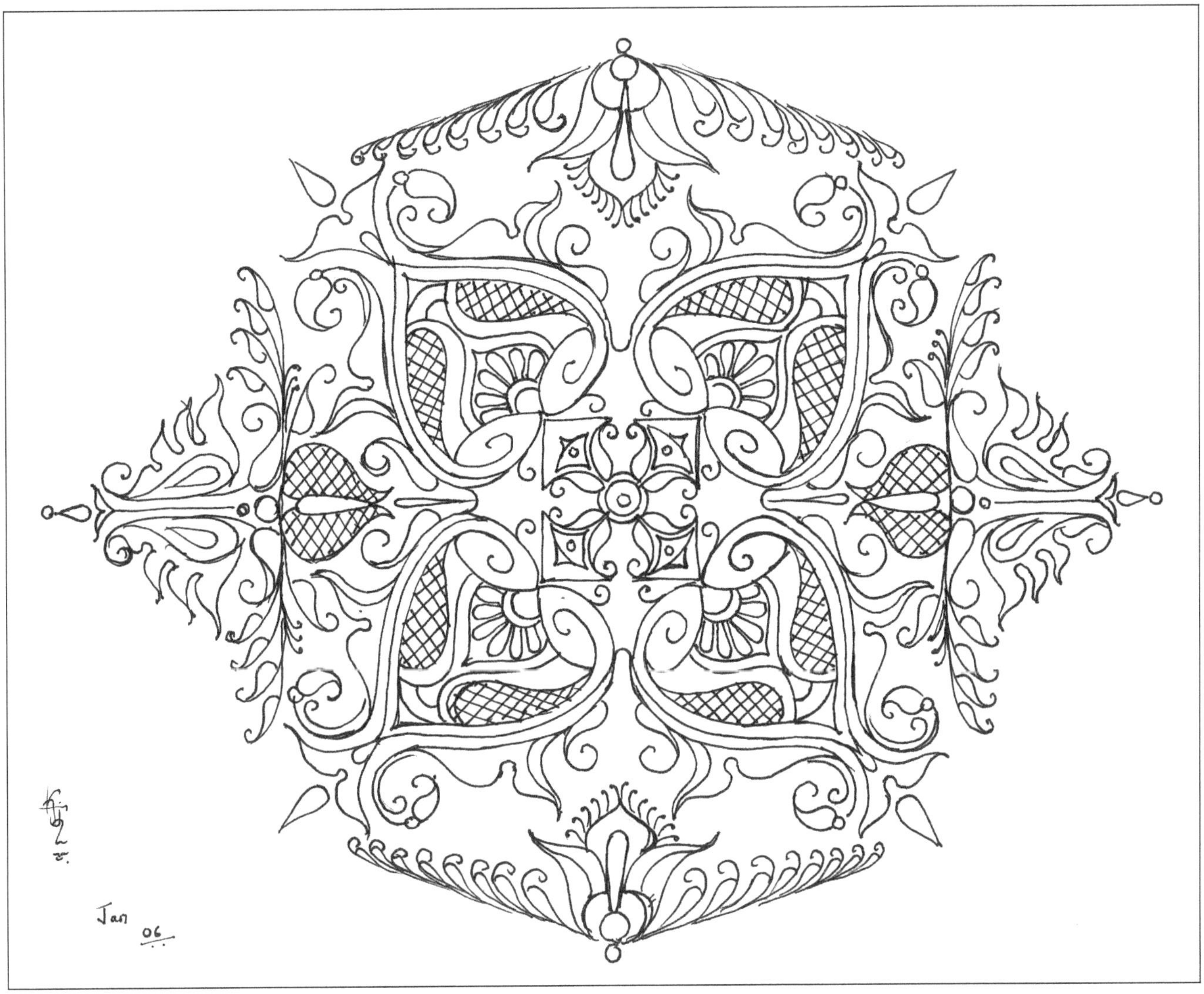

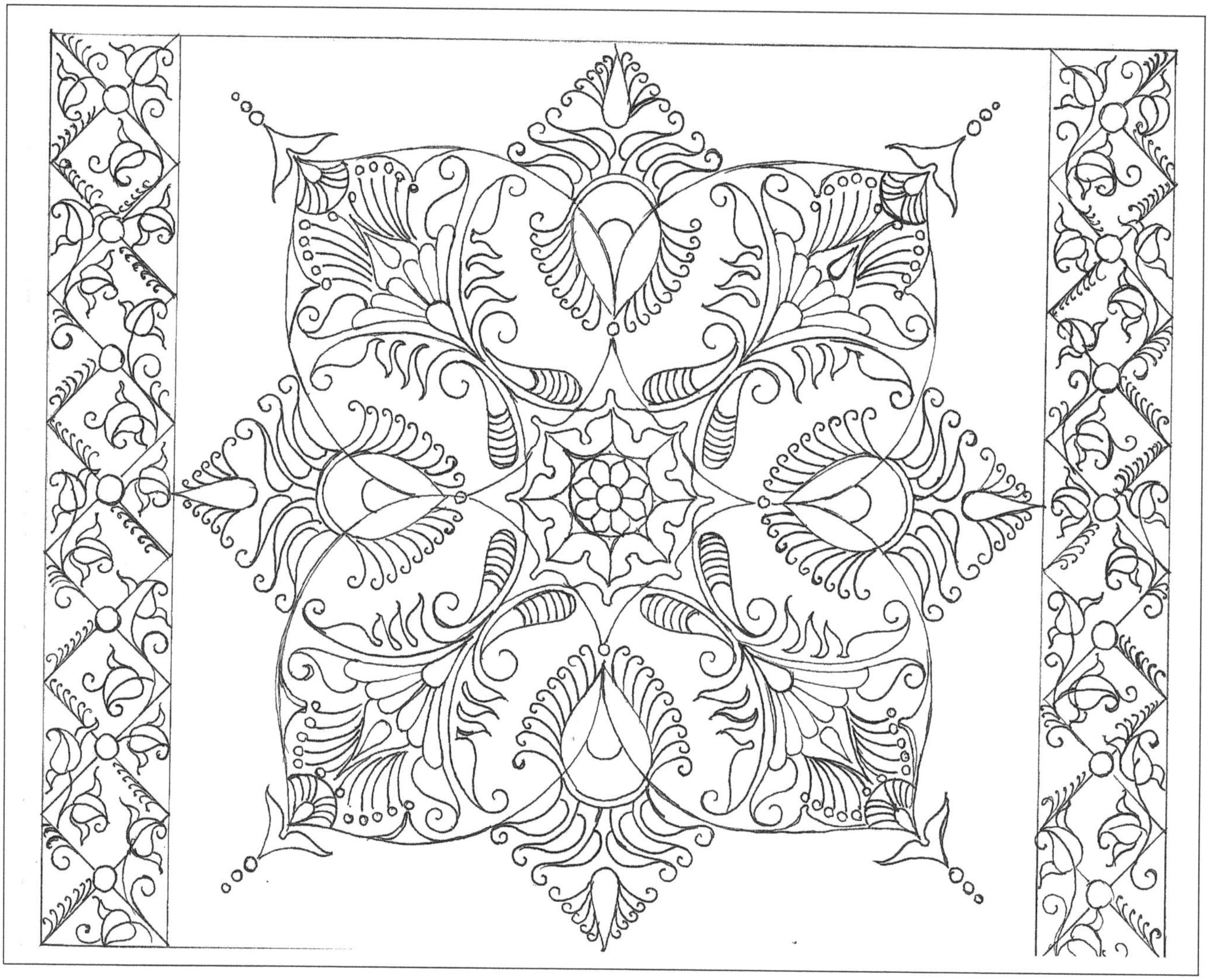

Diamond

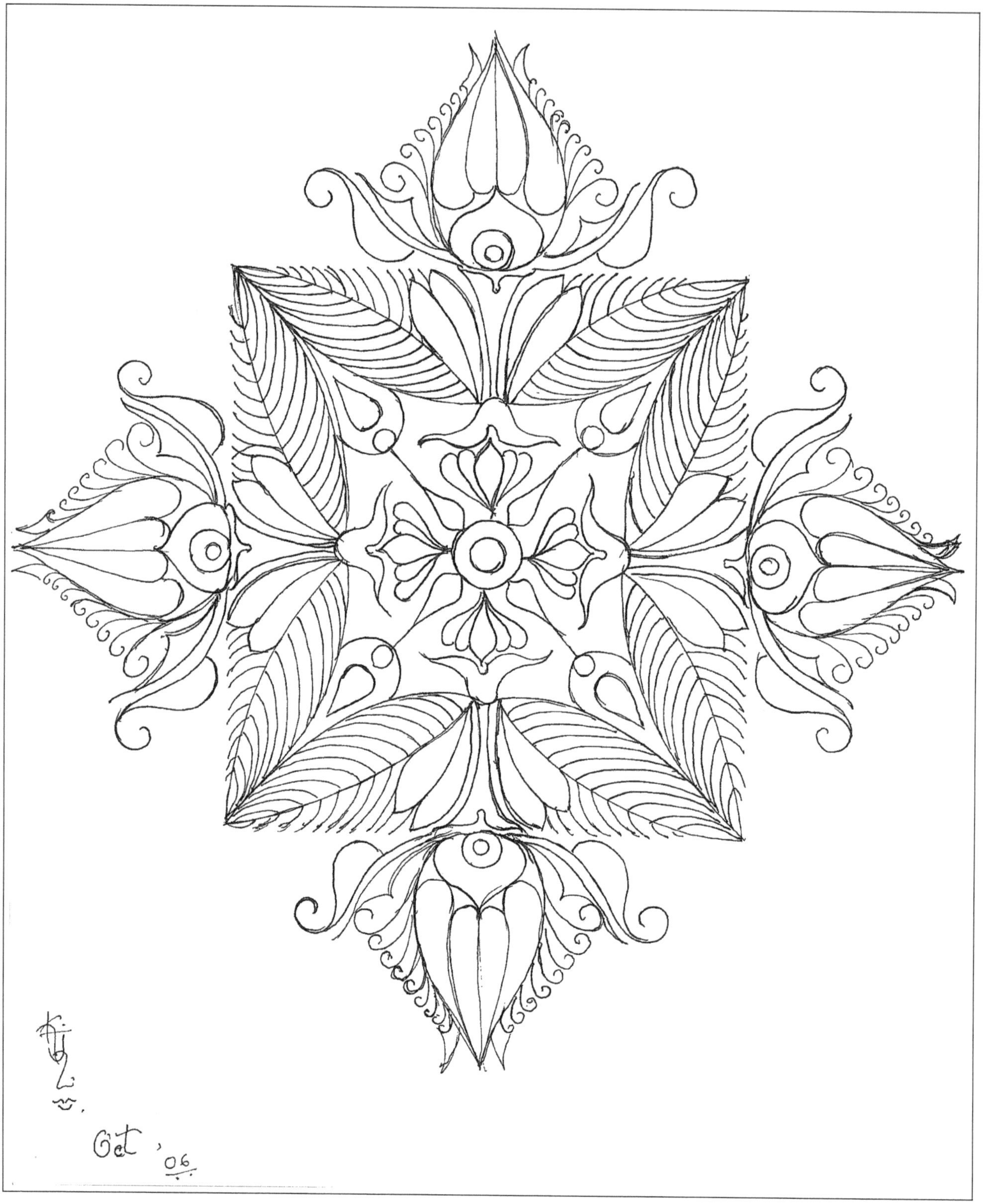

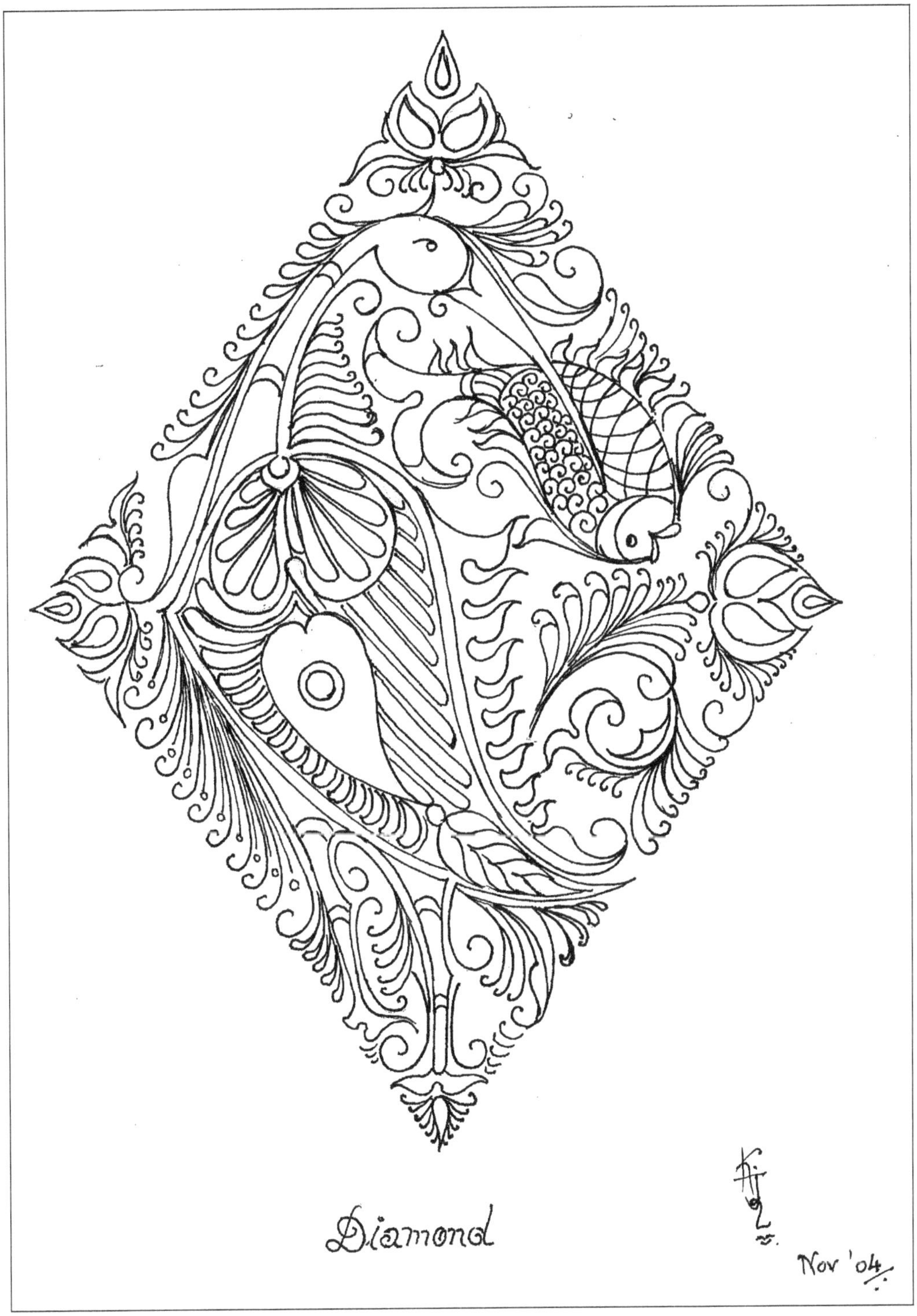
Diamond
Nov '04

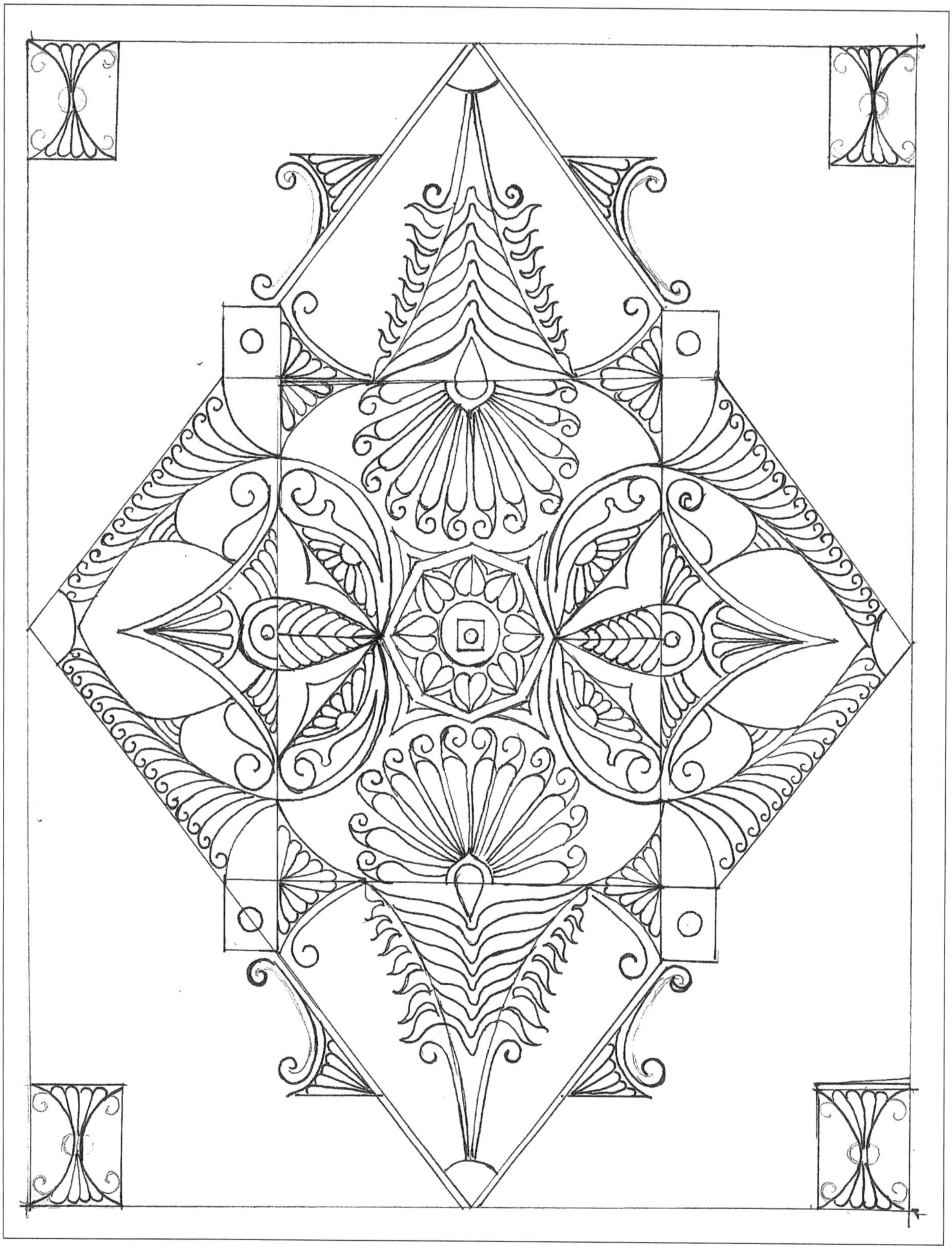

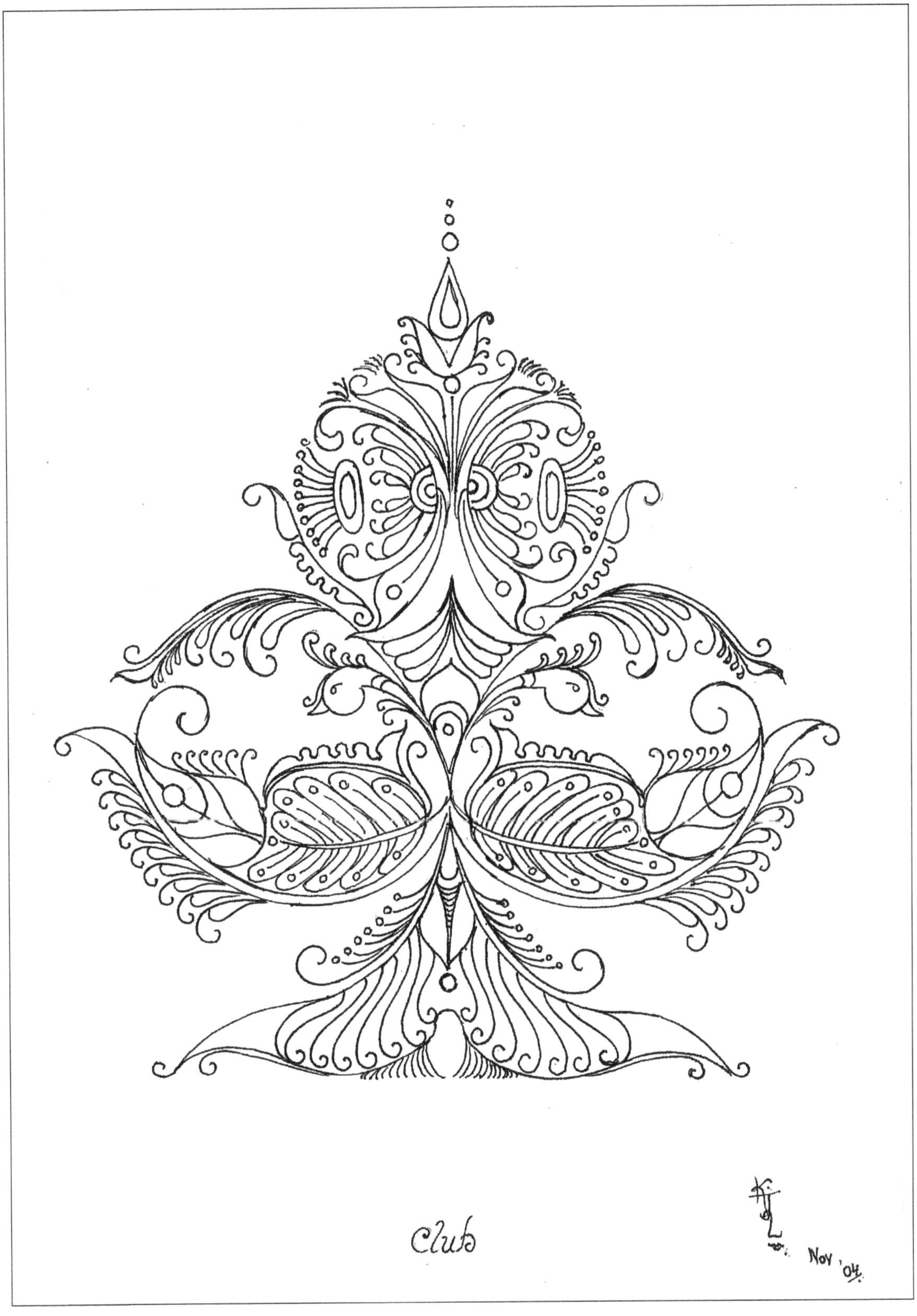
Club
Nov '04.

Triangle

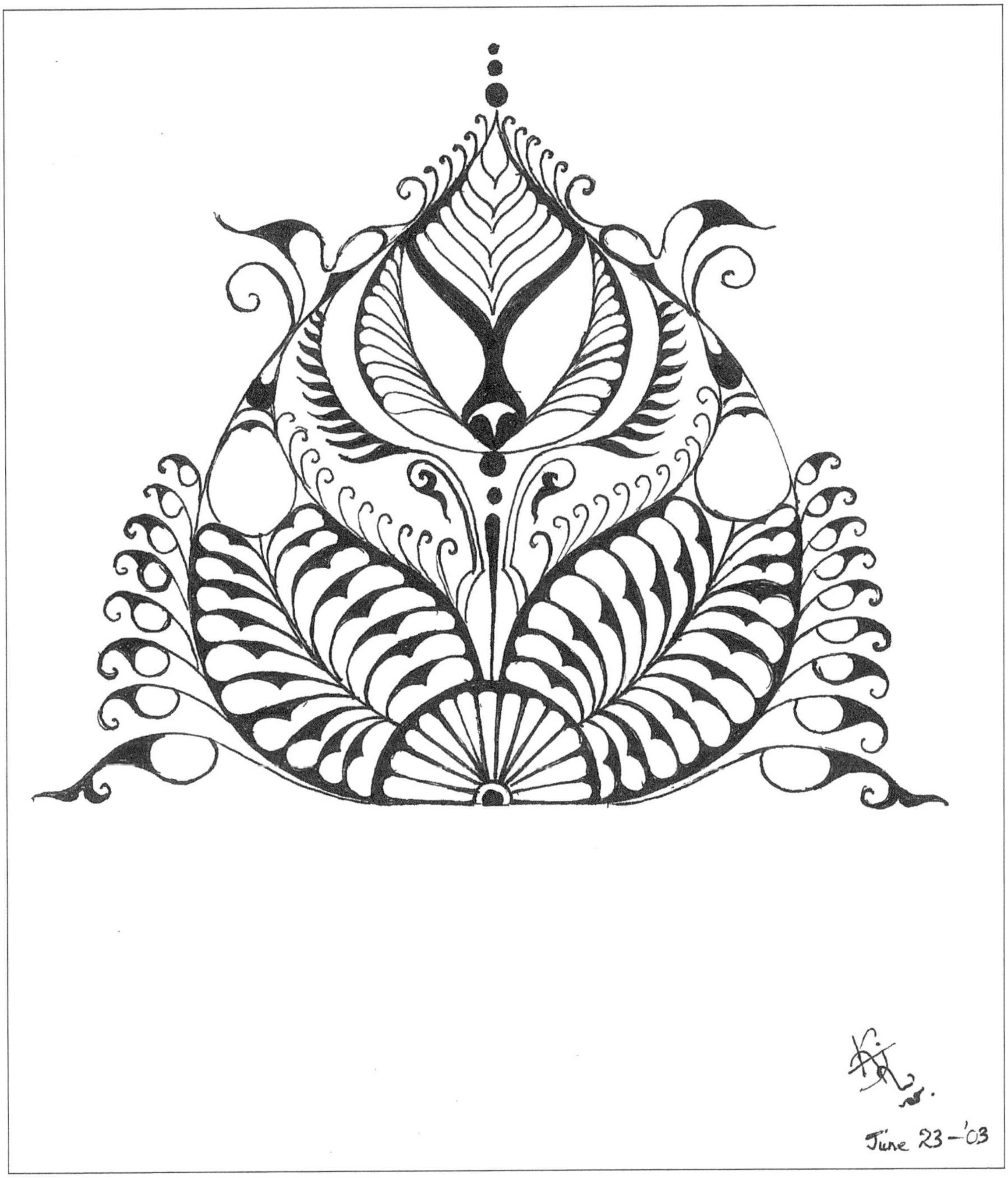
June 23 – '03

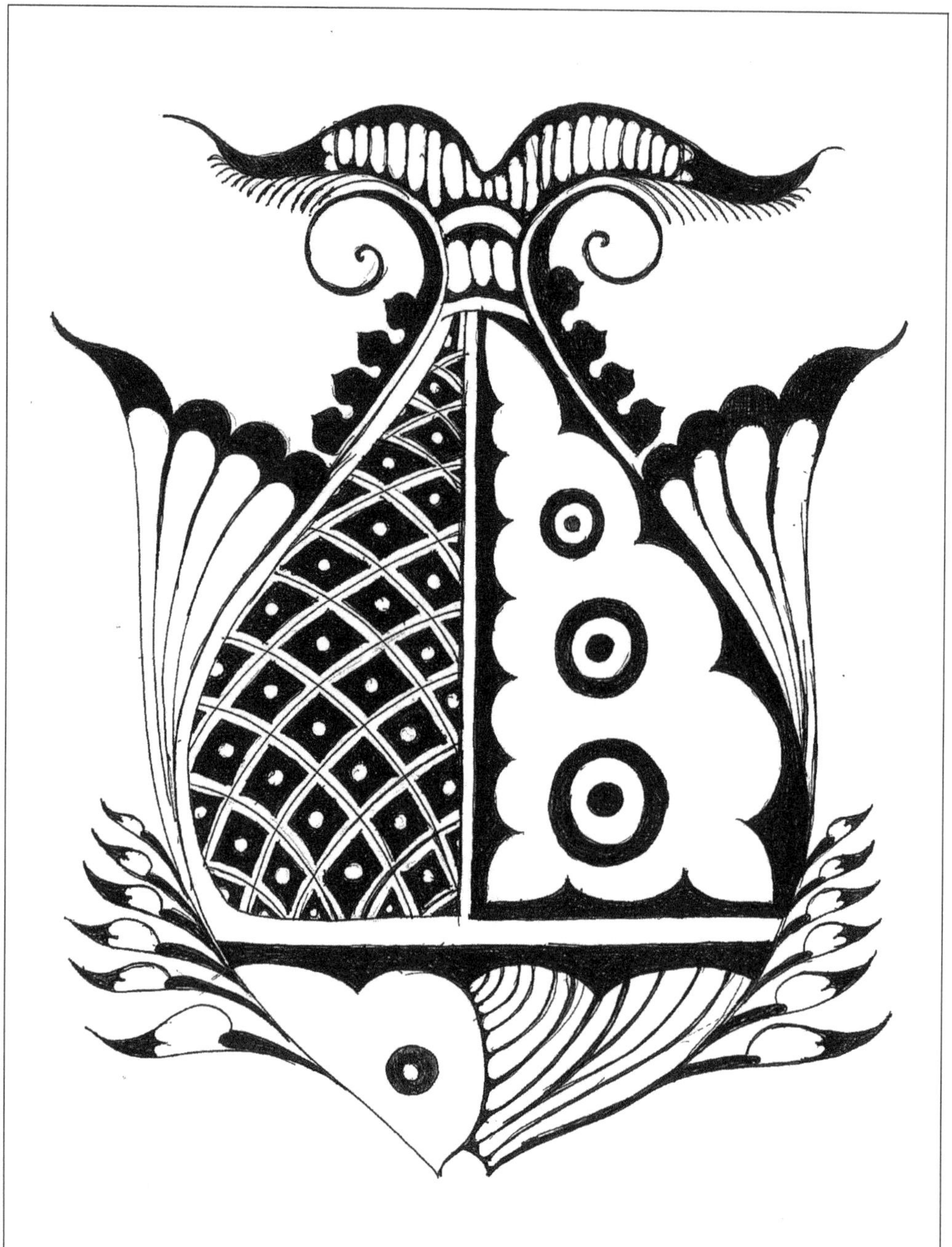

Oval

OVAL

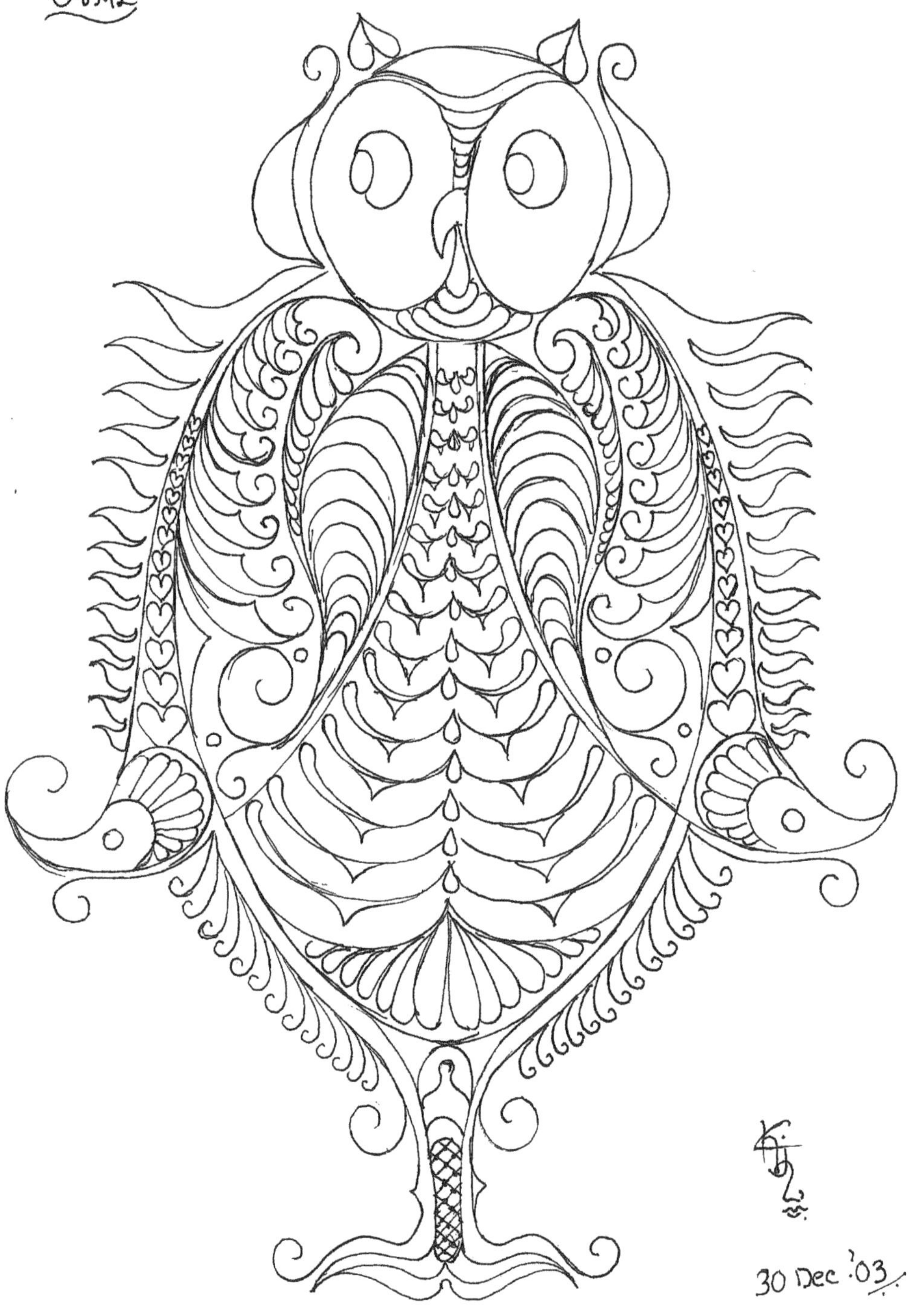

30 Dec '03

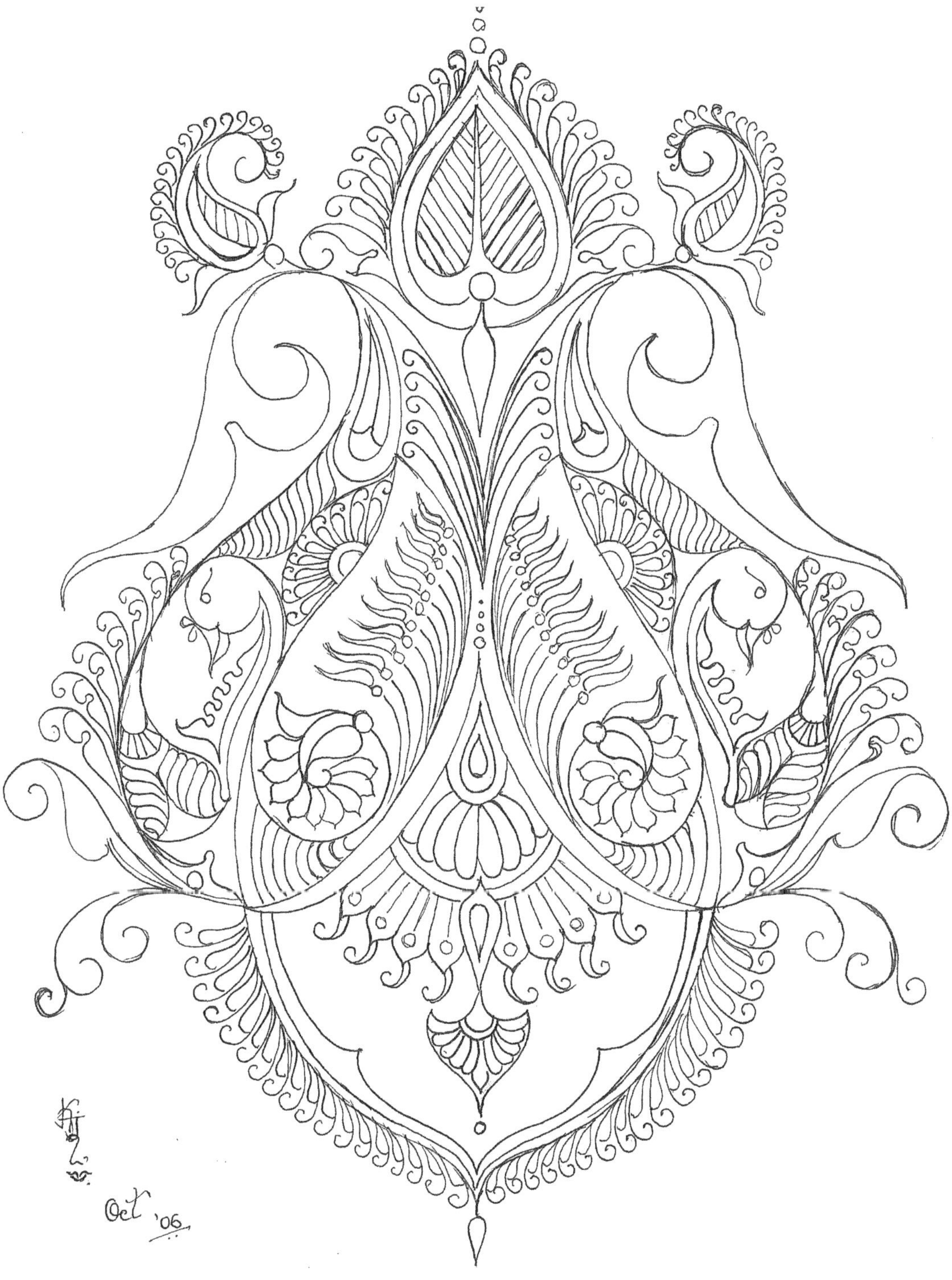
Oct '06

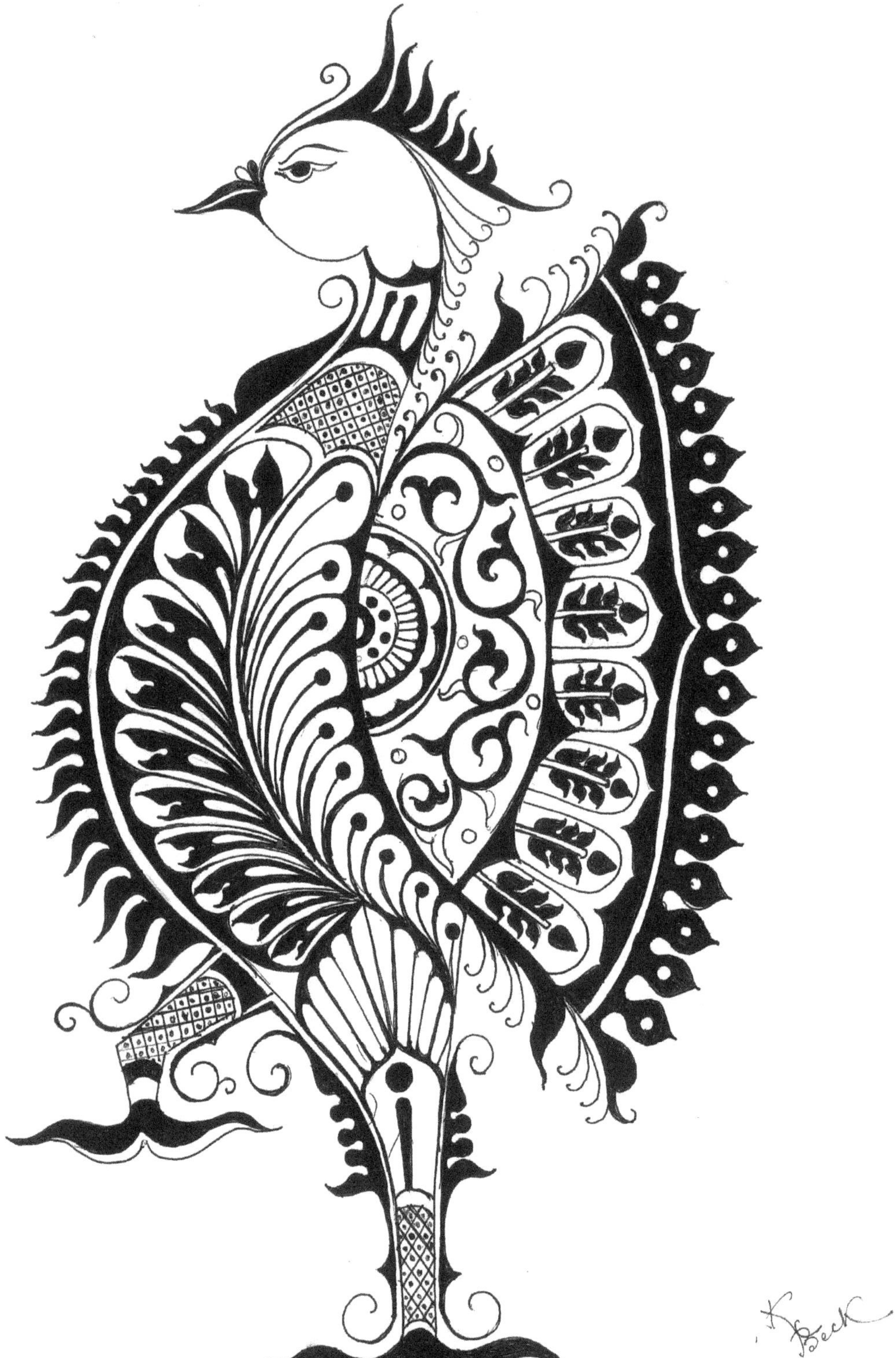

Fruit

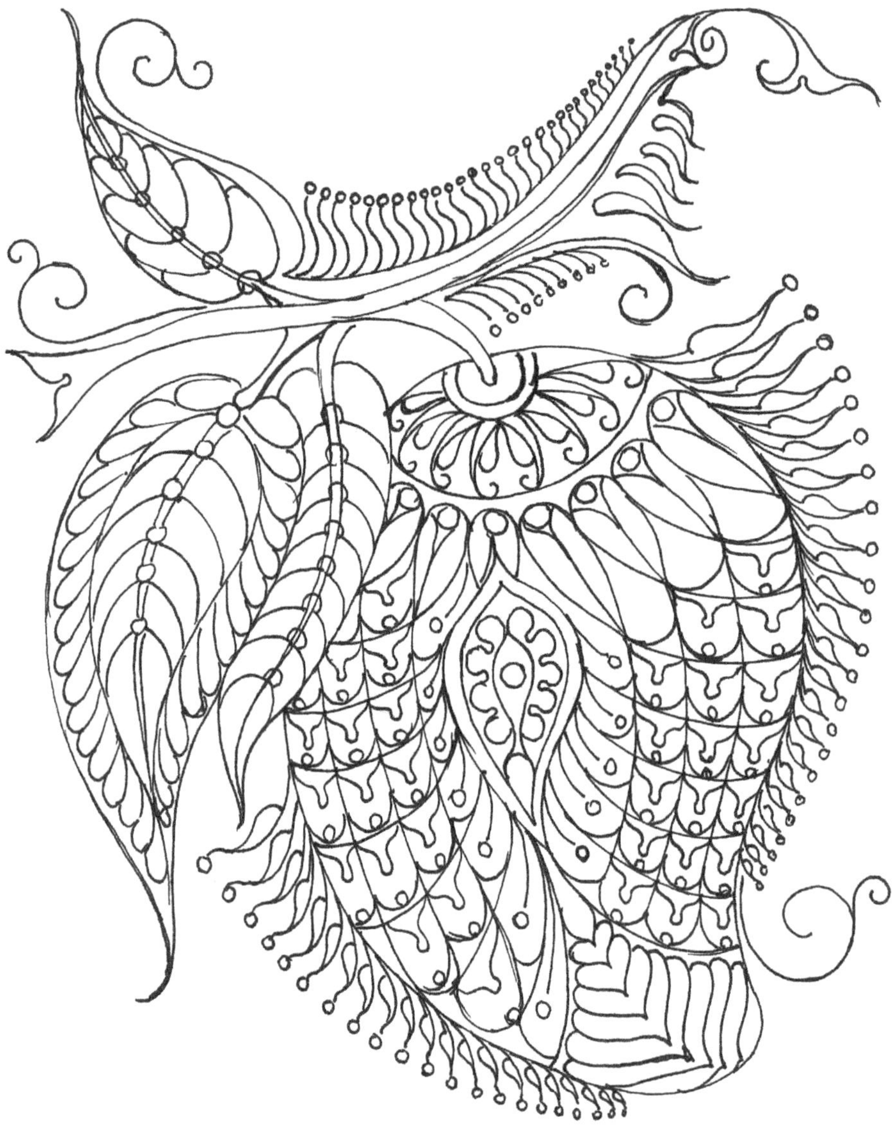

Mango For The King

5 Feb 06

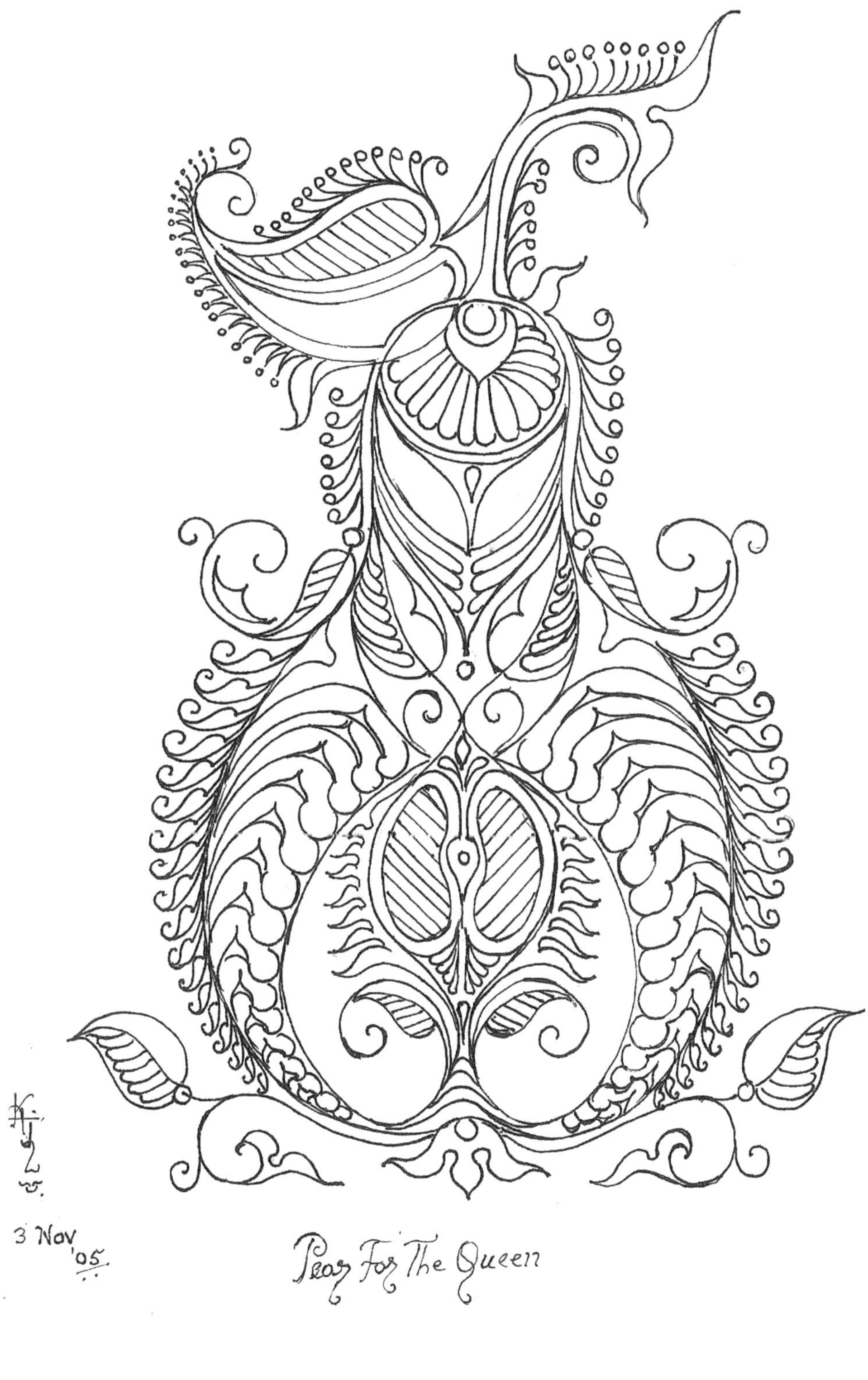
3 Nov '05.
Pear For The Queen

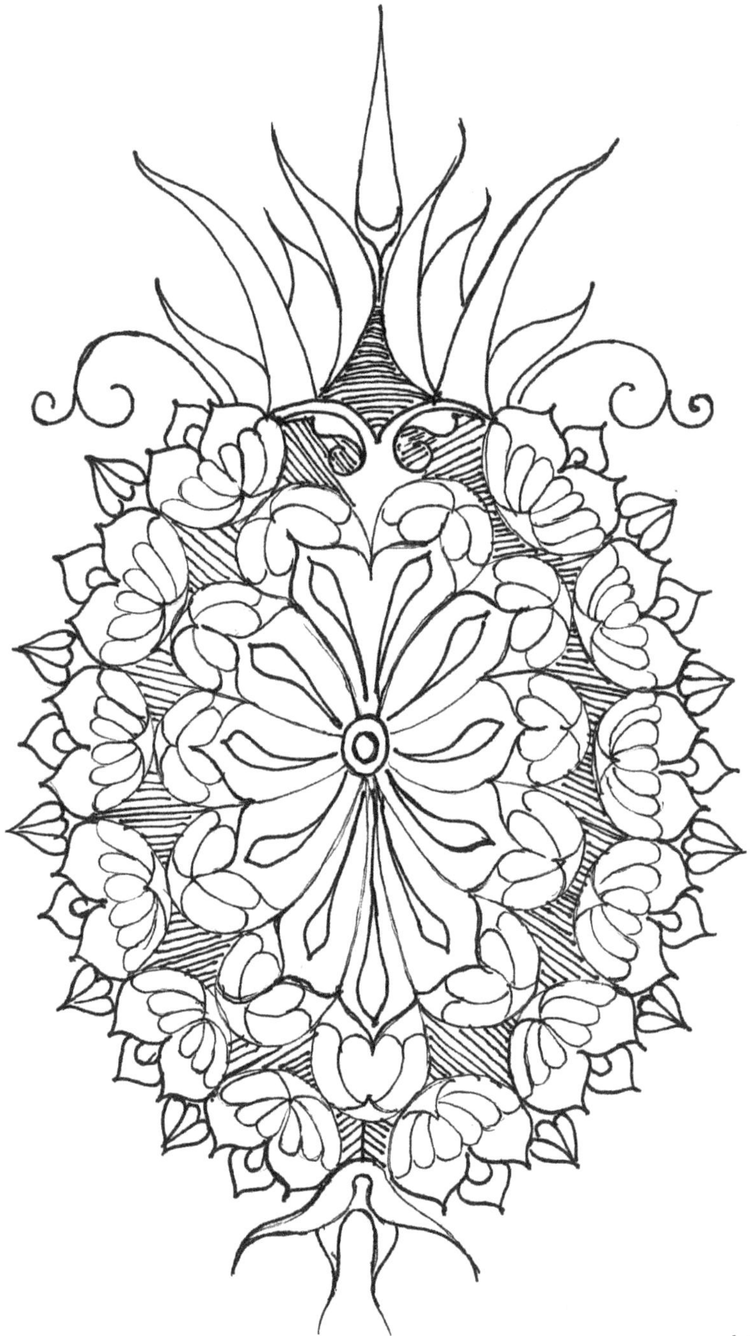

Pineapple

Jan. 06

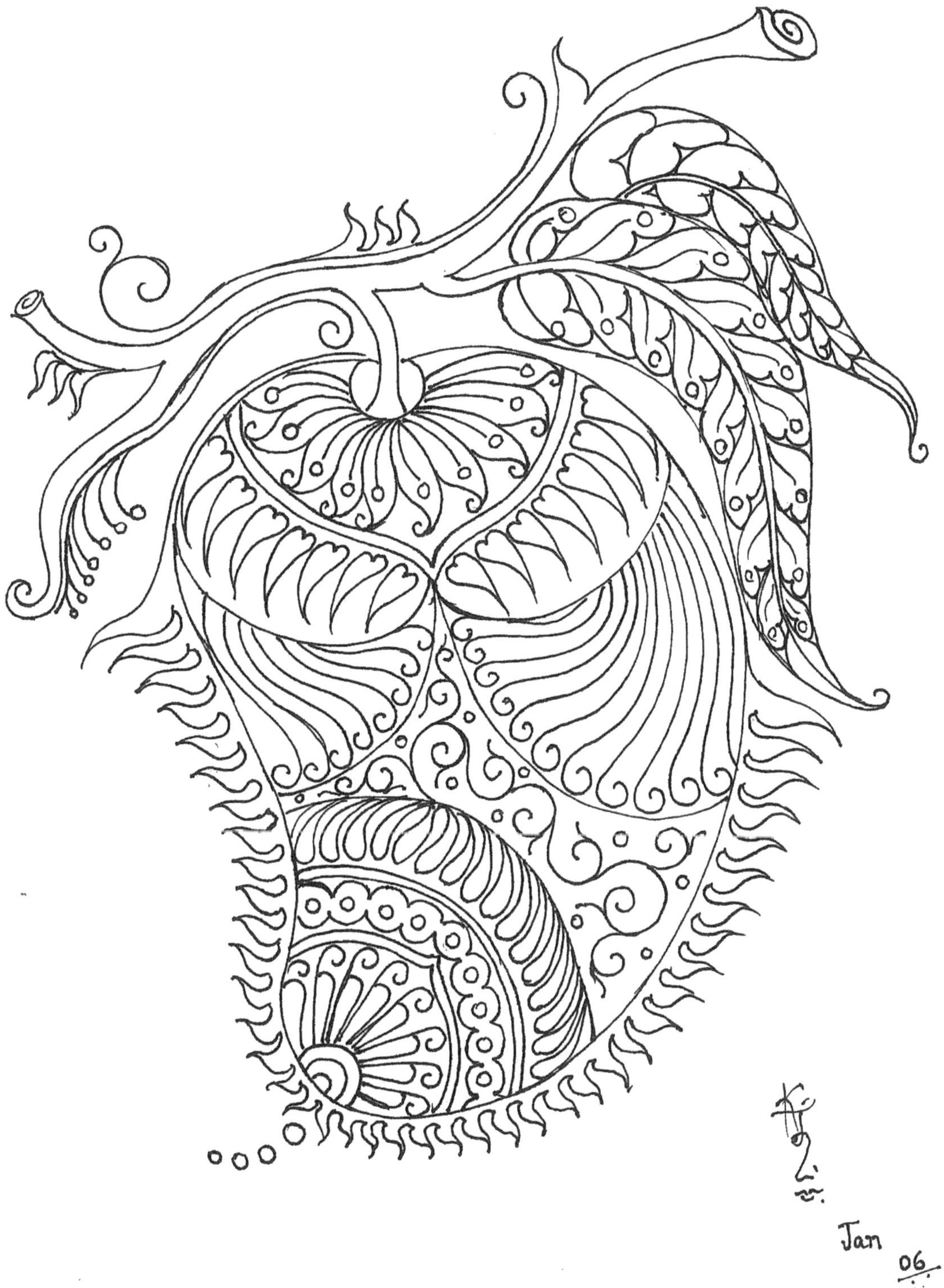
Jan
06

Vegetables

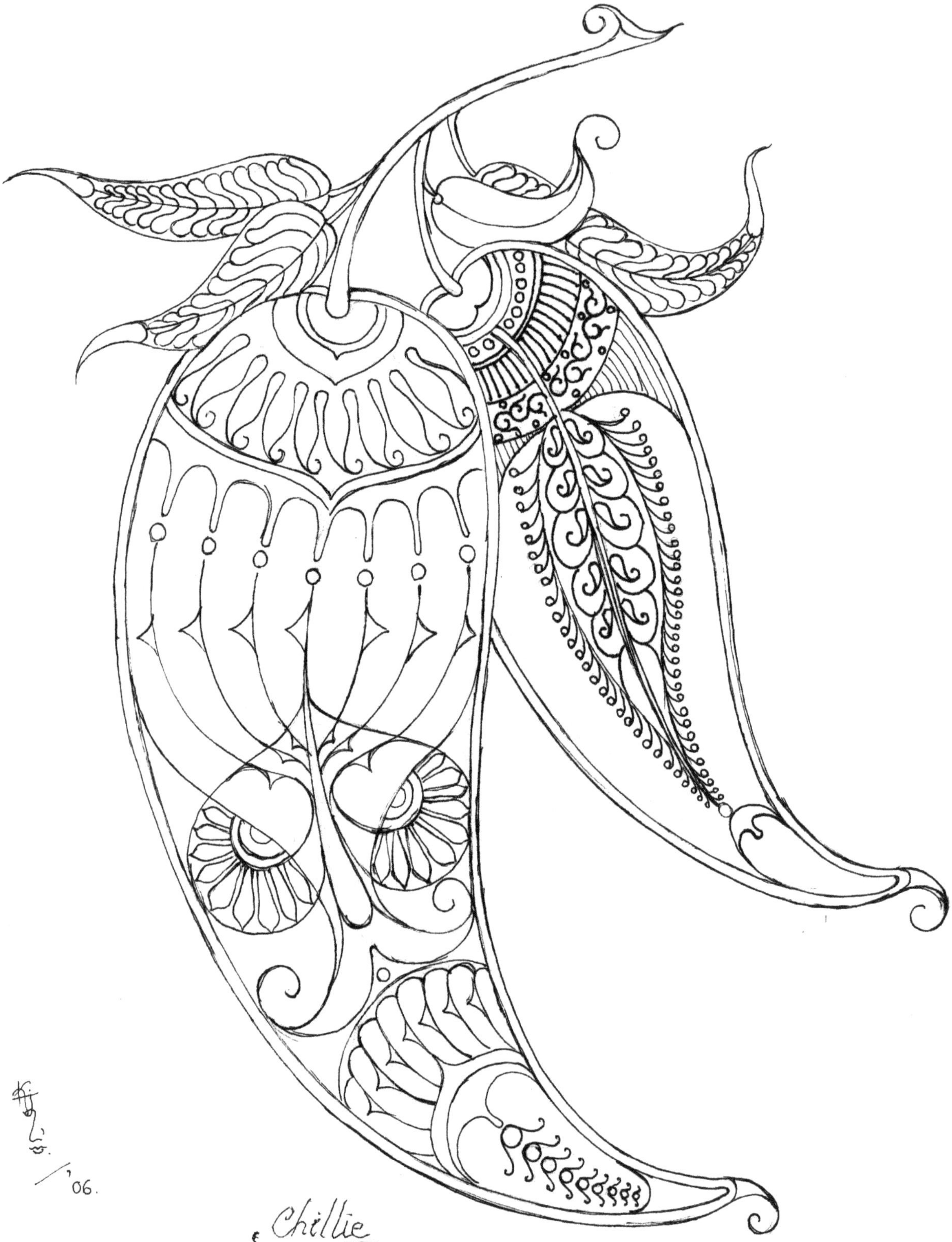

Chillie

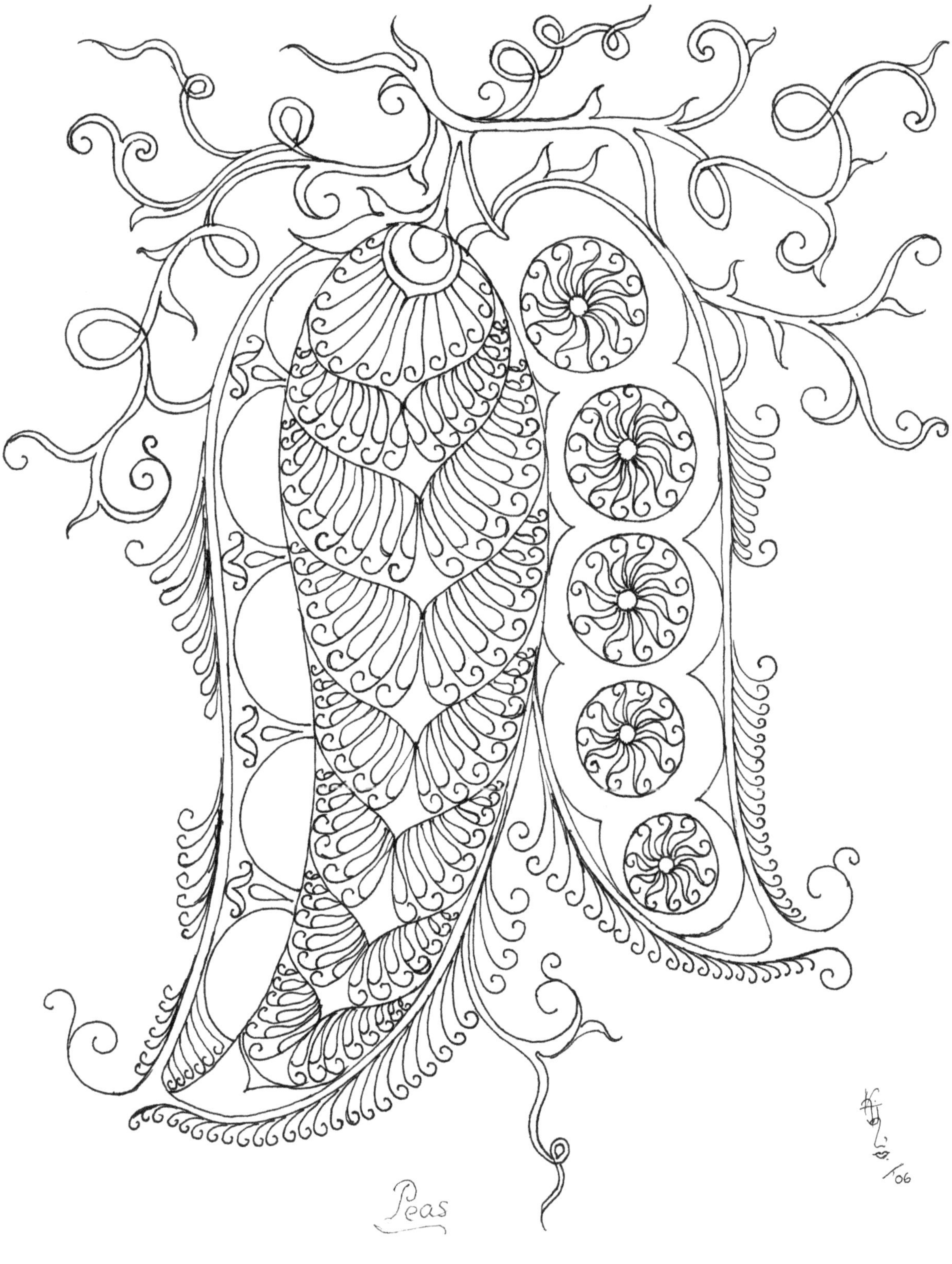

Peas

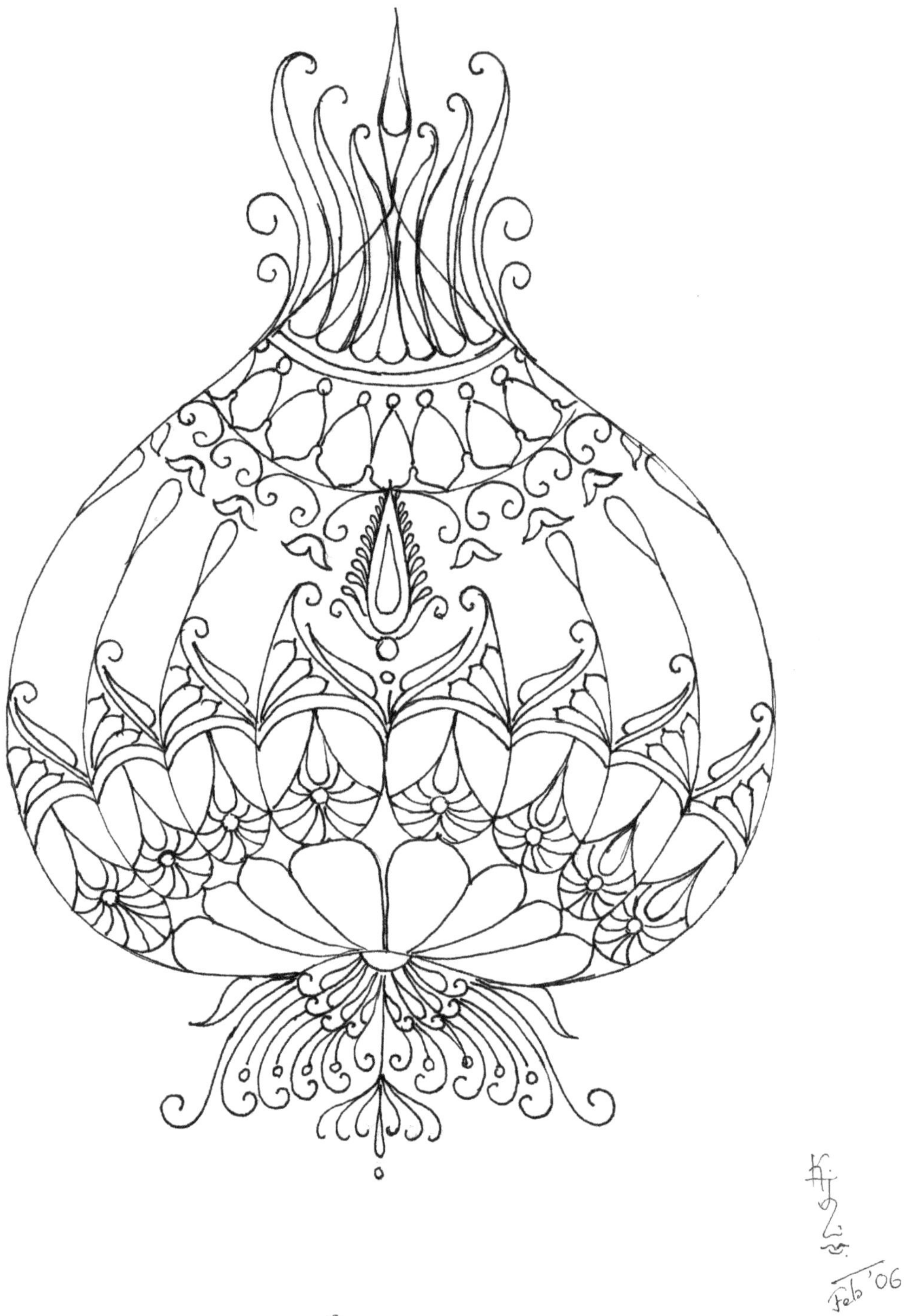

Onion

Birds

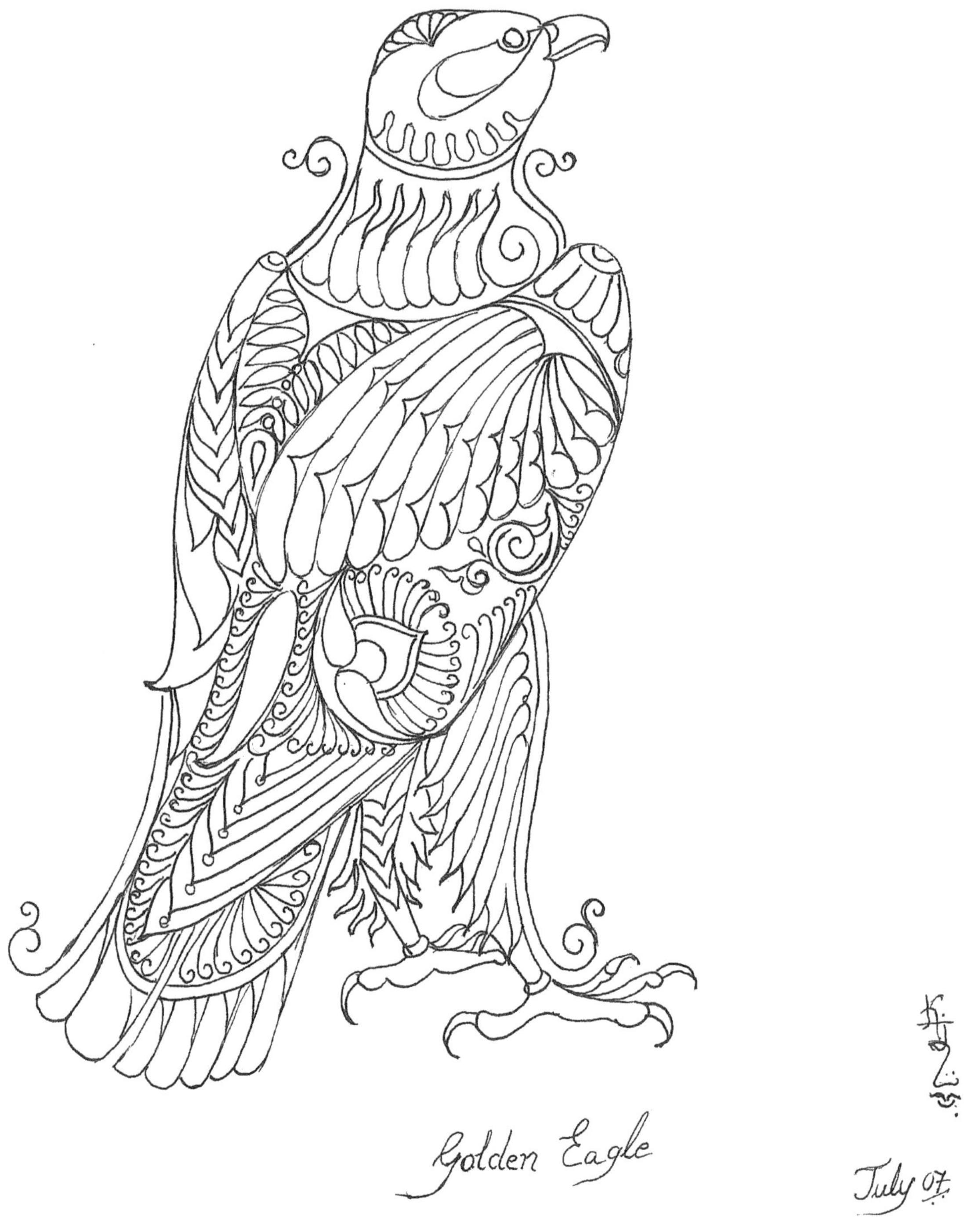
Golden Eagle
July 07

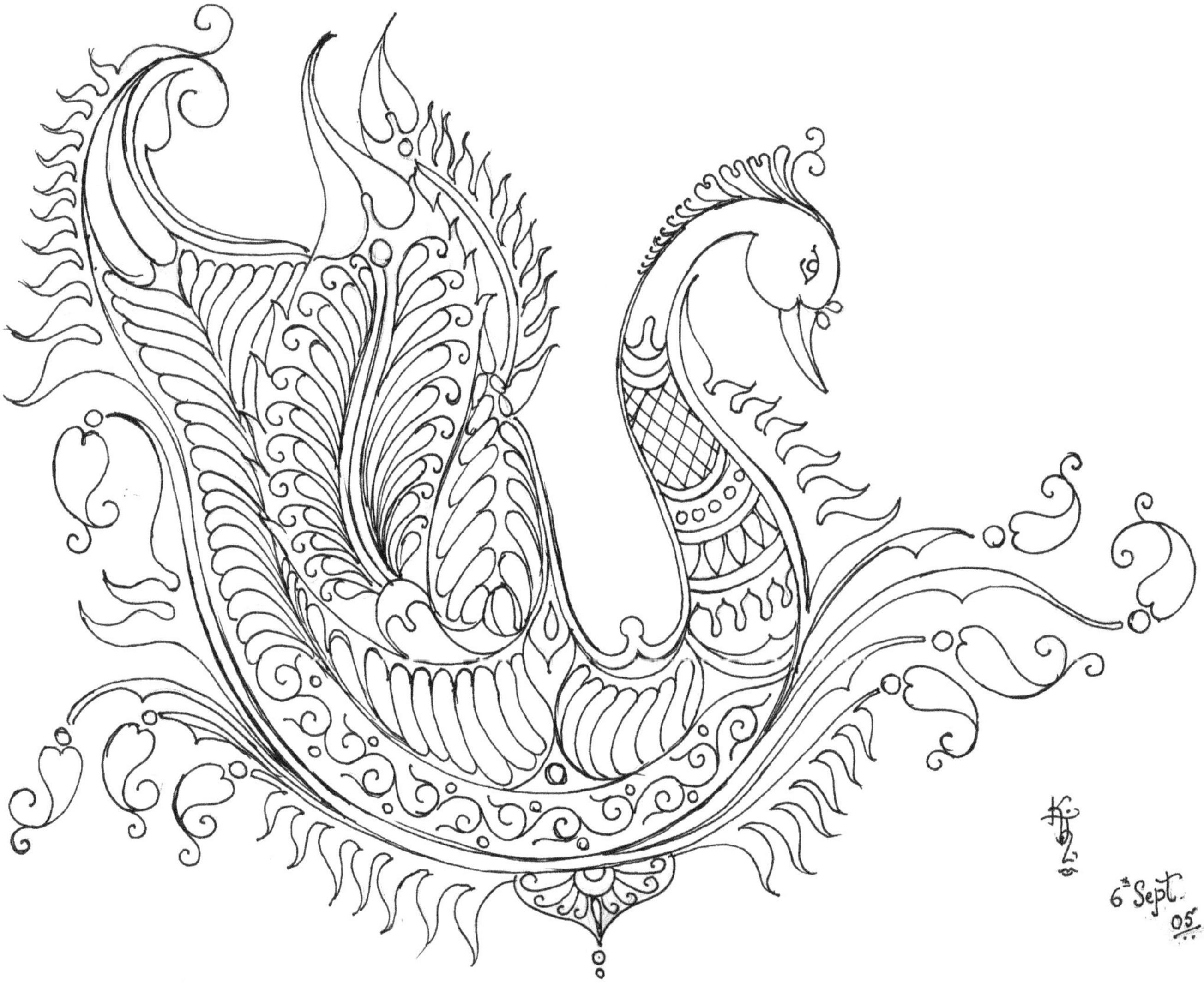
6th Sept.
05.

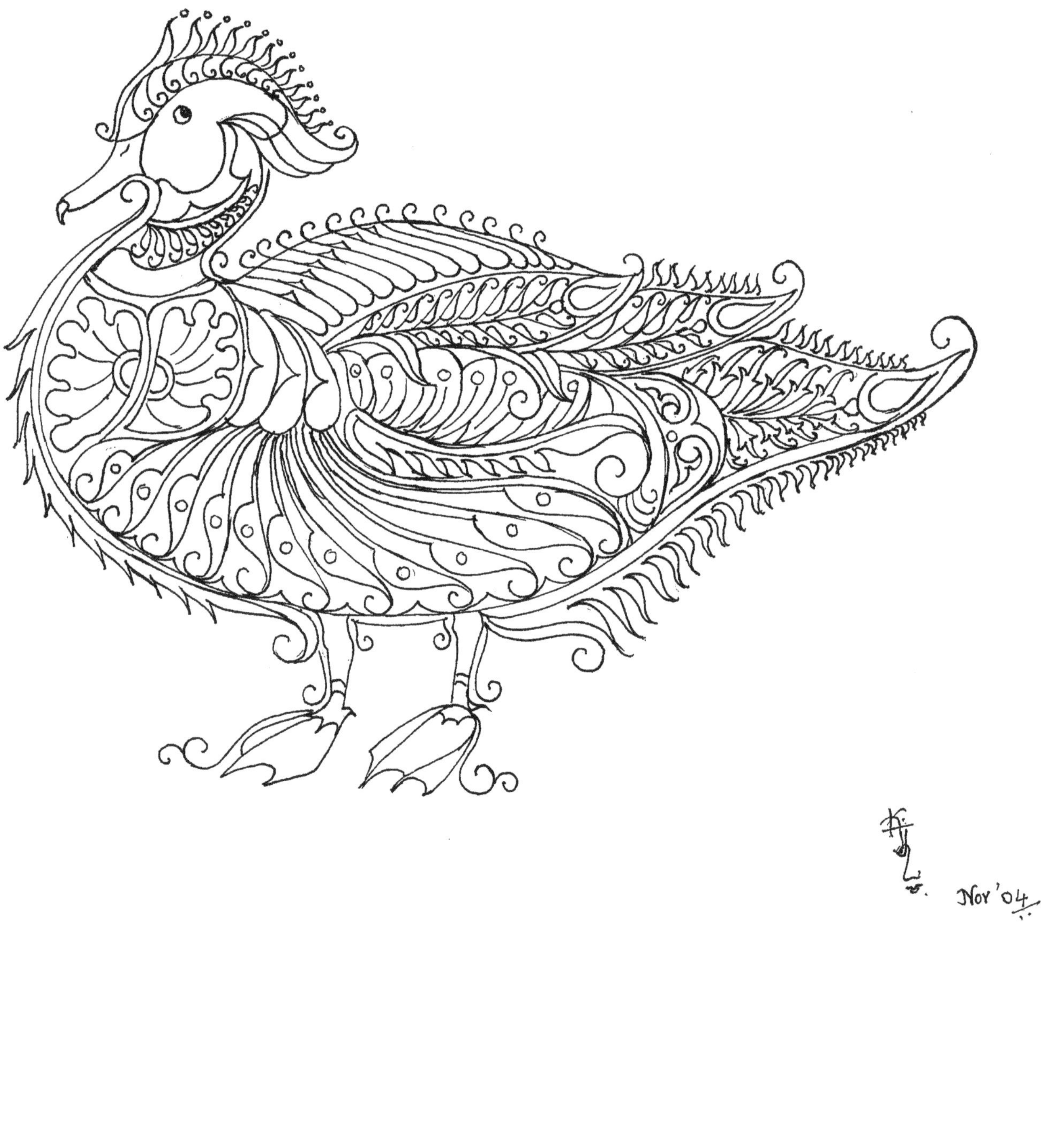
Nov '04

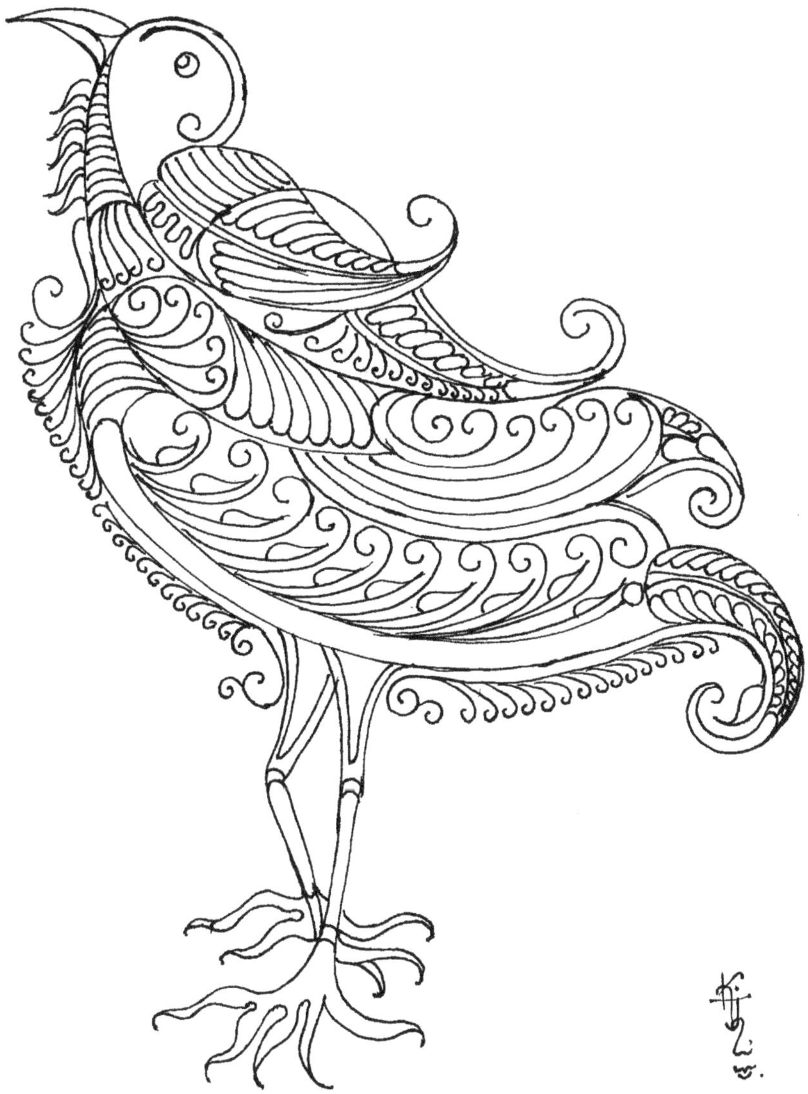

Calcutta Crow

7 Feb 06

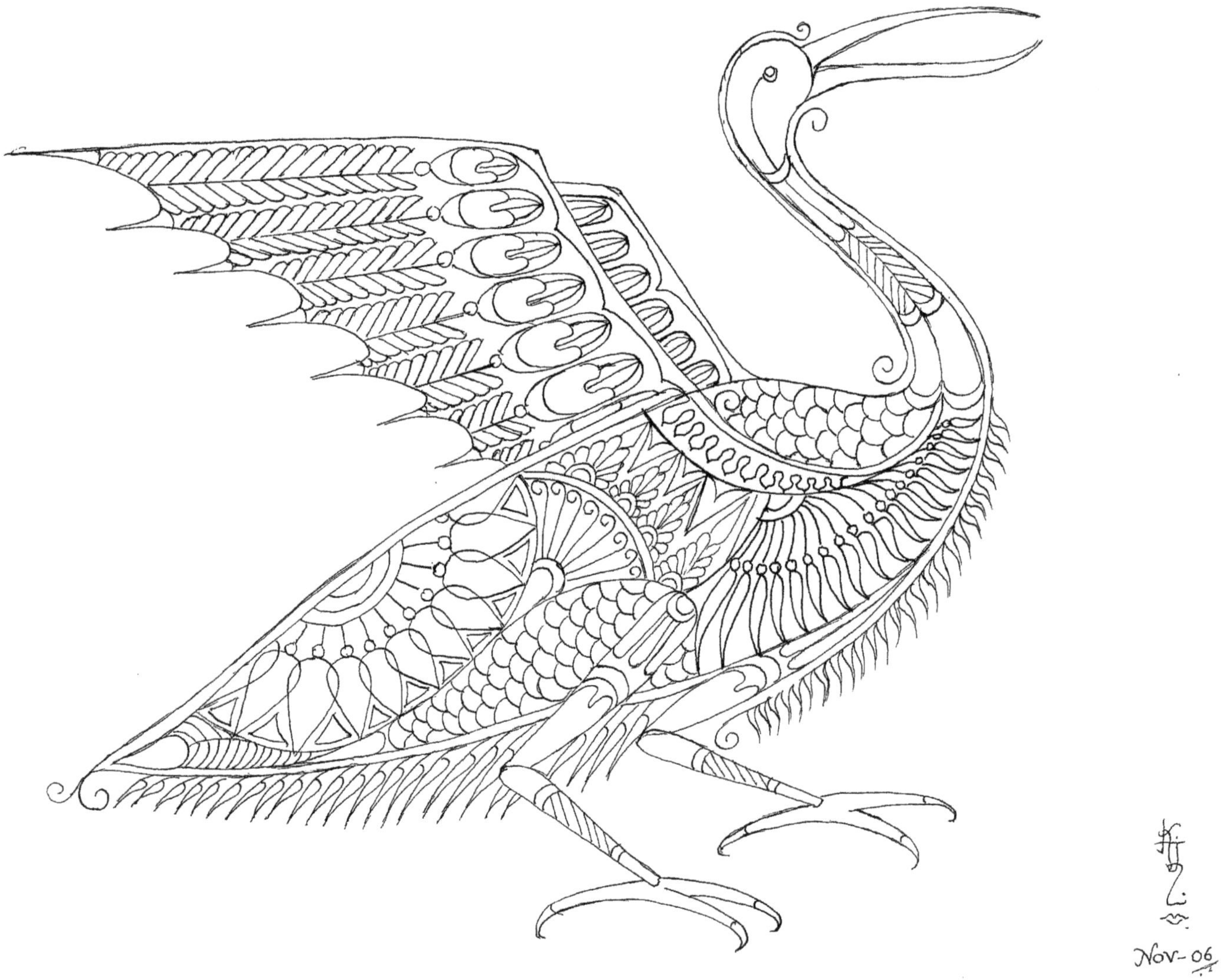
Nov-06

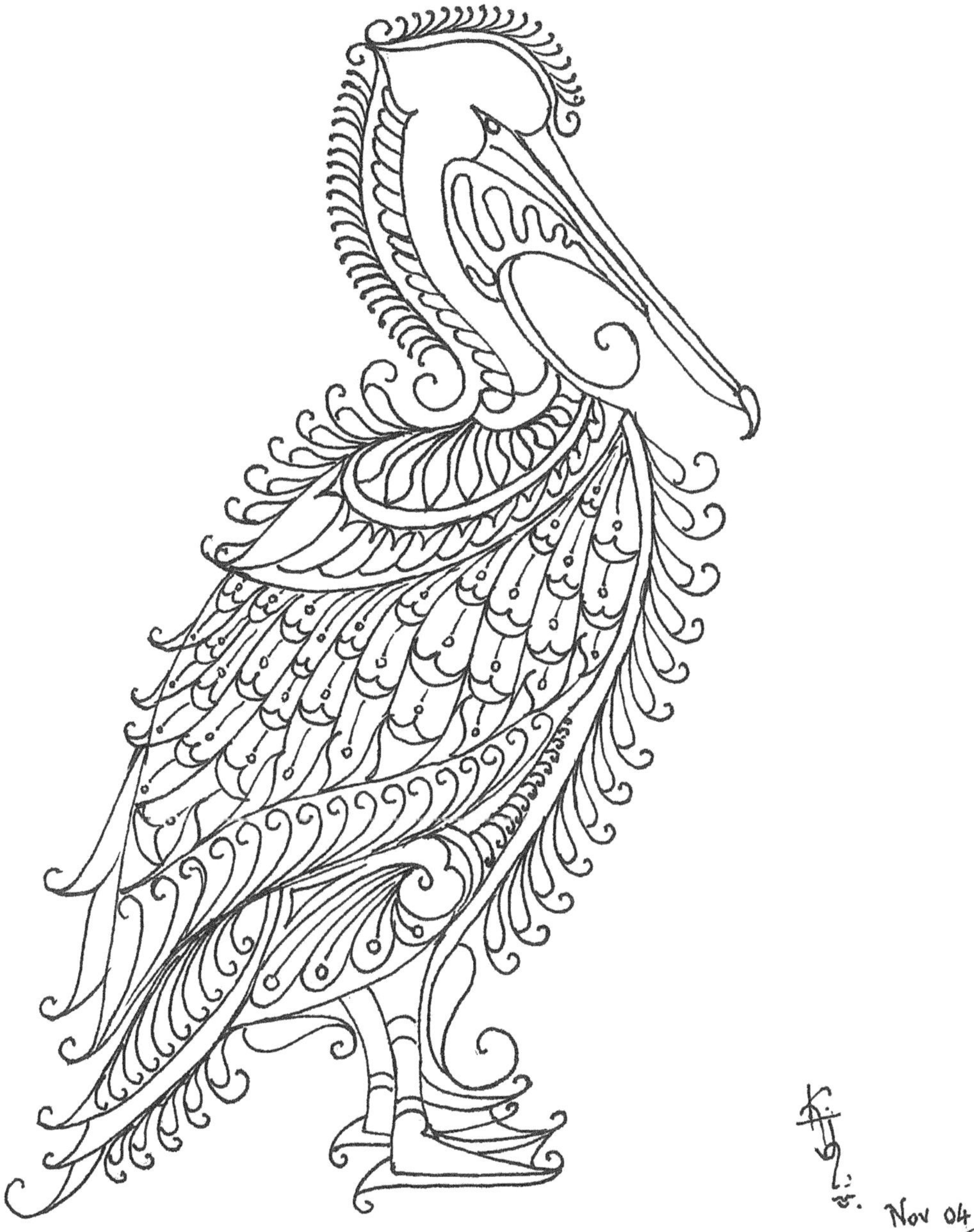
Nov 04

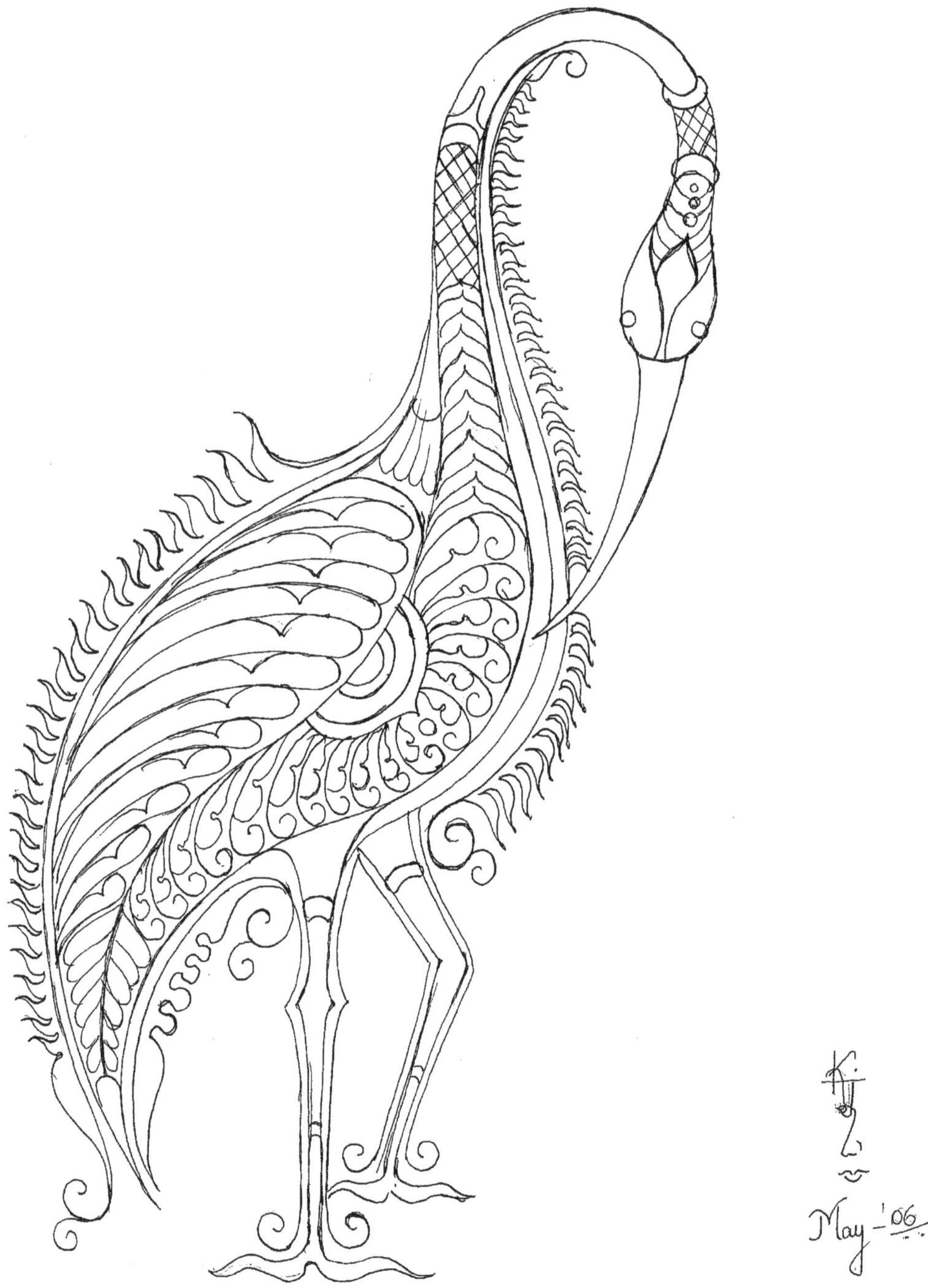
May-'06

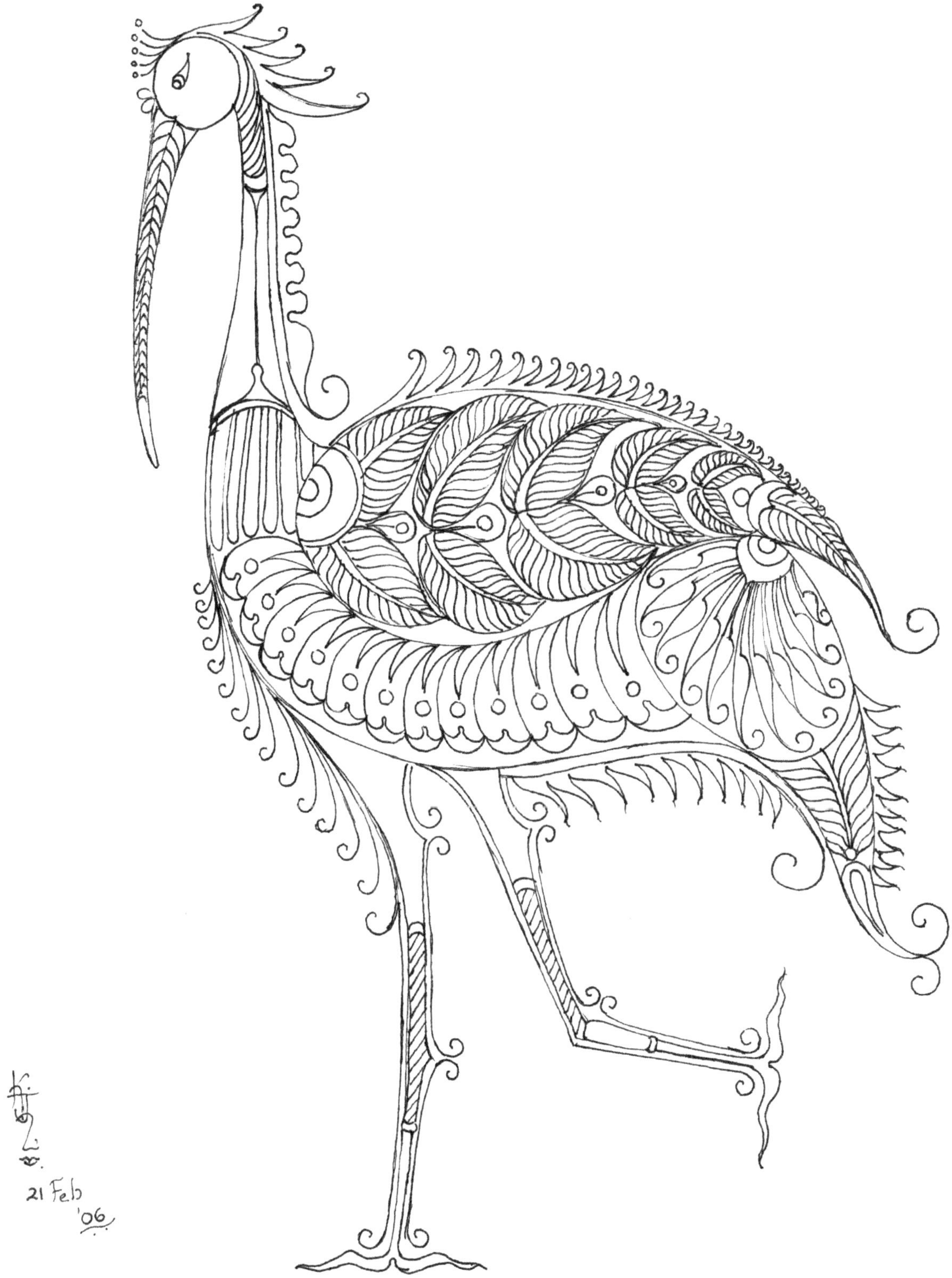
21 Feb
'06

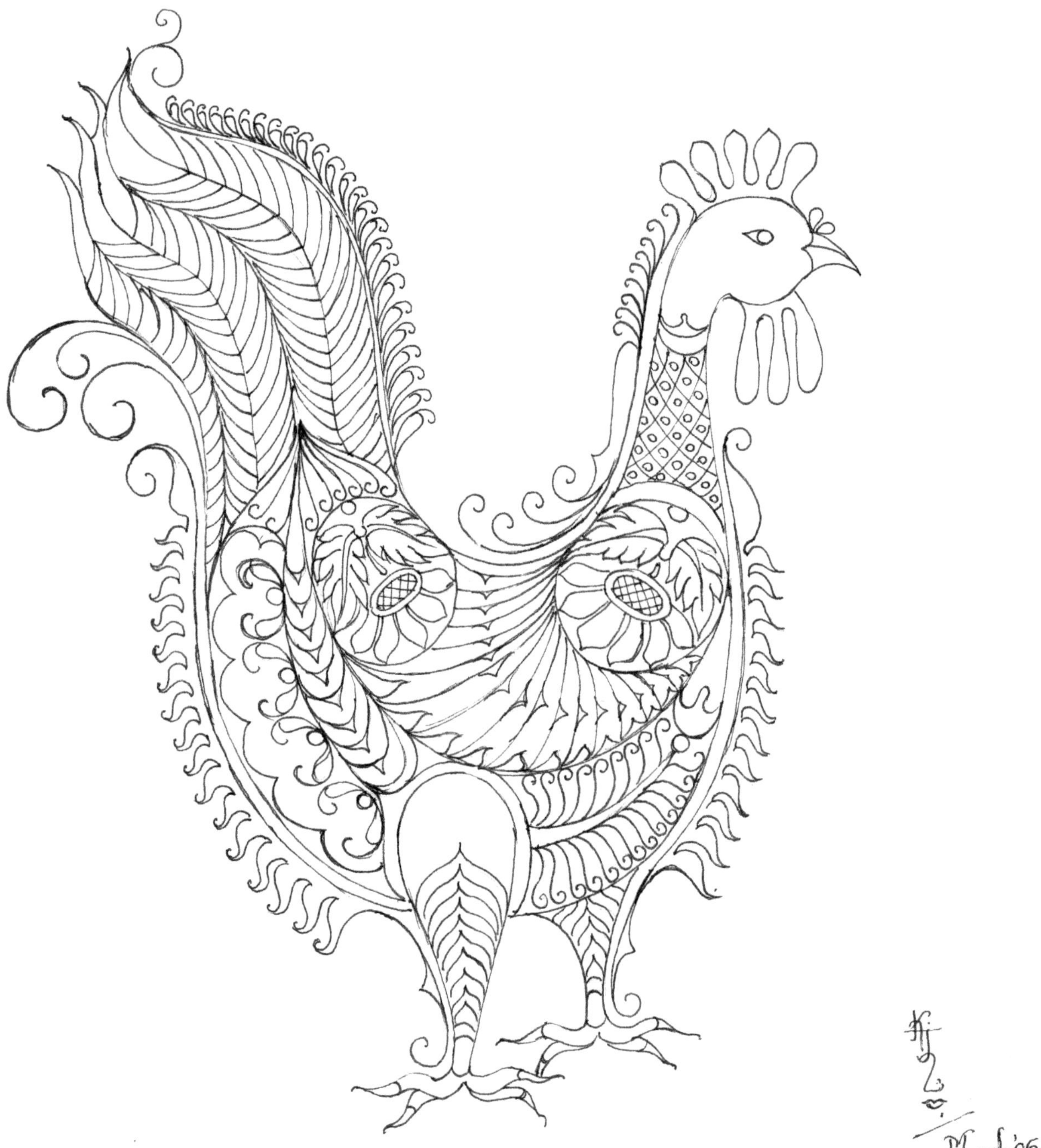

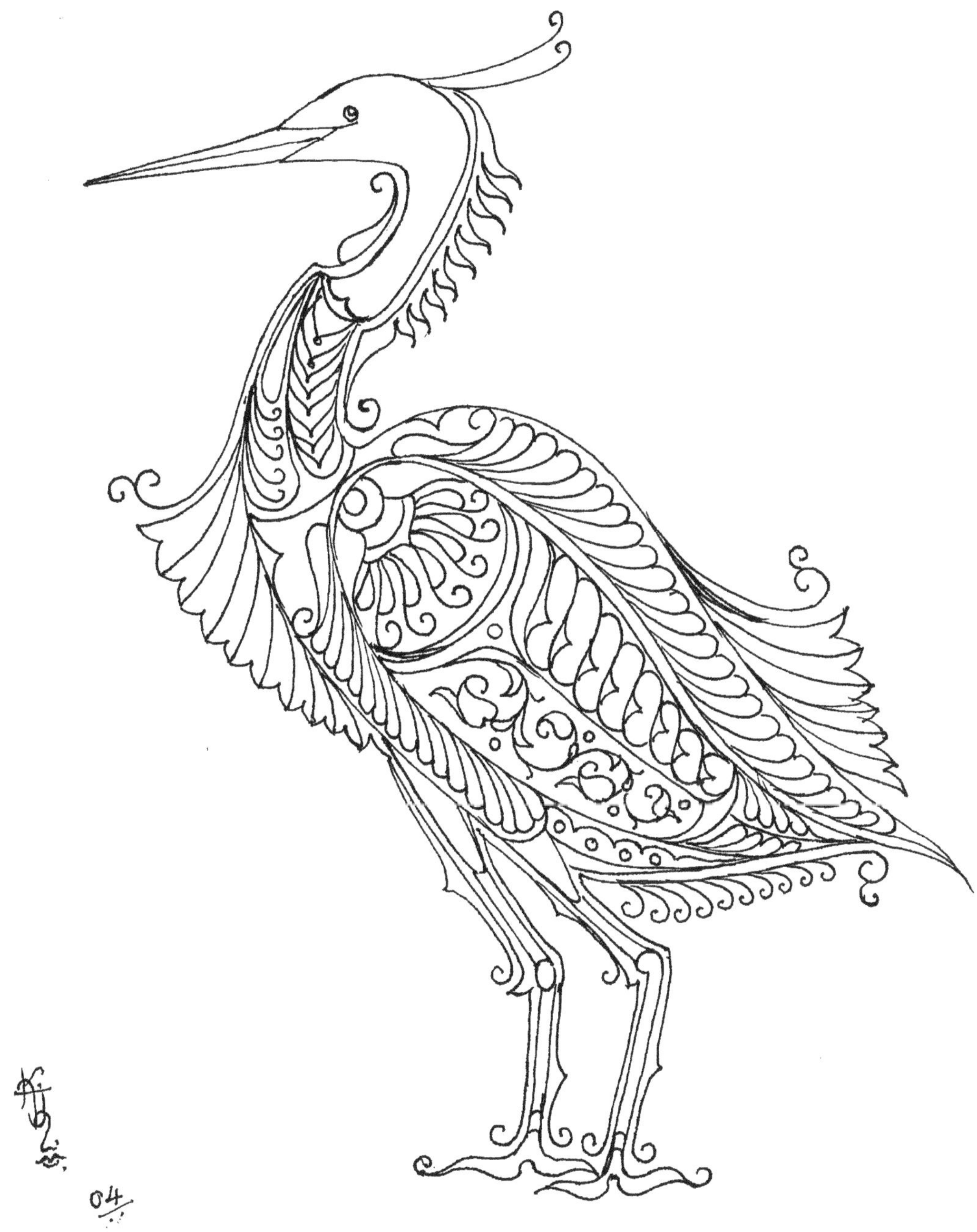

Animals

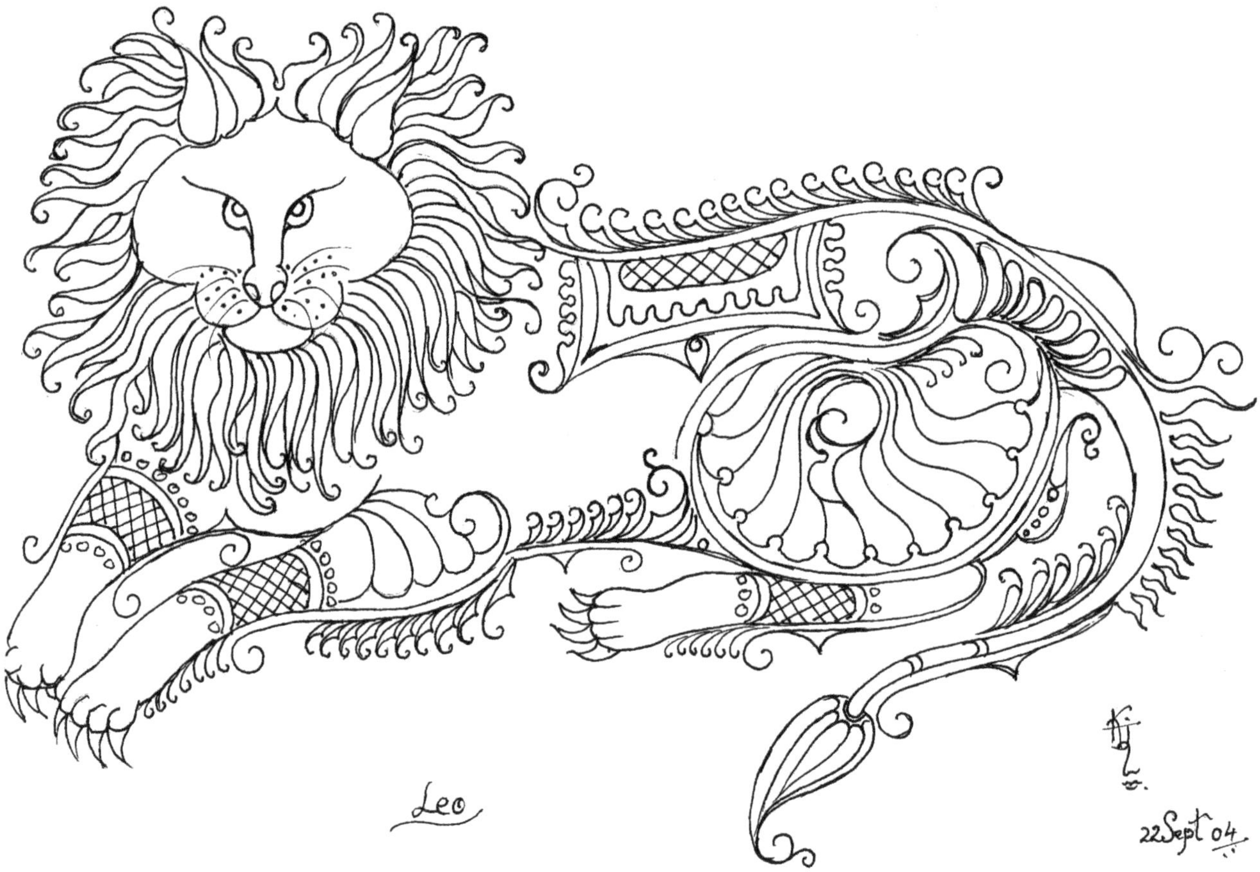

Leo

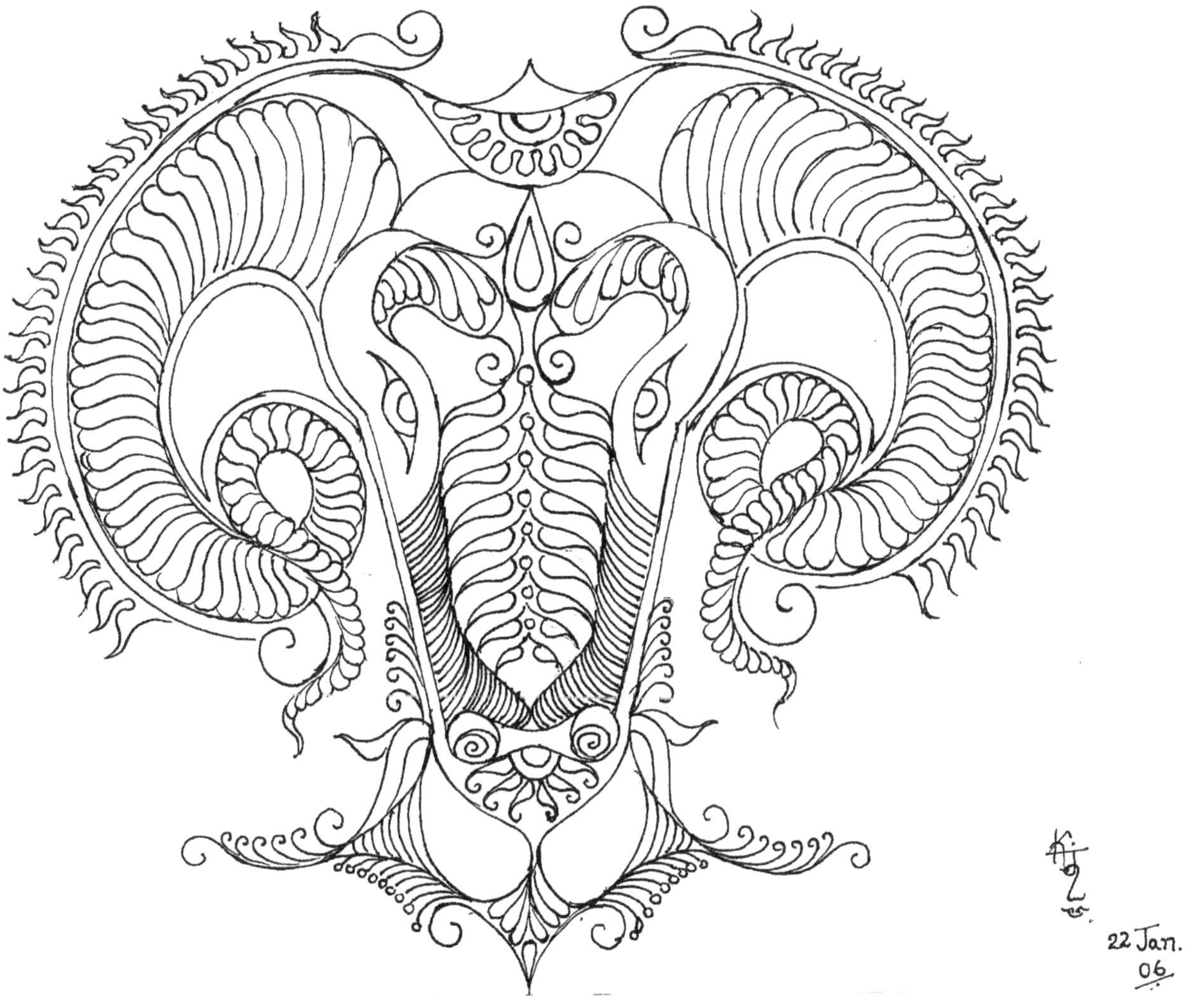
22 Jan.
06

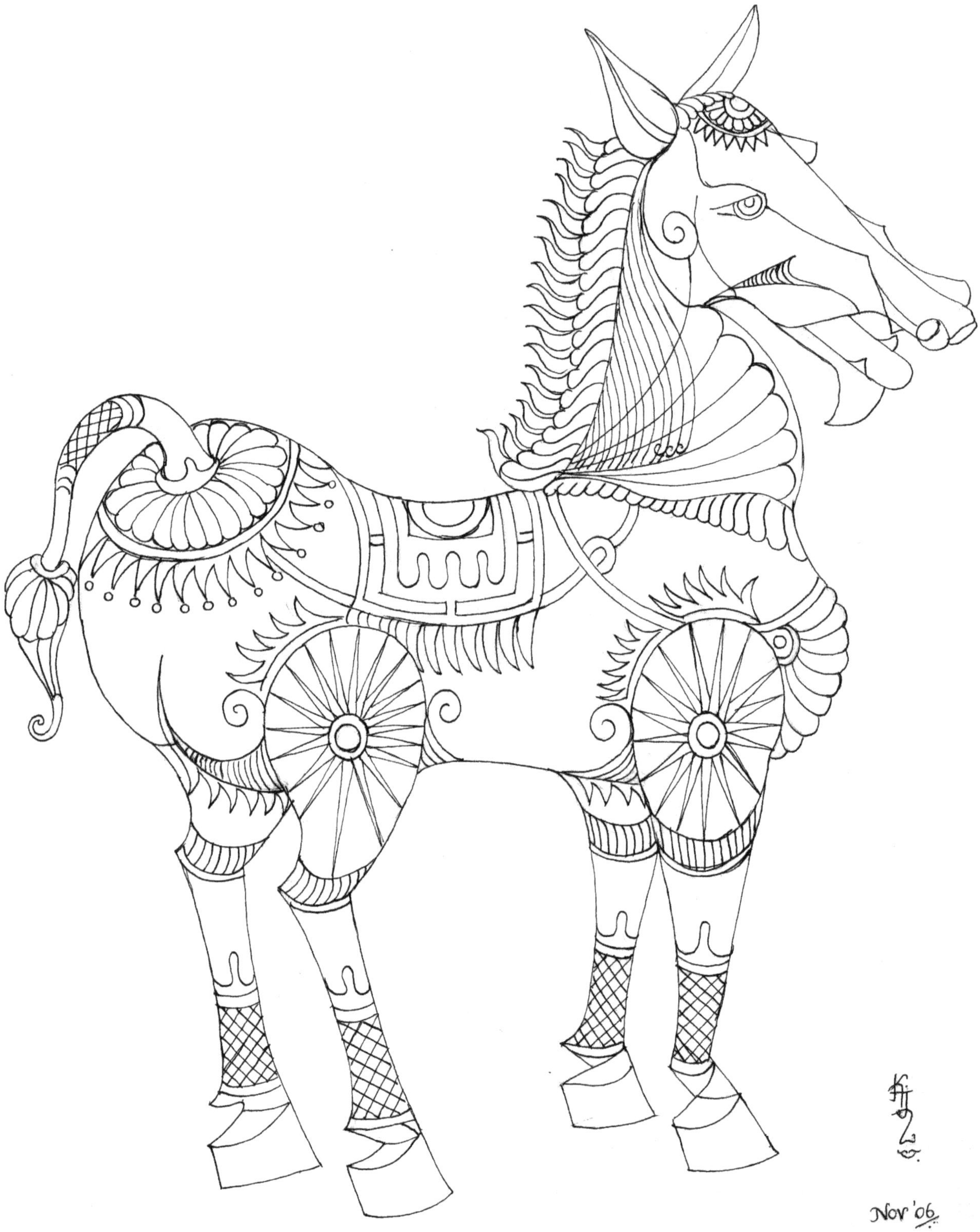
Nov '06

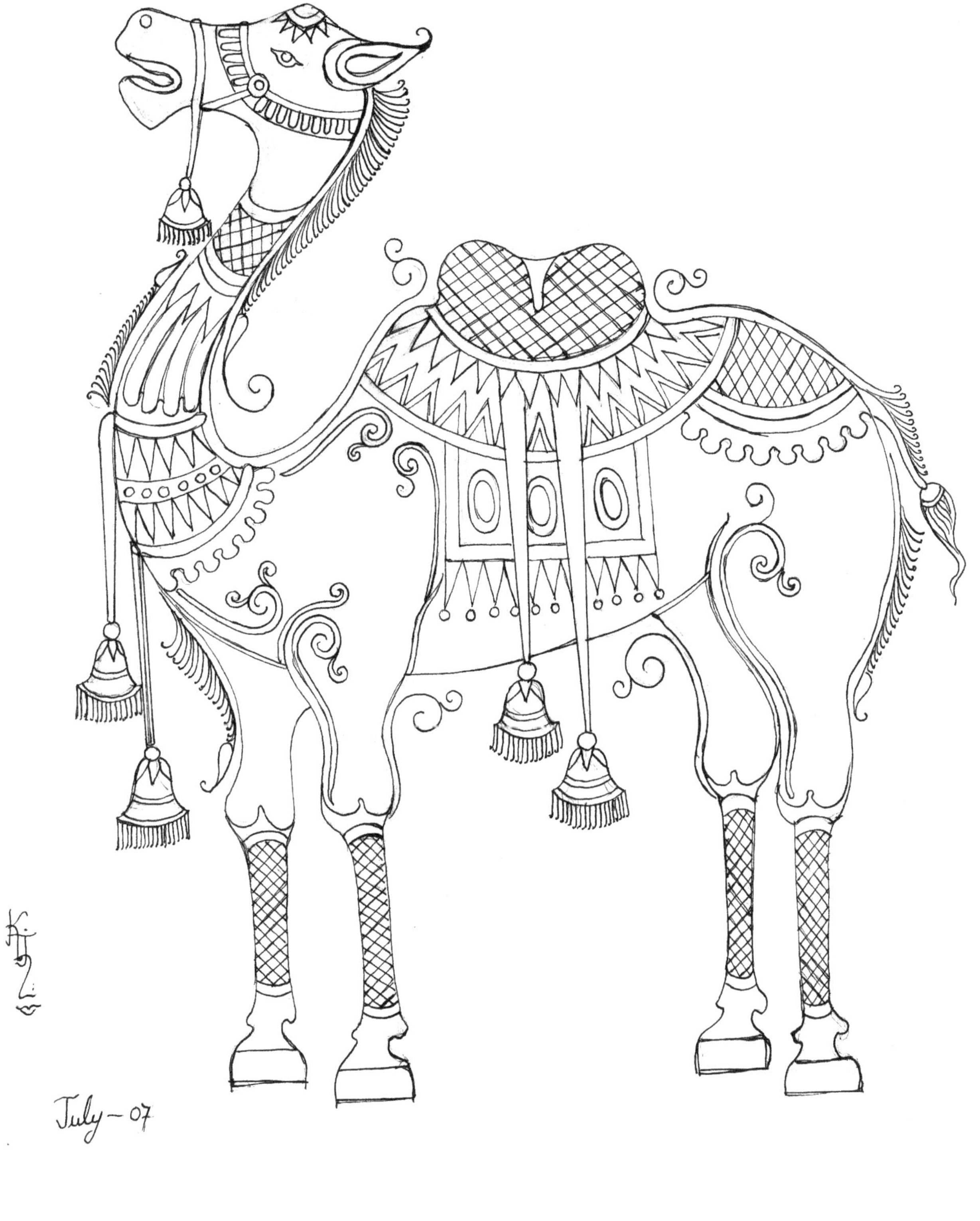
July – 07

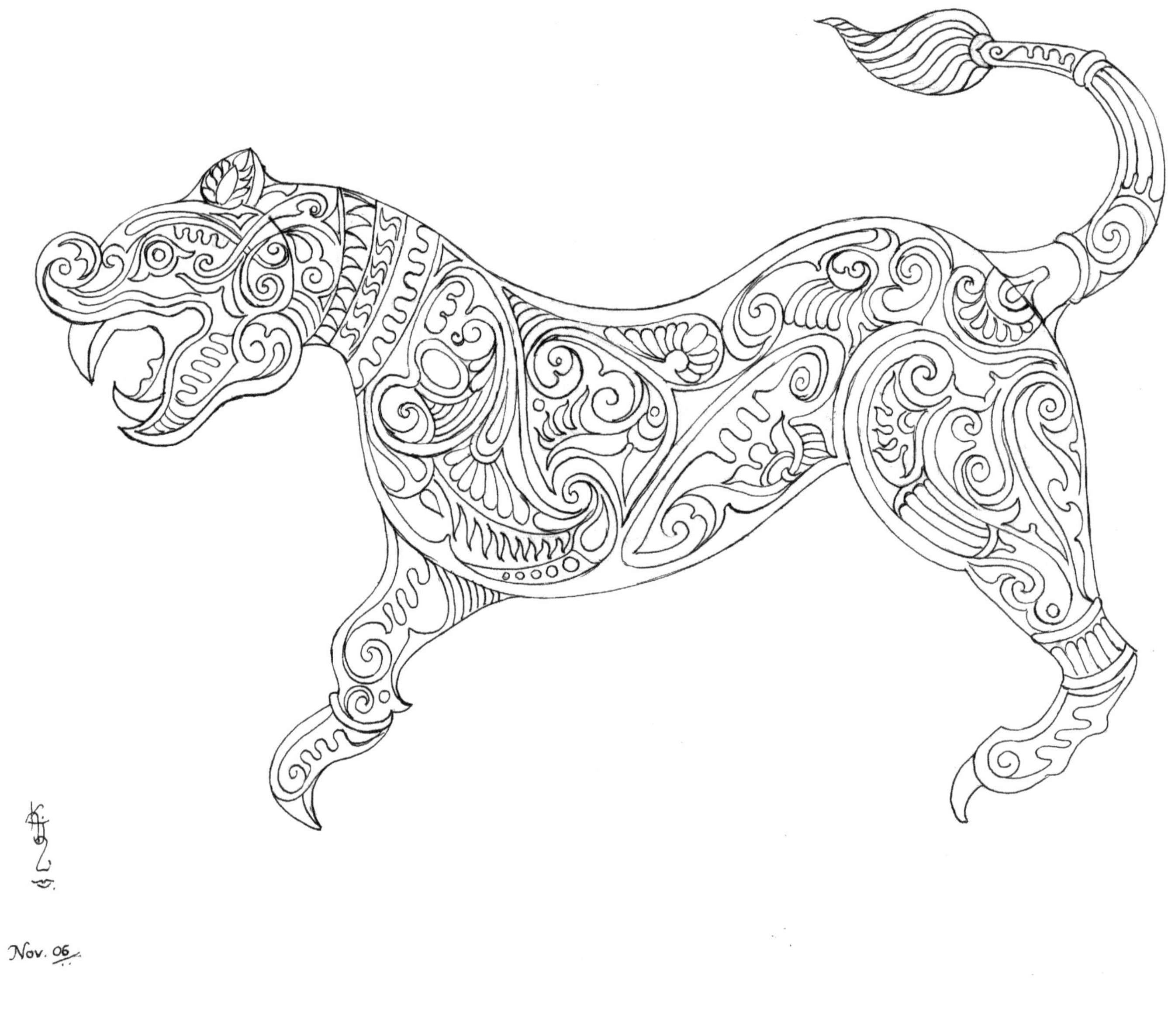

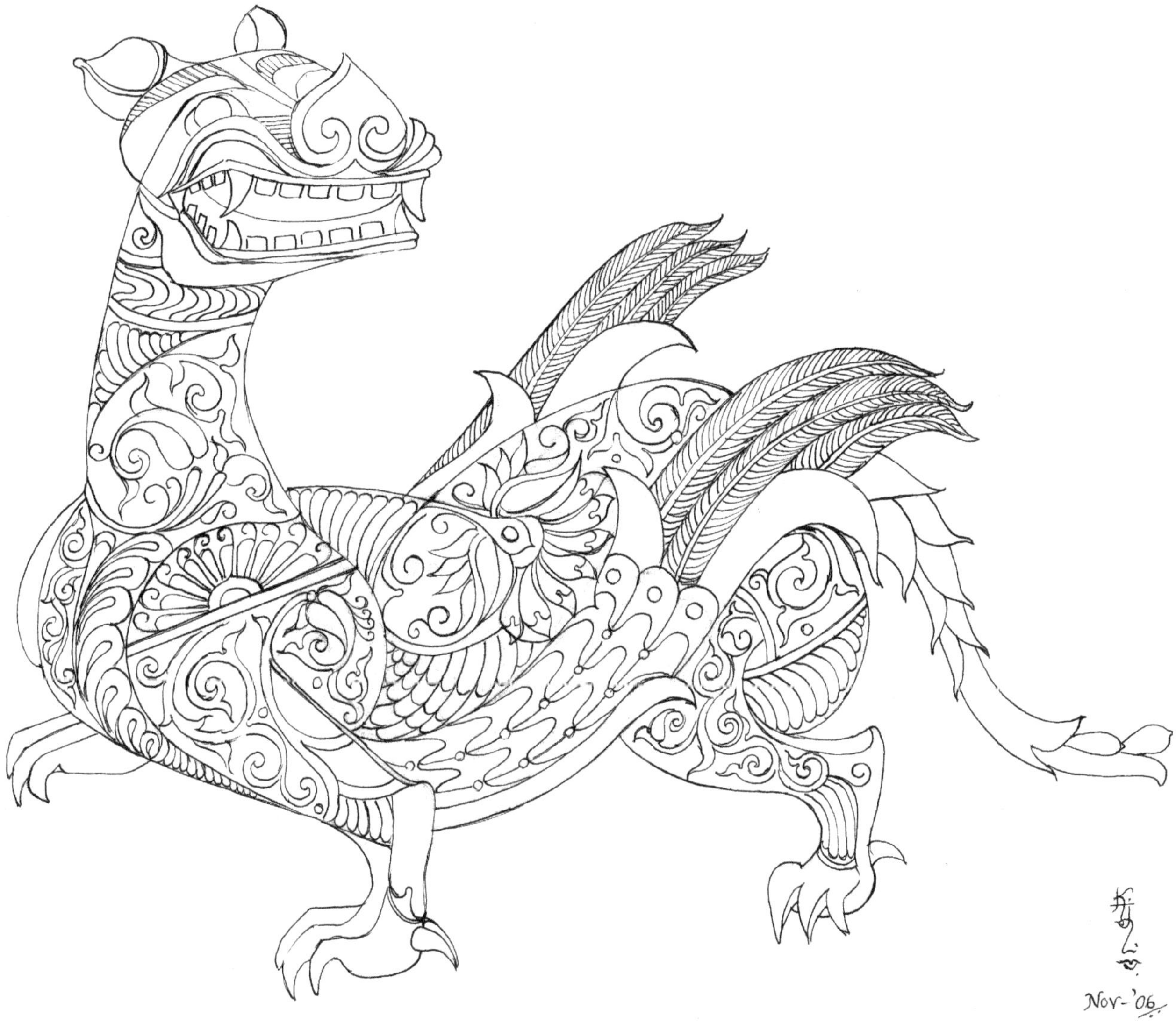

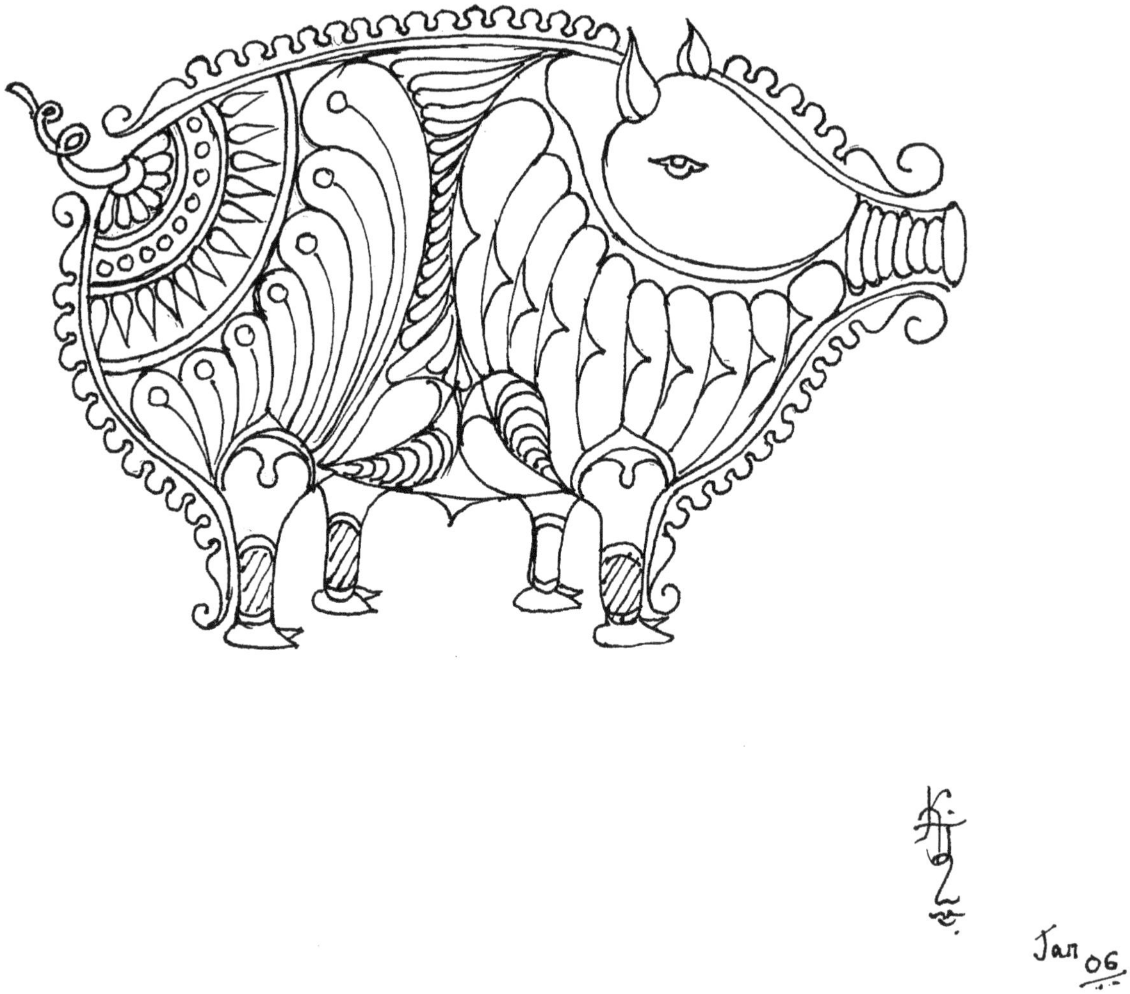
Jan 06

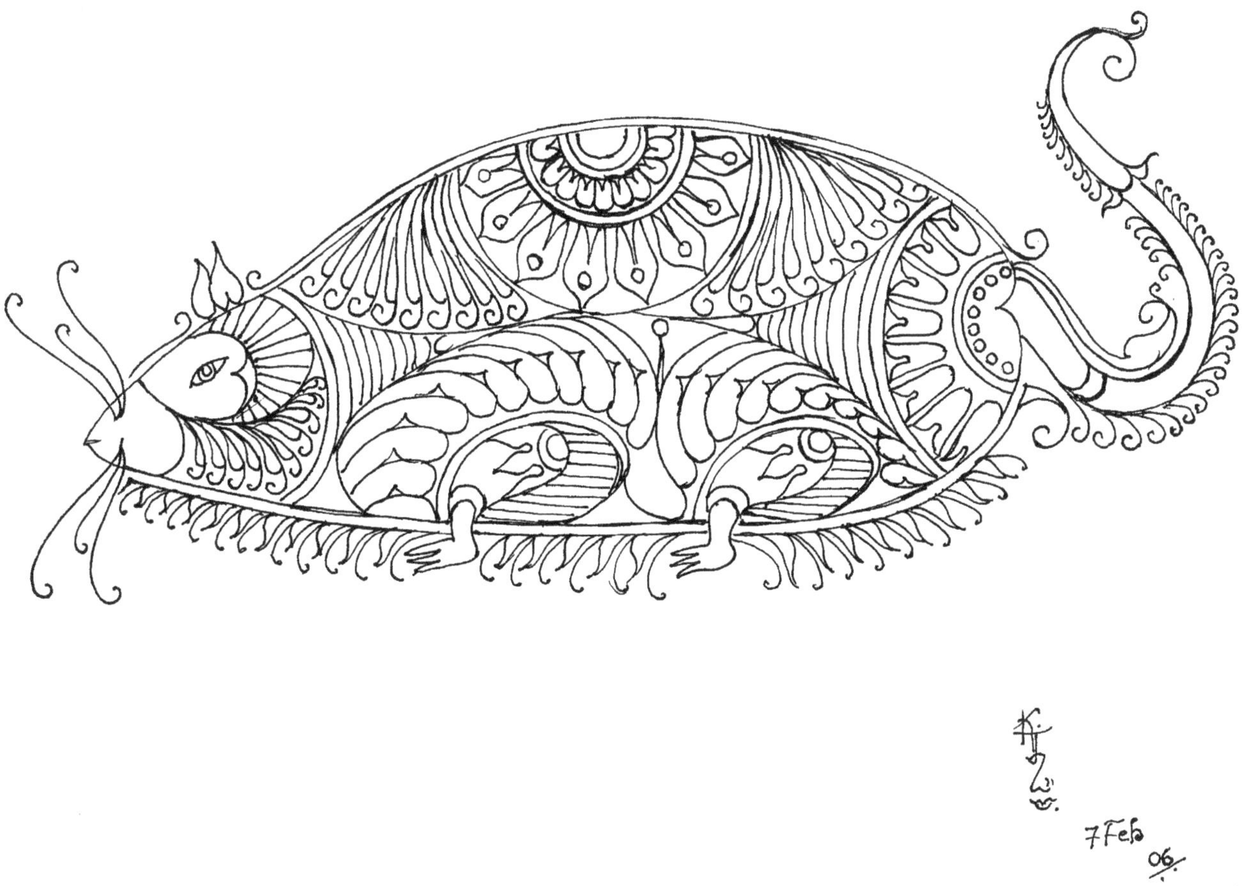
7 Feb
06

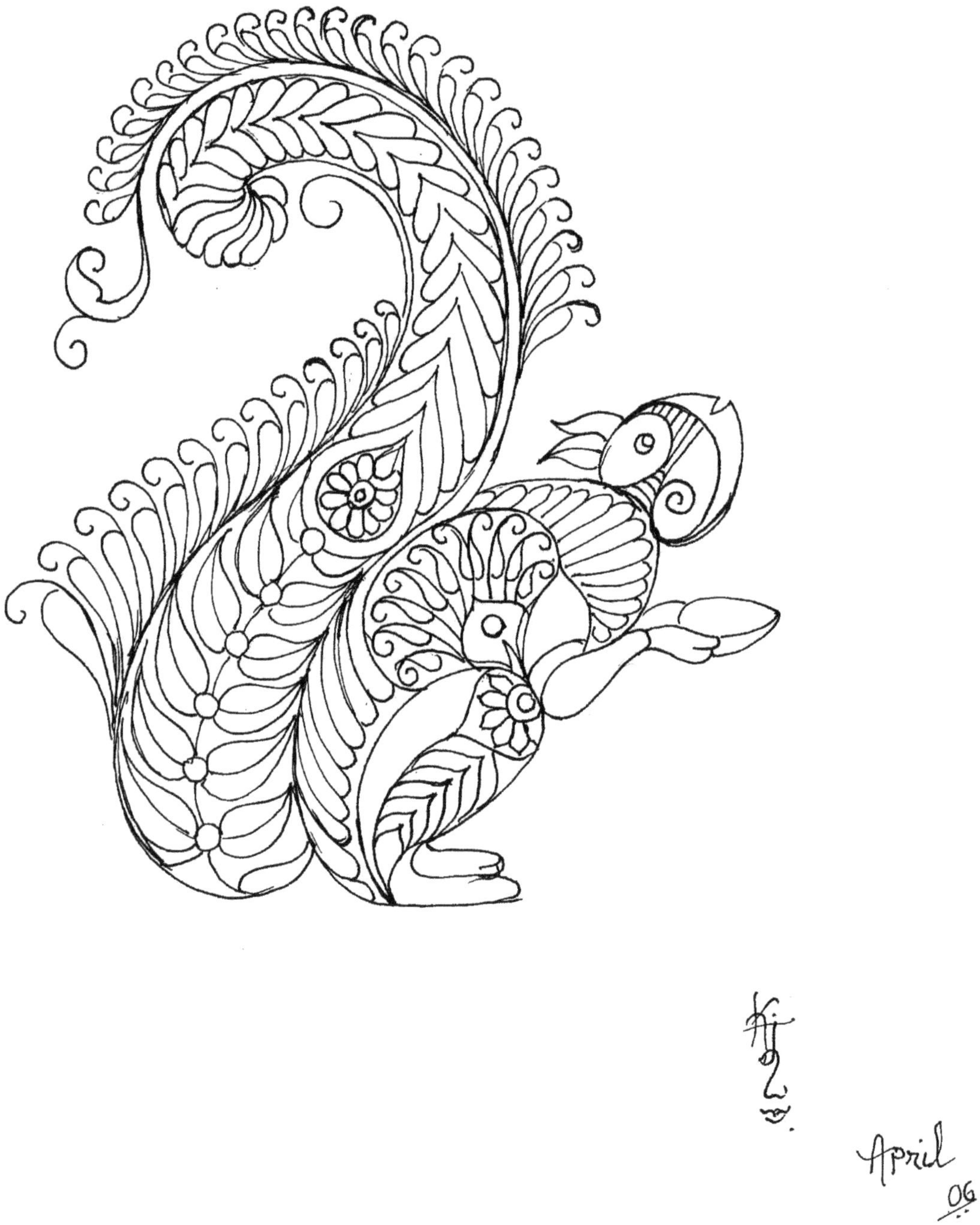
April
06

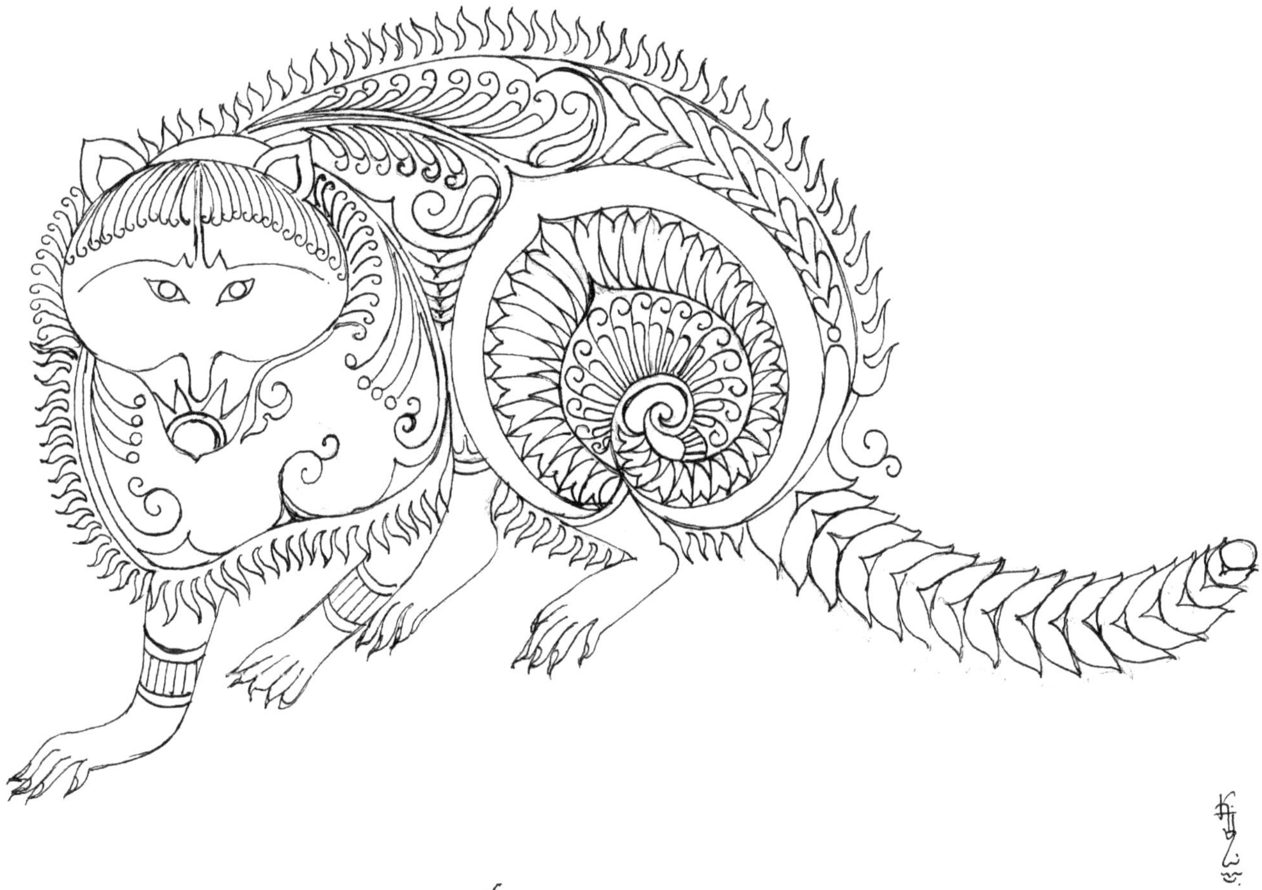

Raccoon

July 07

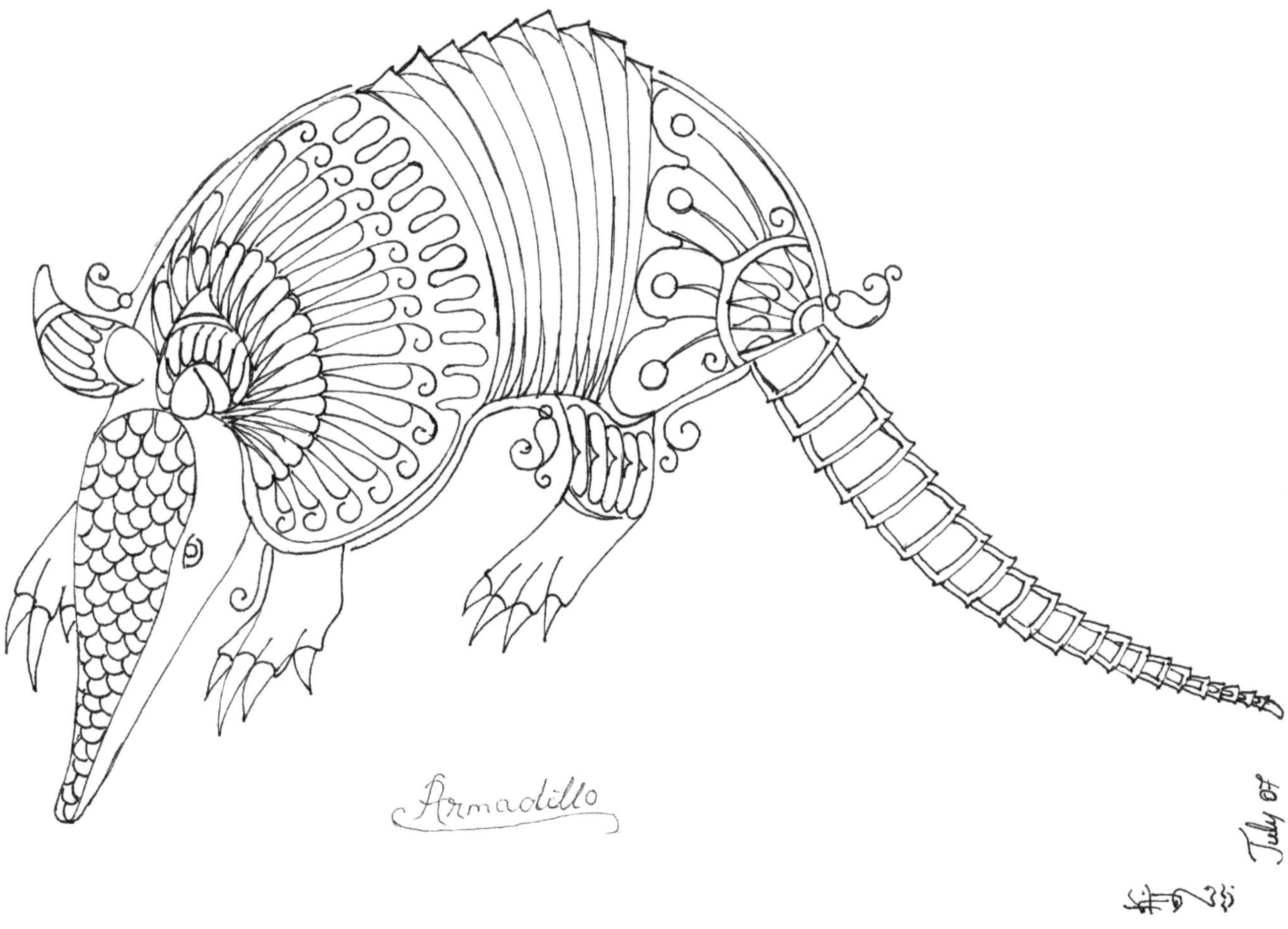
Armadillo
July 07

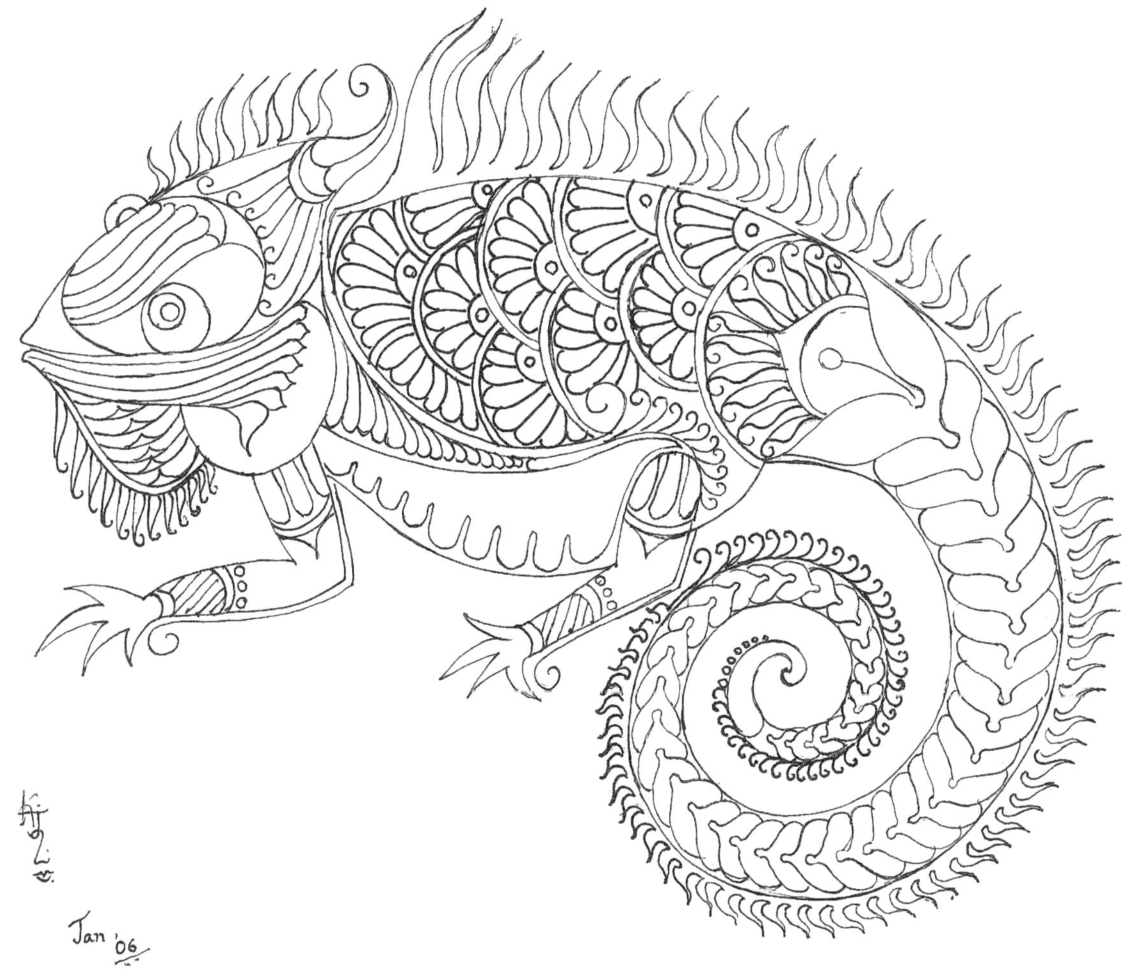

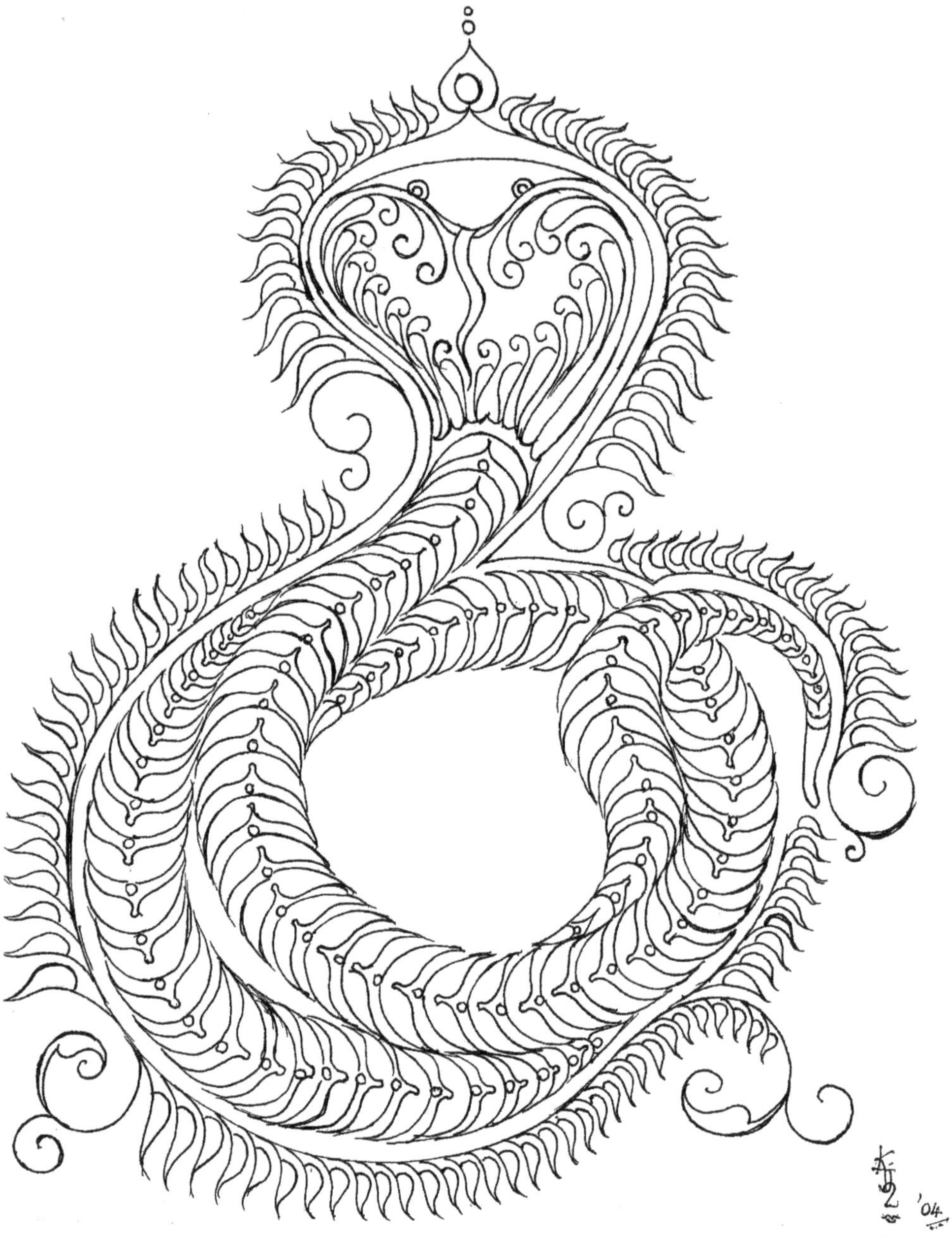

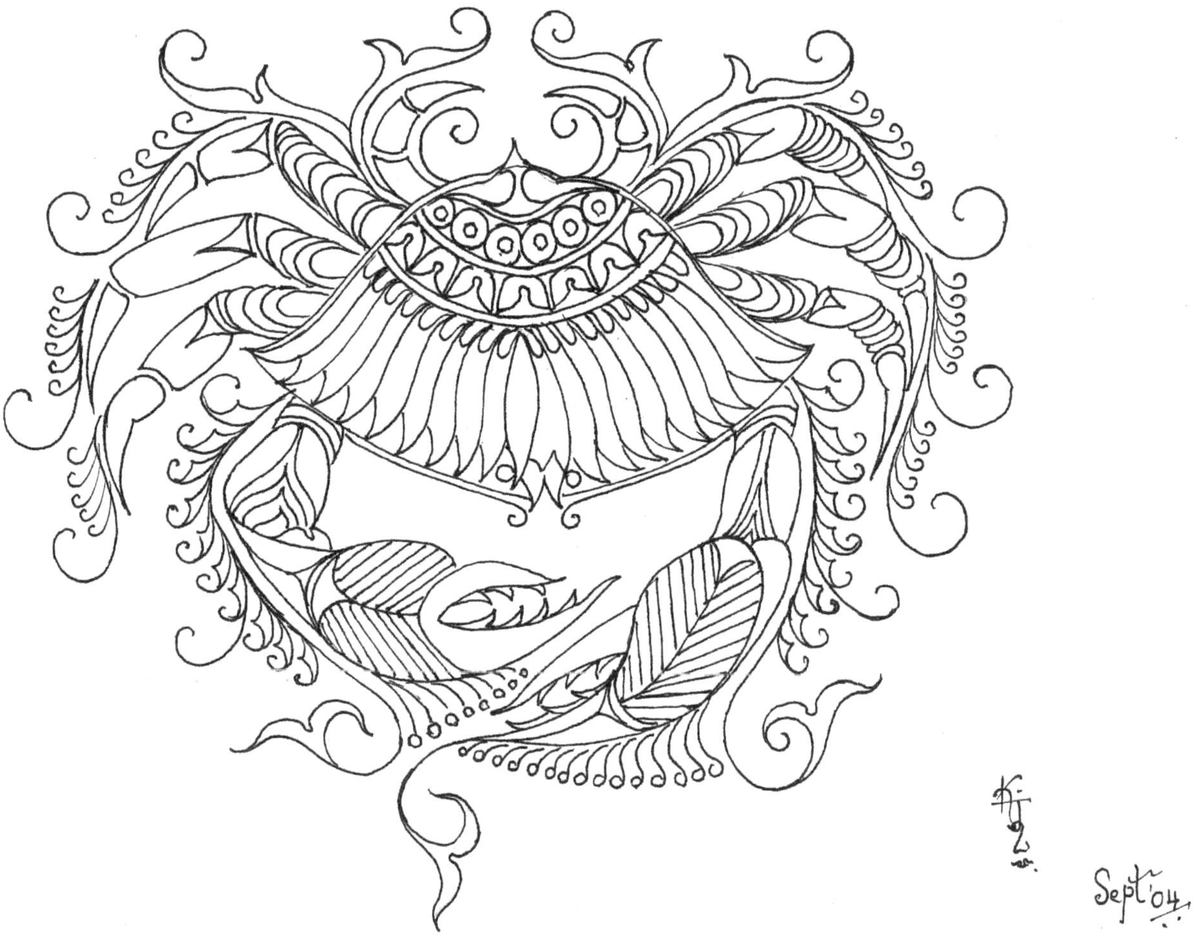
Sept '04

Insects

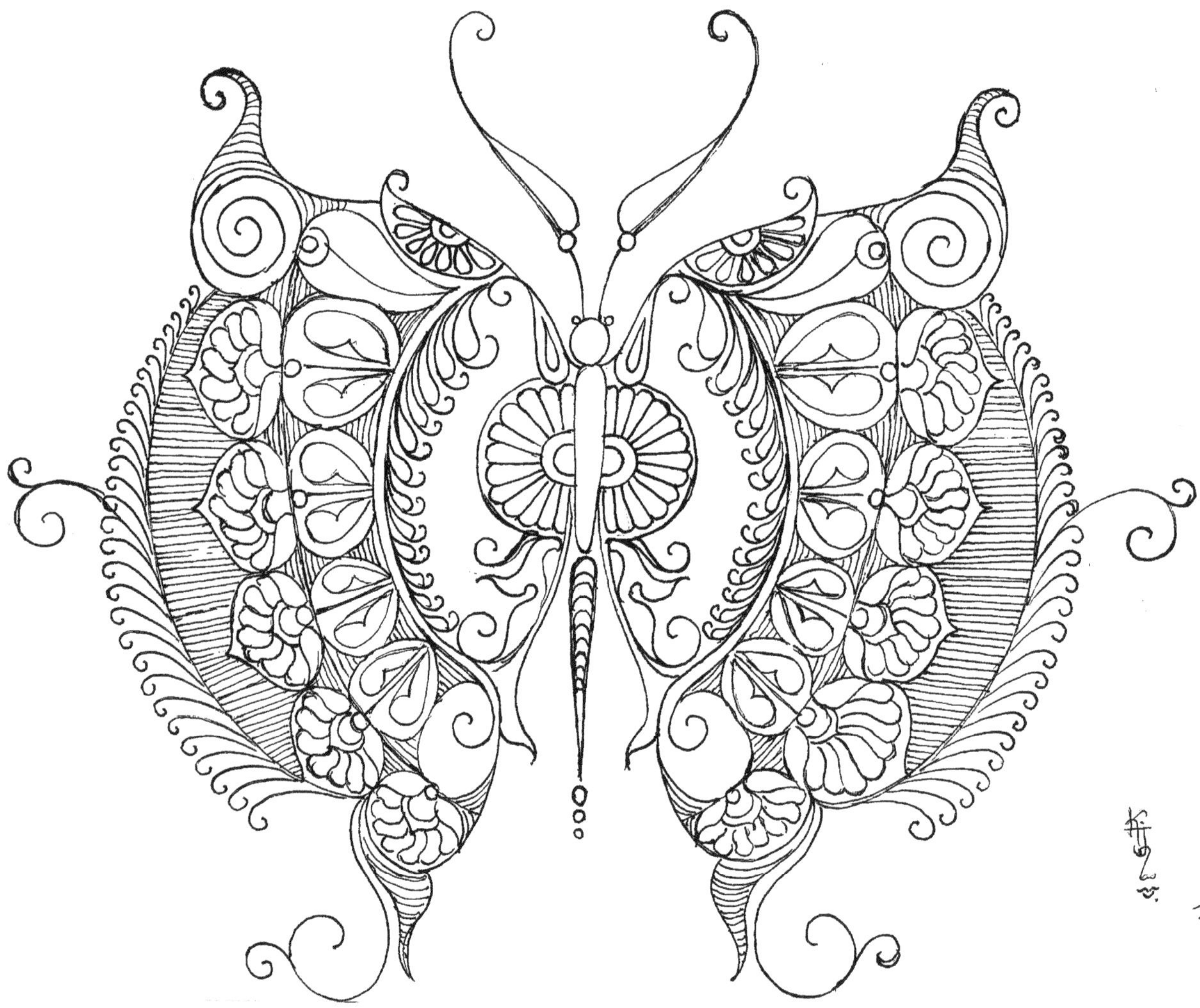

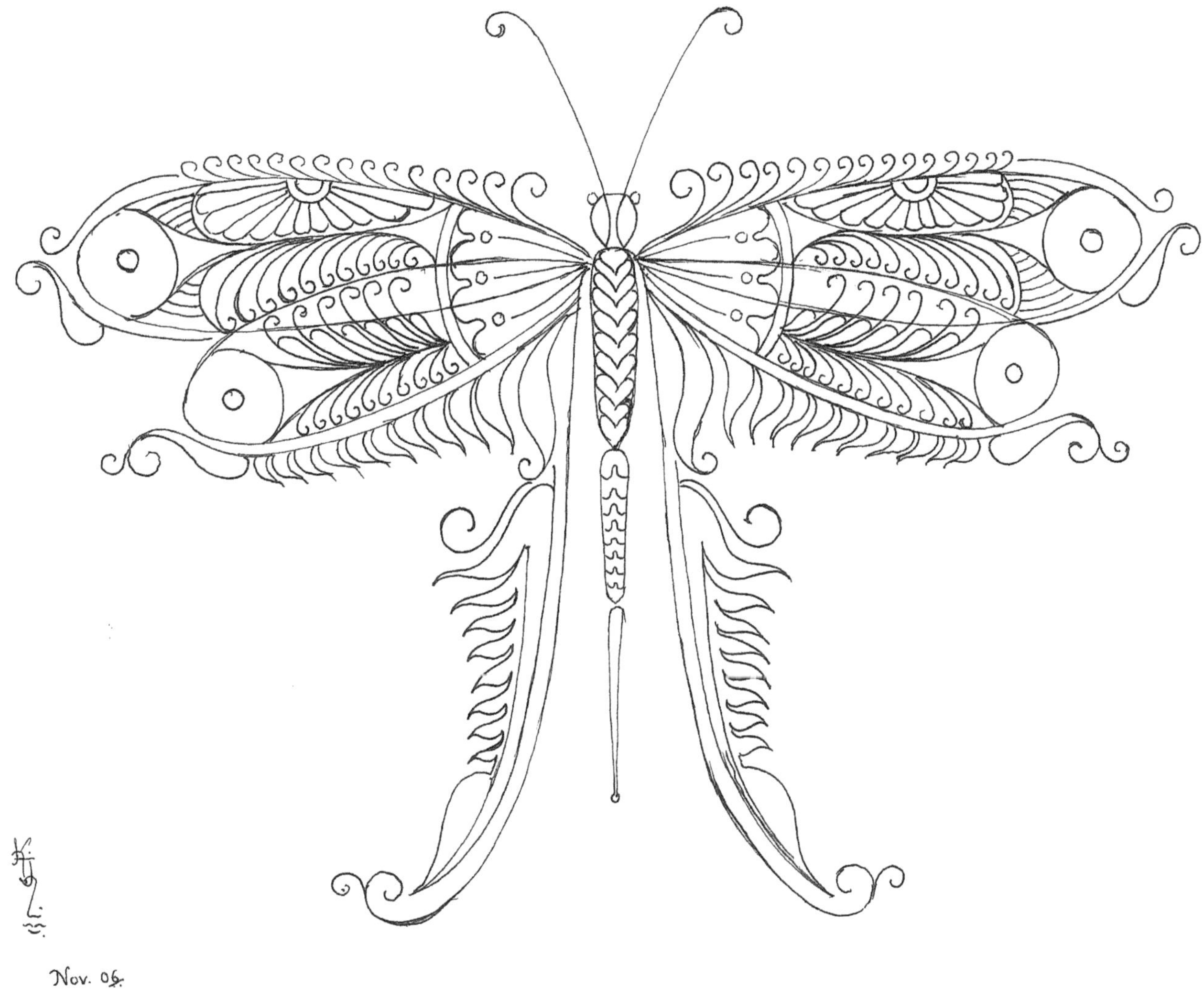
Nov. 06.

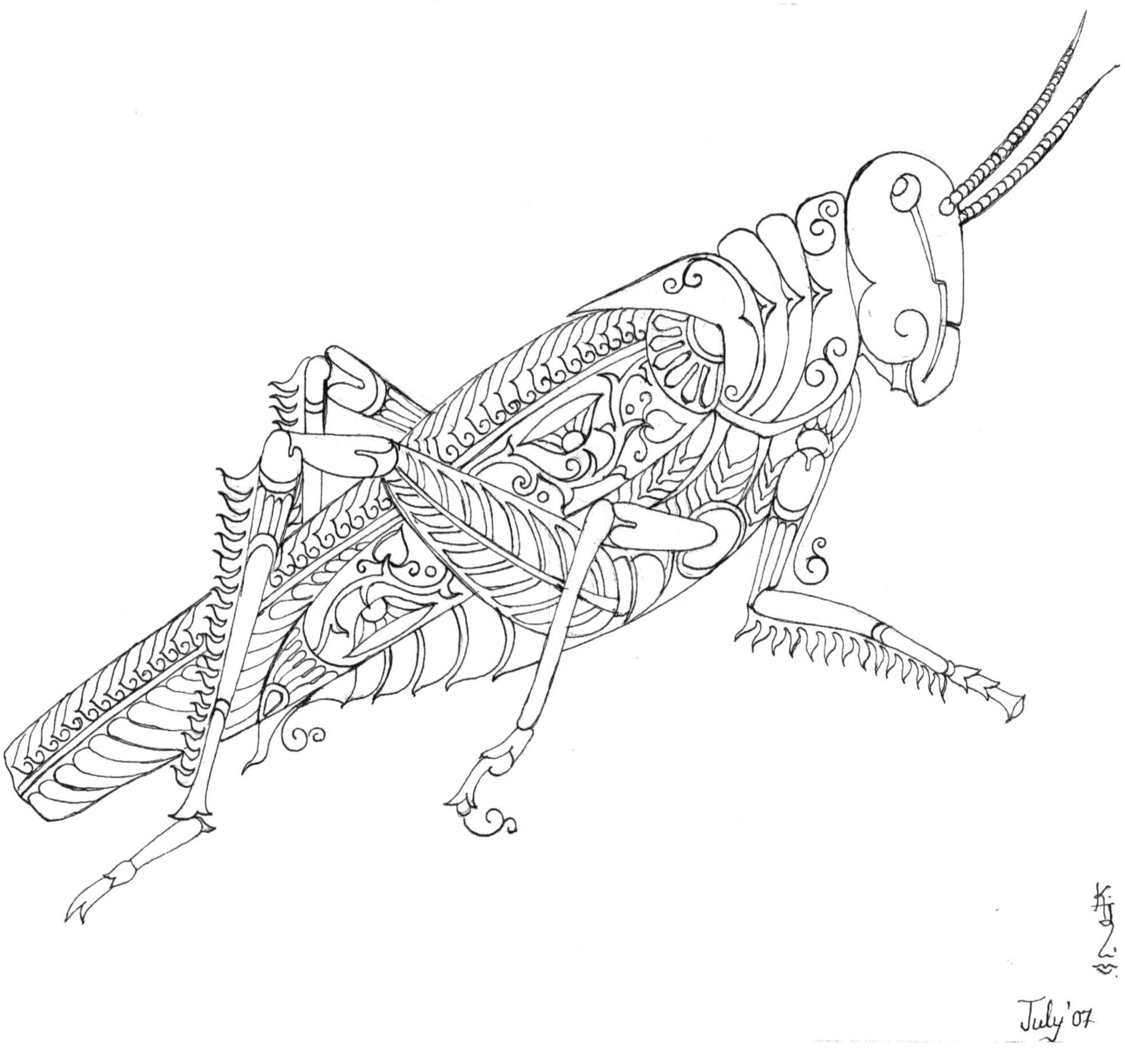
July '07

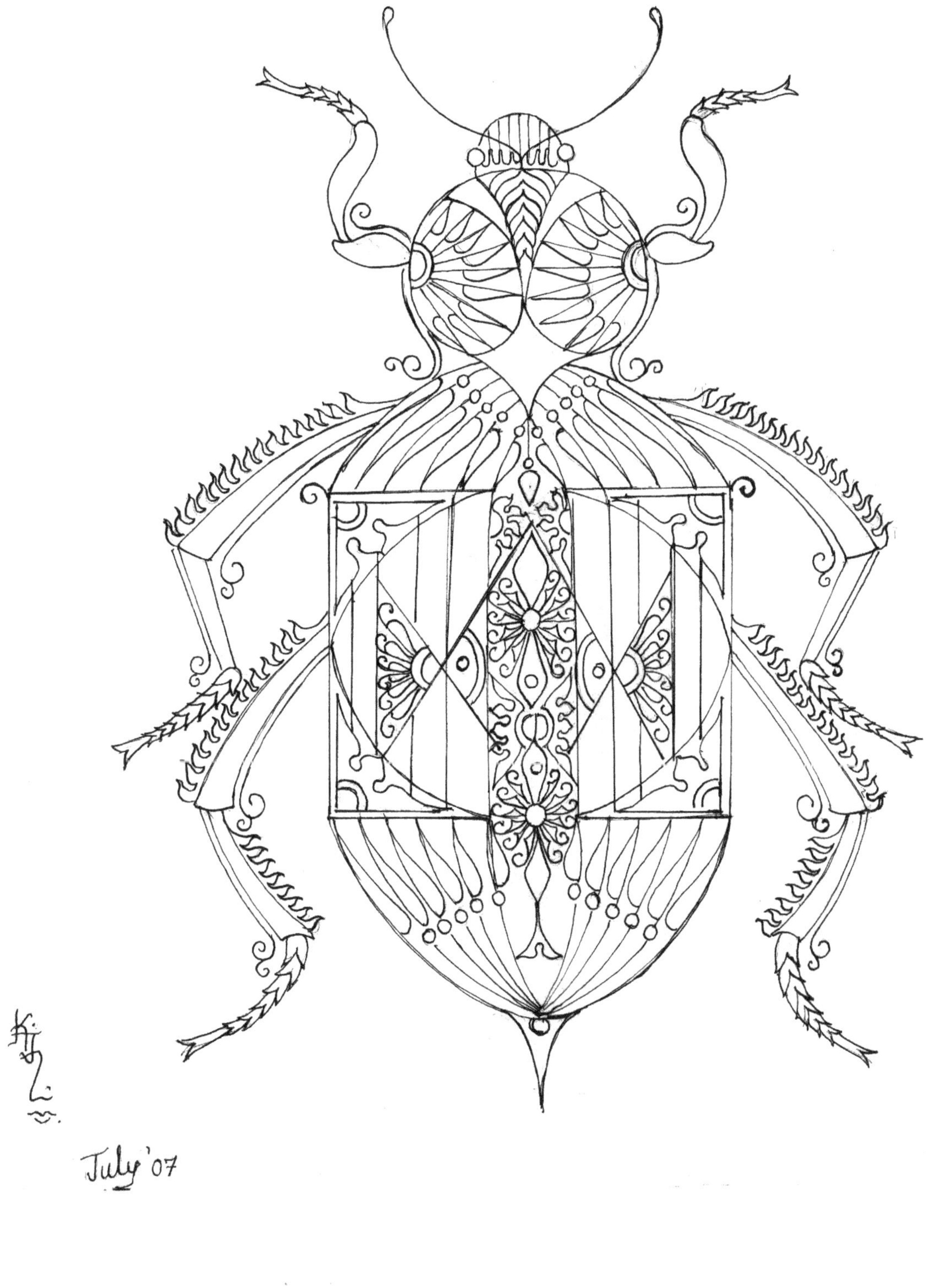
July '07

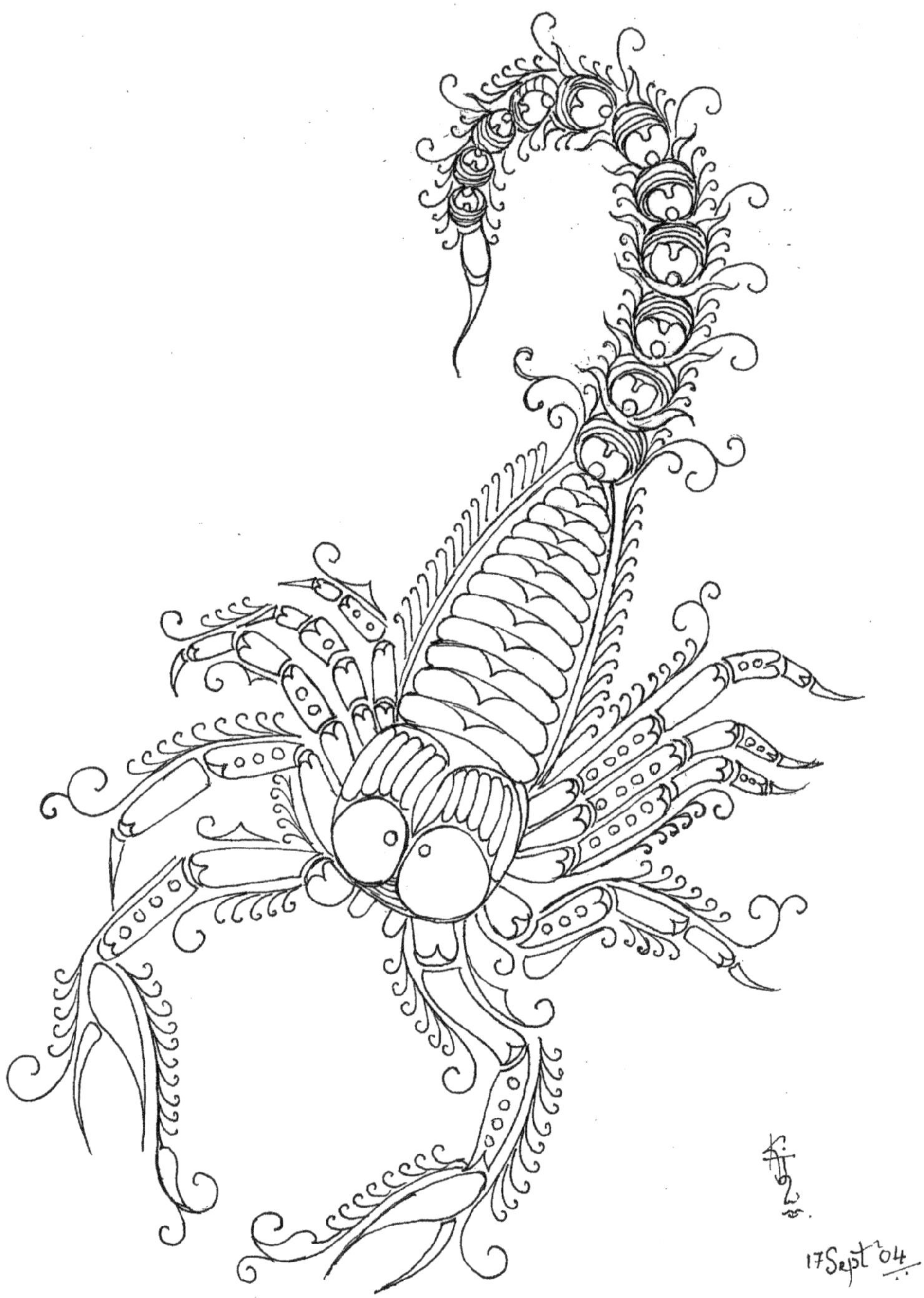
17 Sept '04

Other

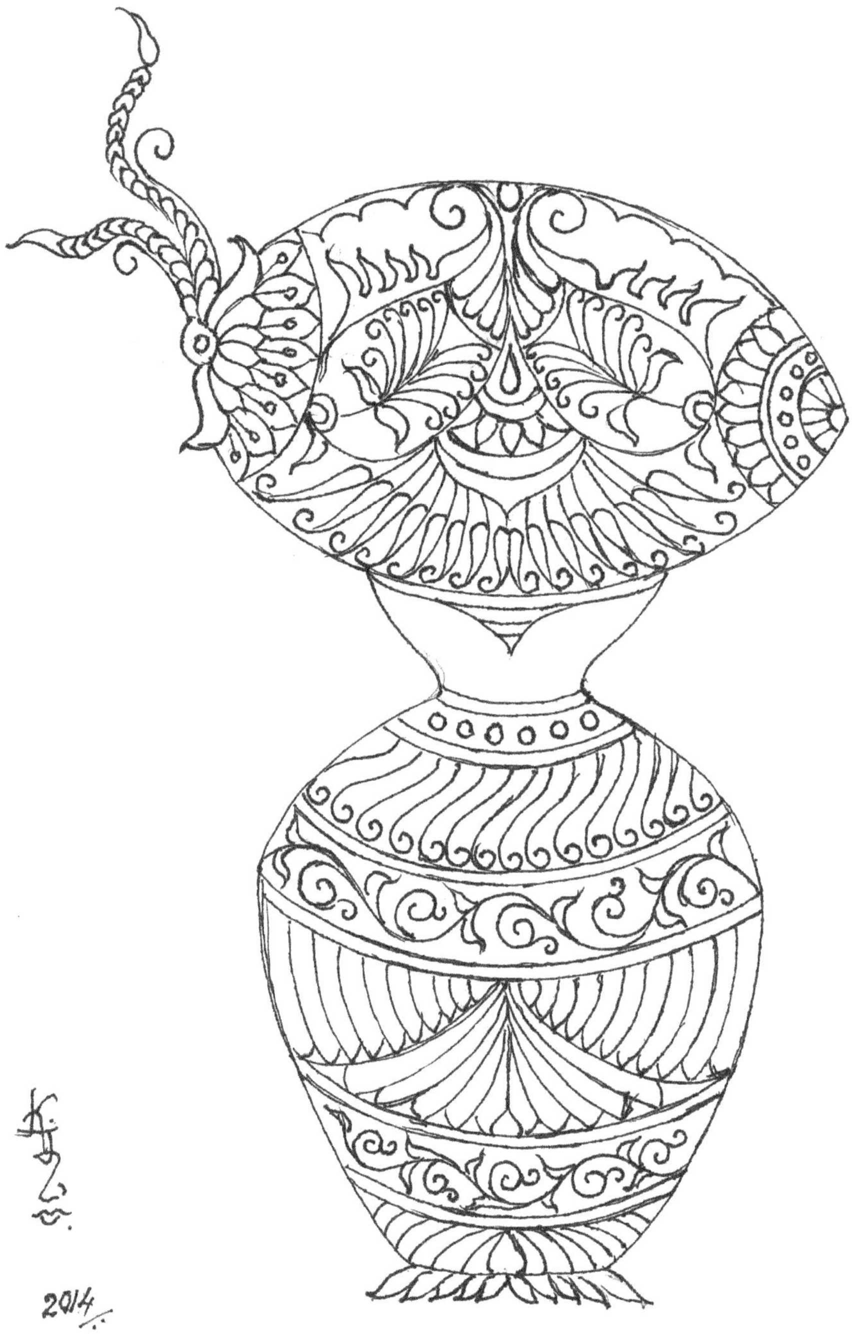
2014

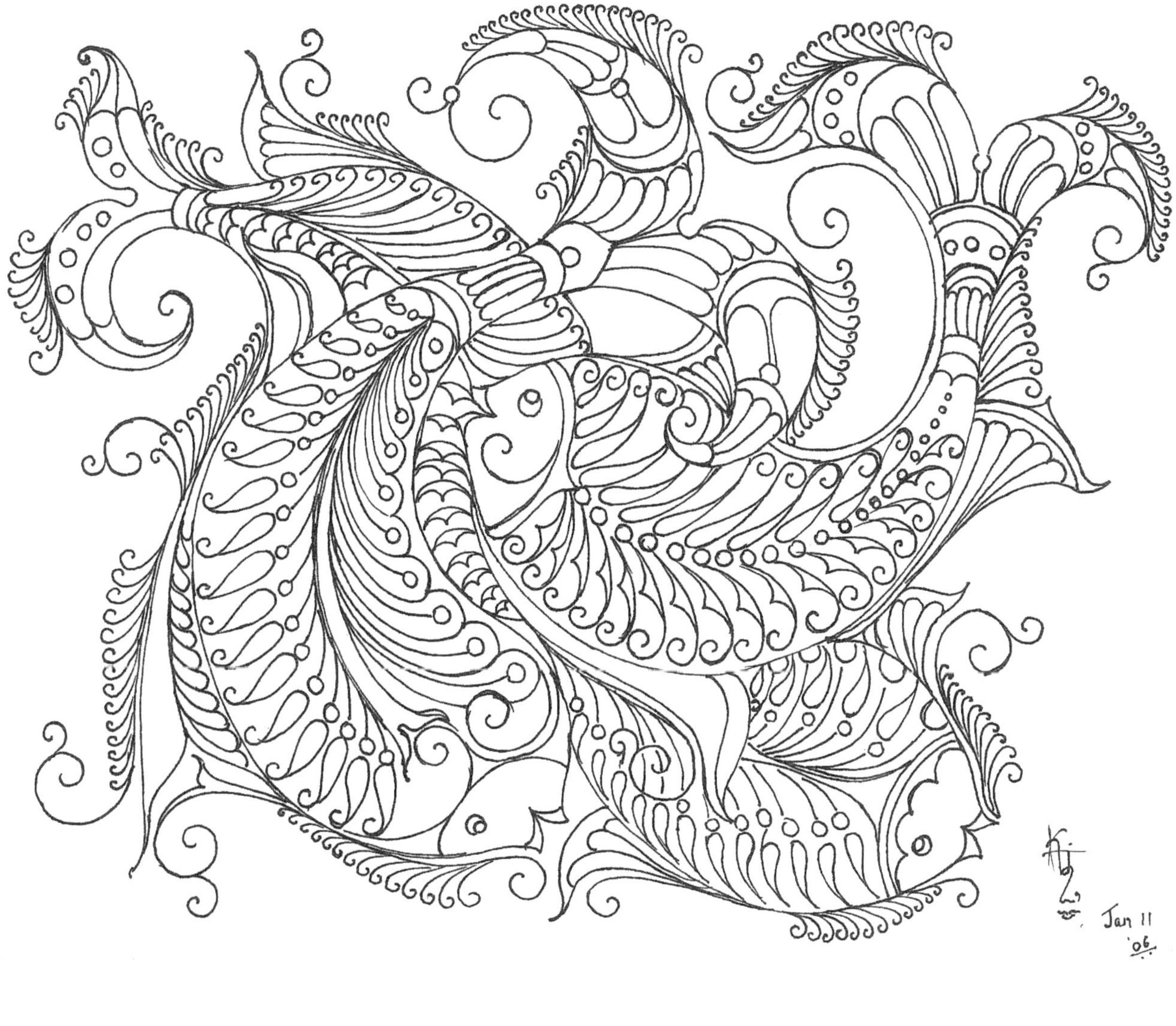
Jan 11
'06

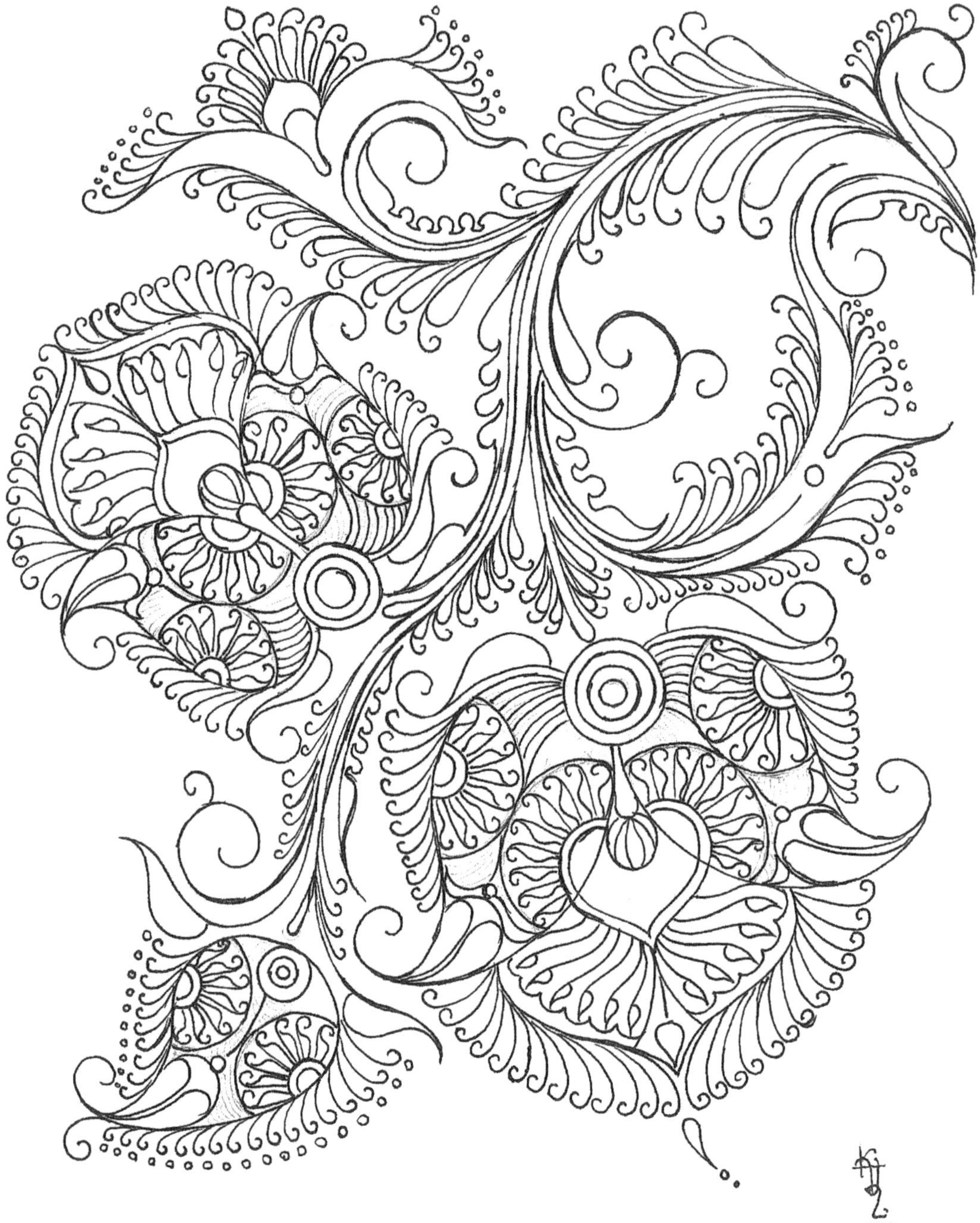

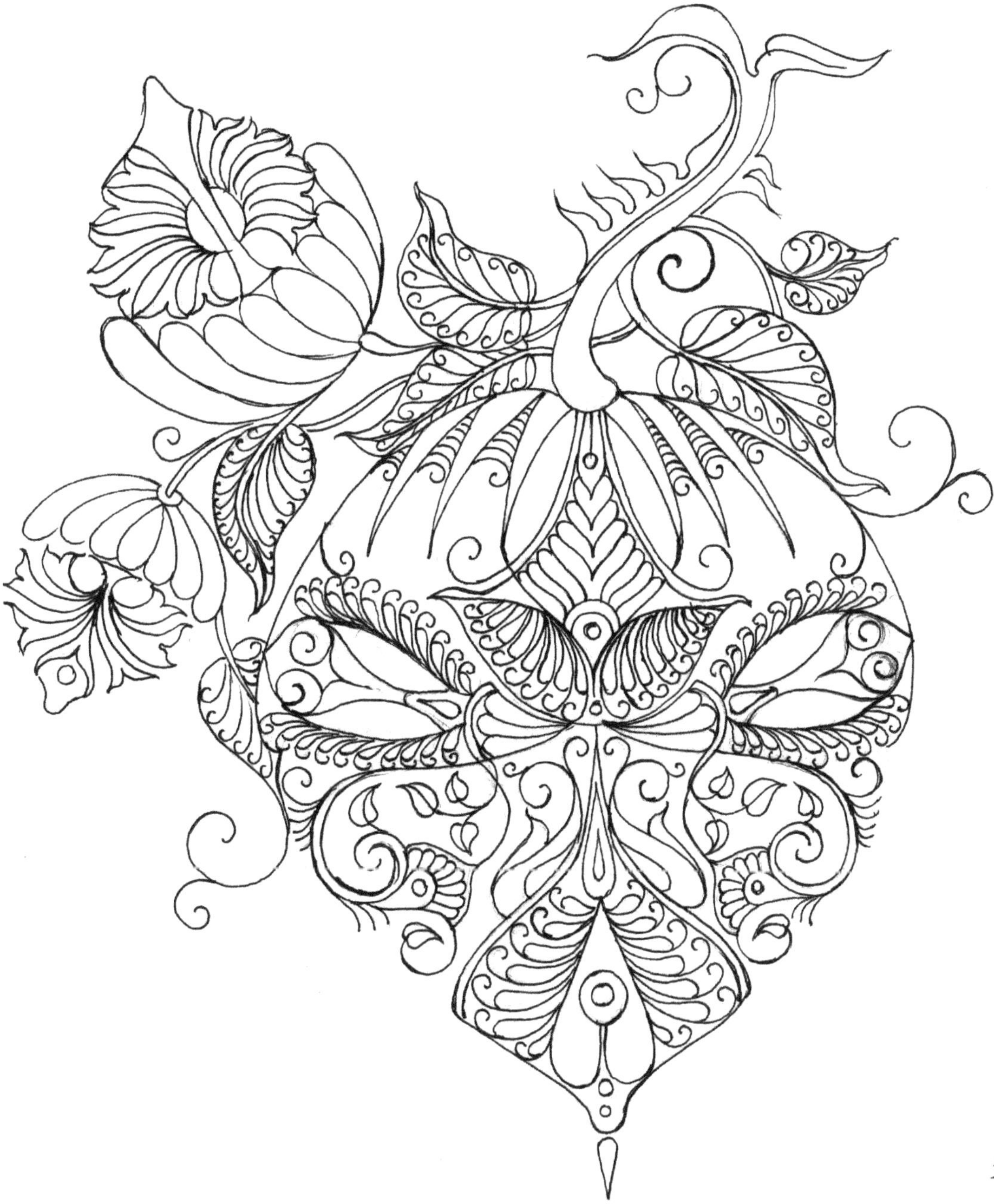

Acorns

26 March '06

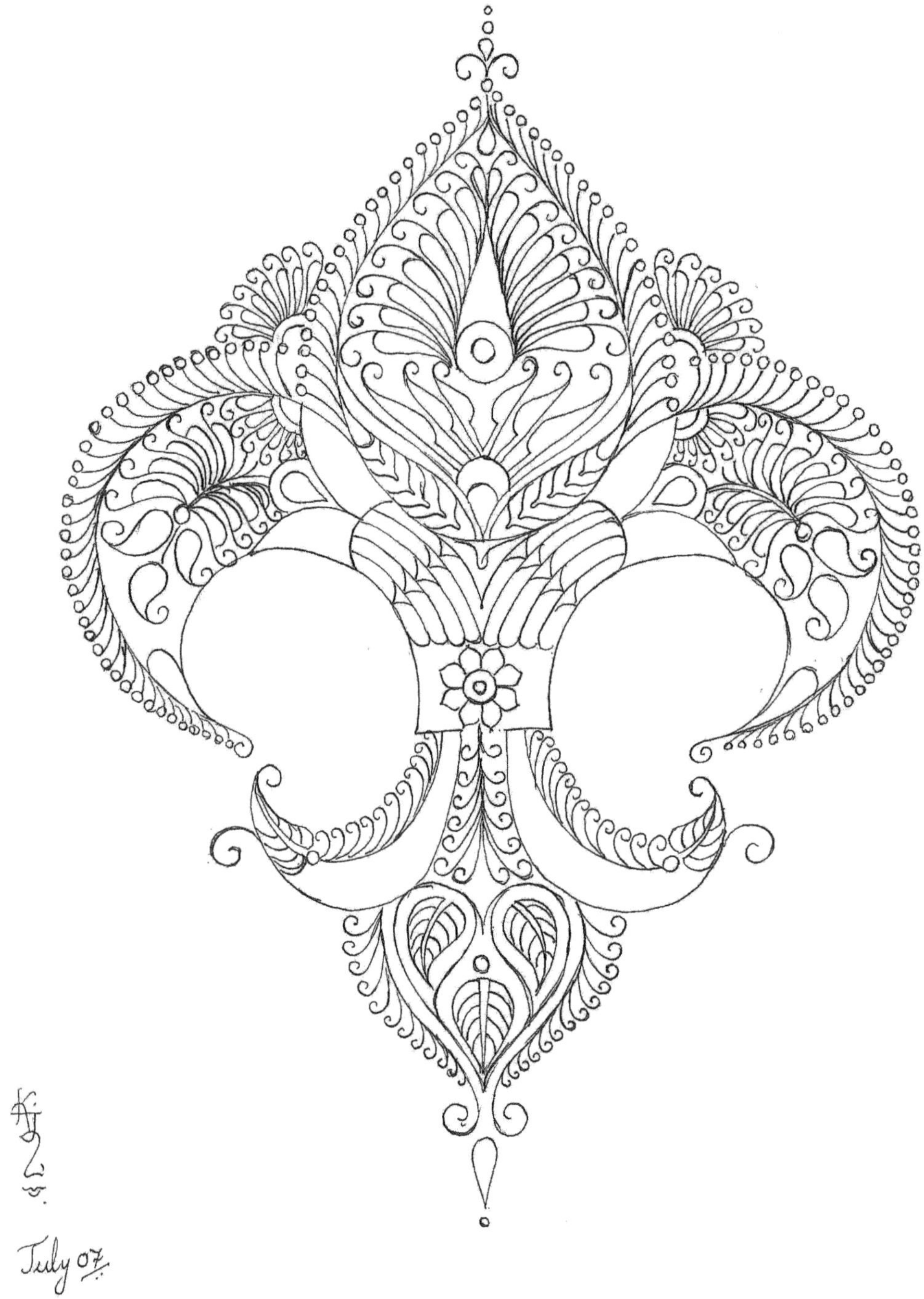
July 07

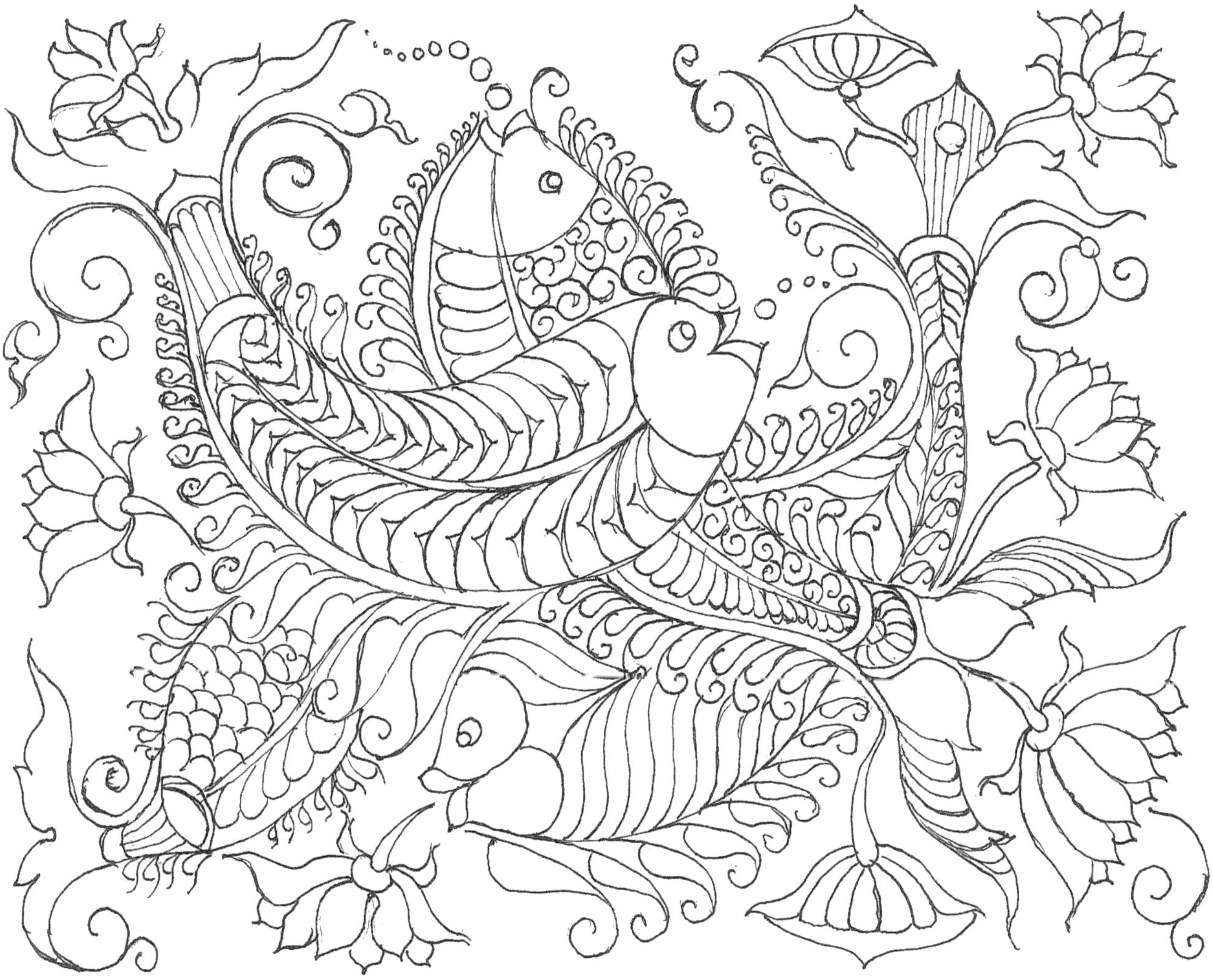

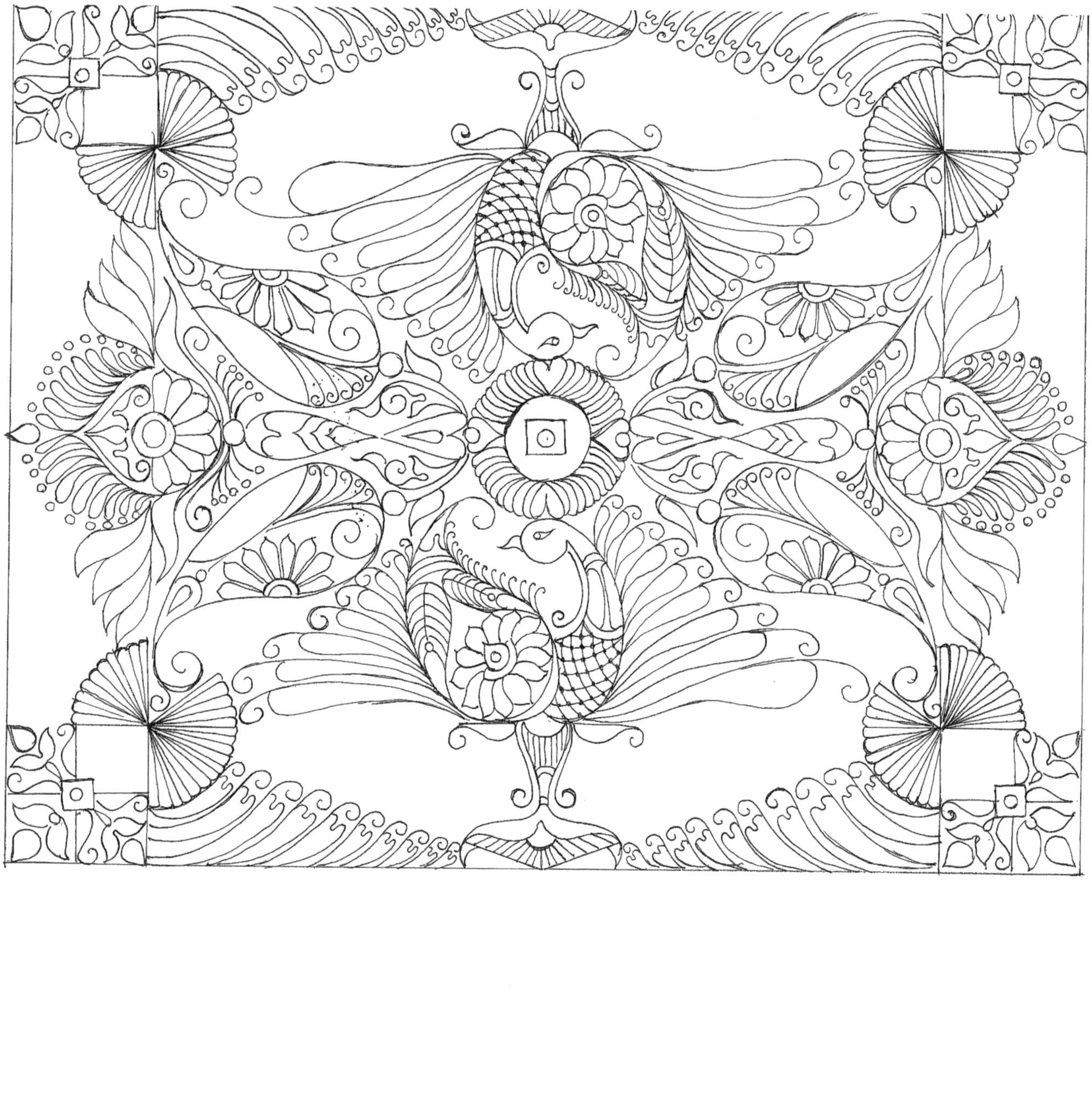

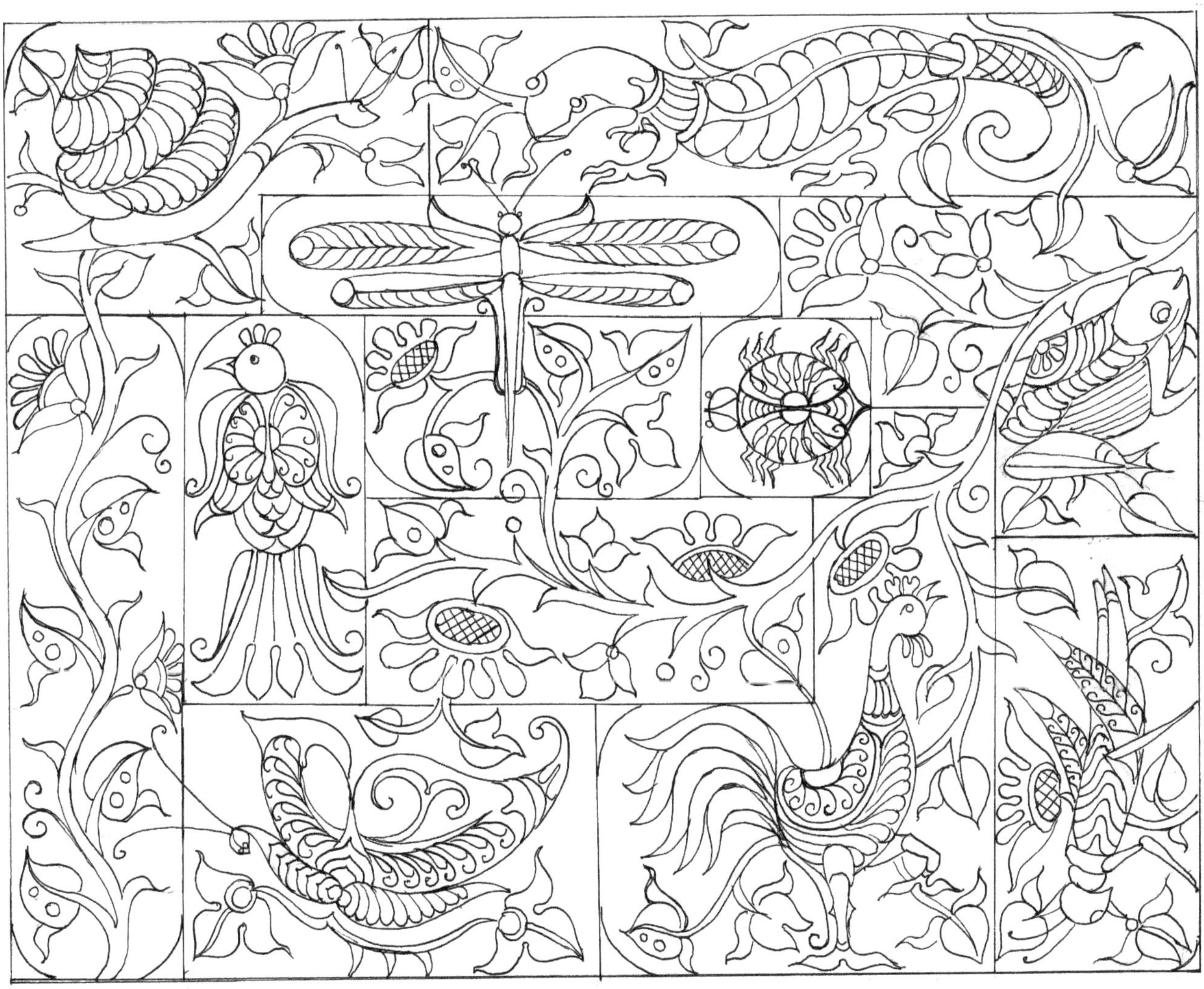

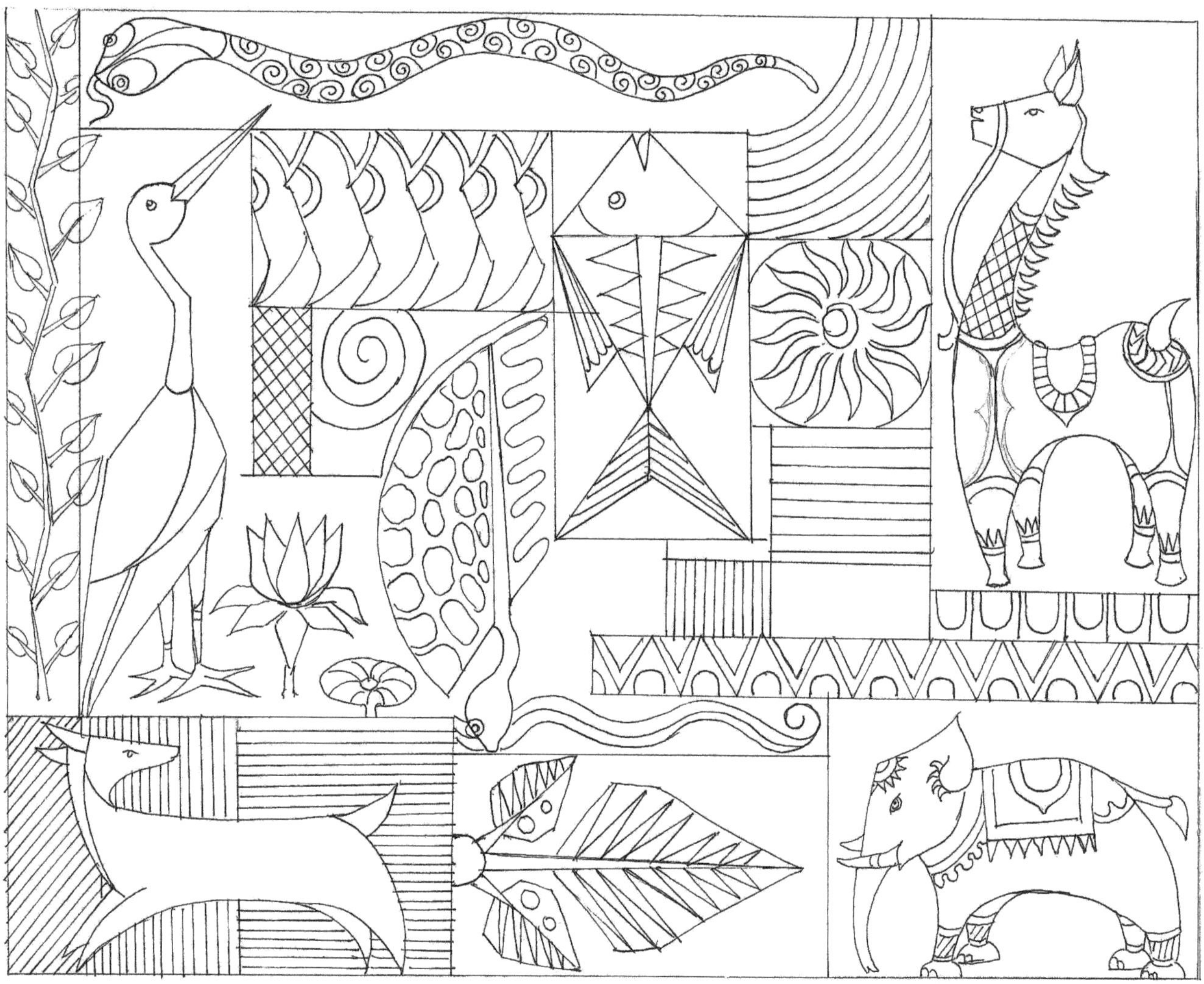

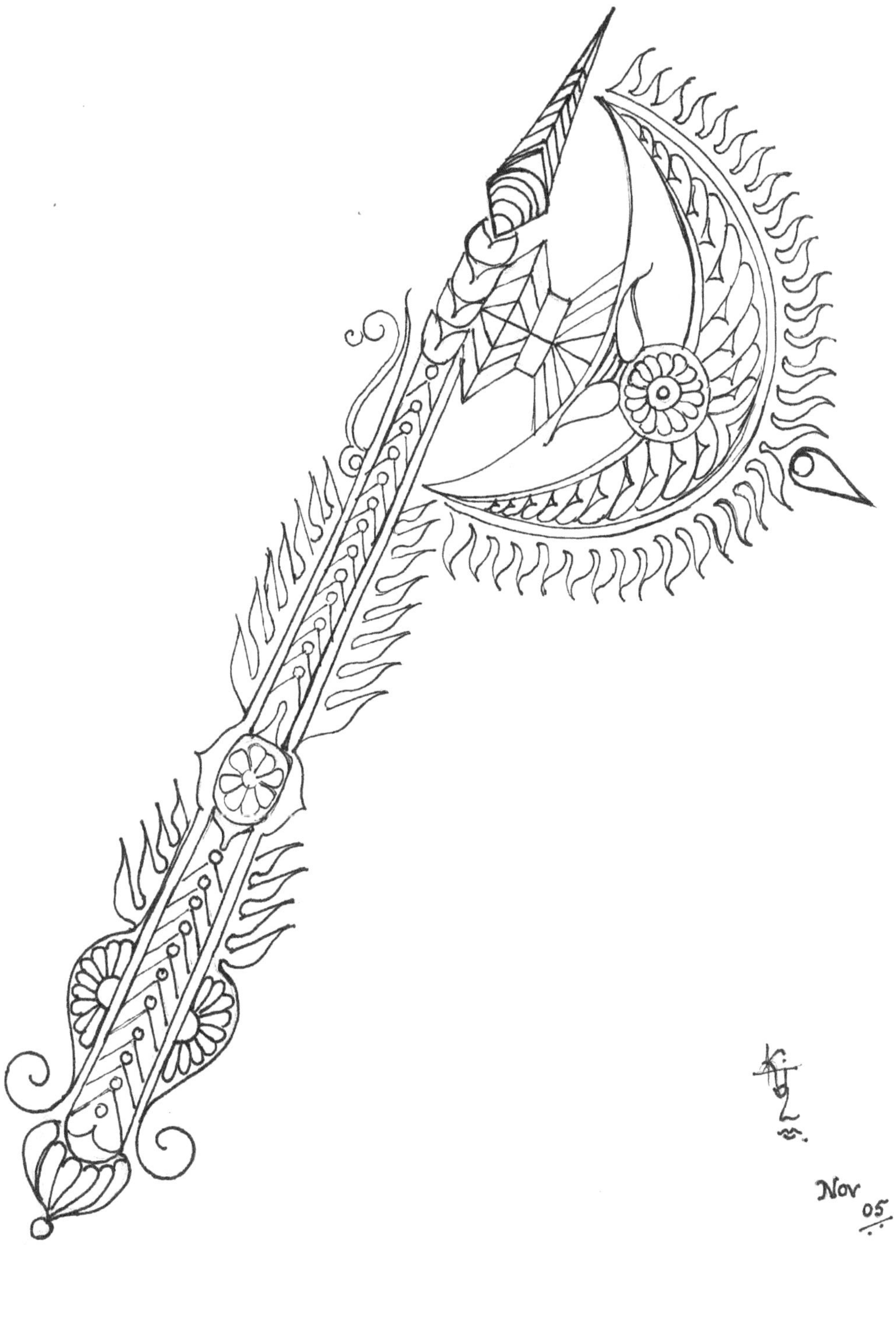
Nov
05

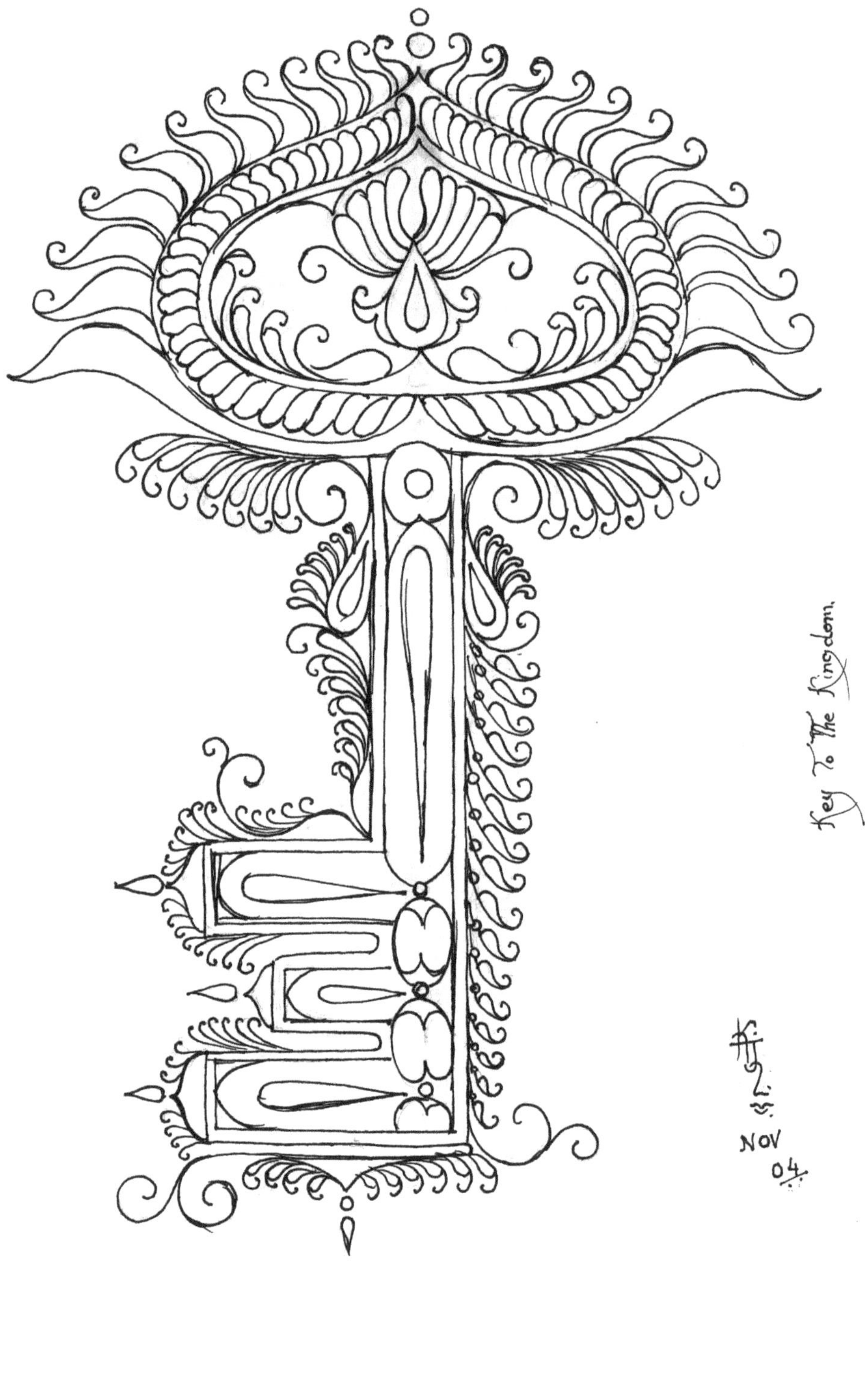
Key To The Kingdom.
NOV
04.

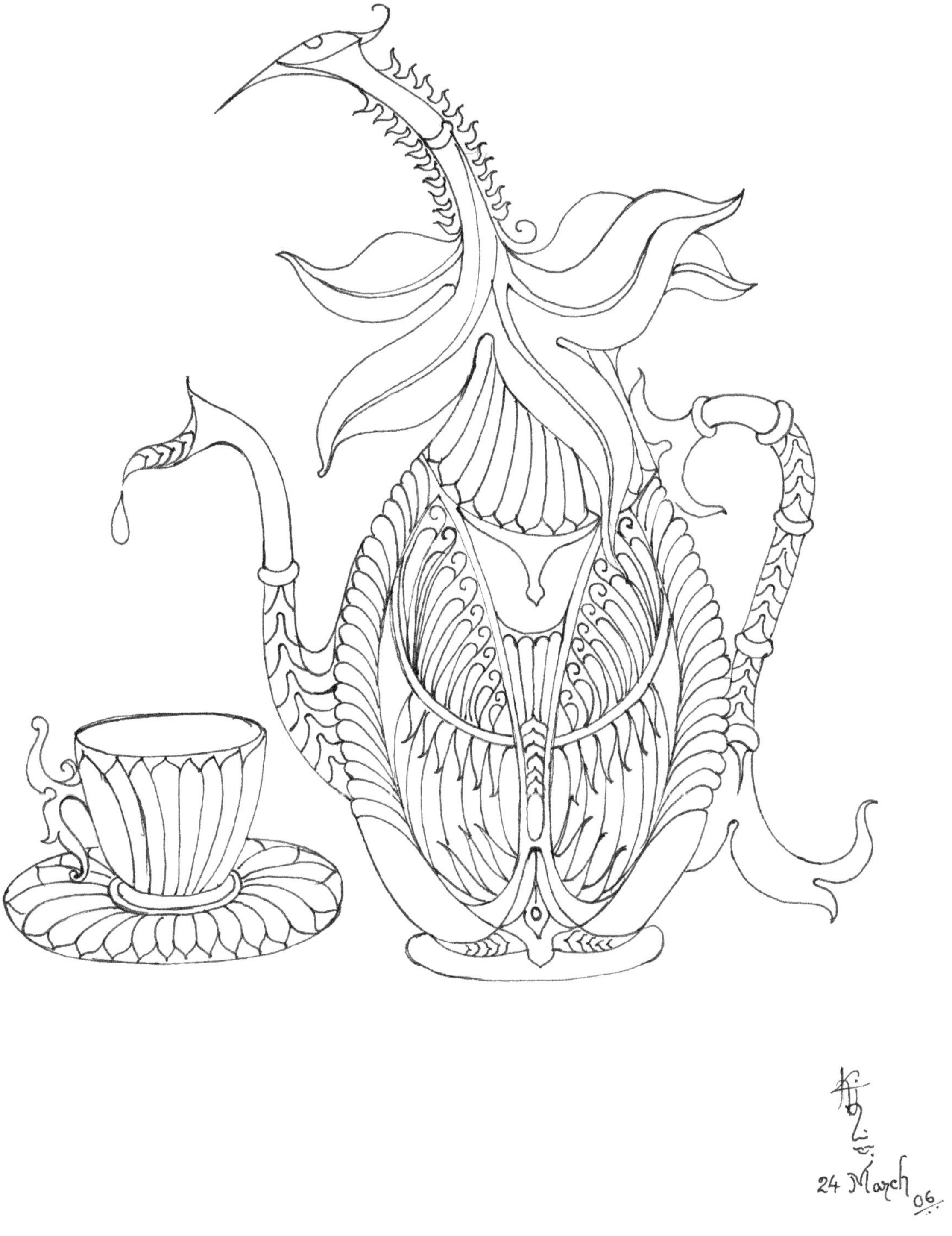

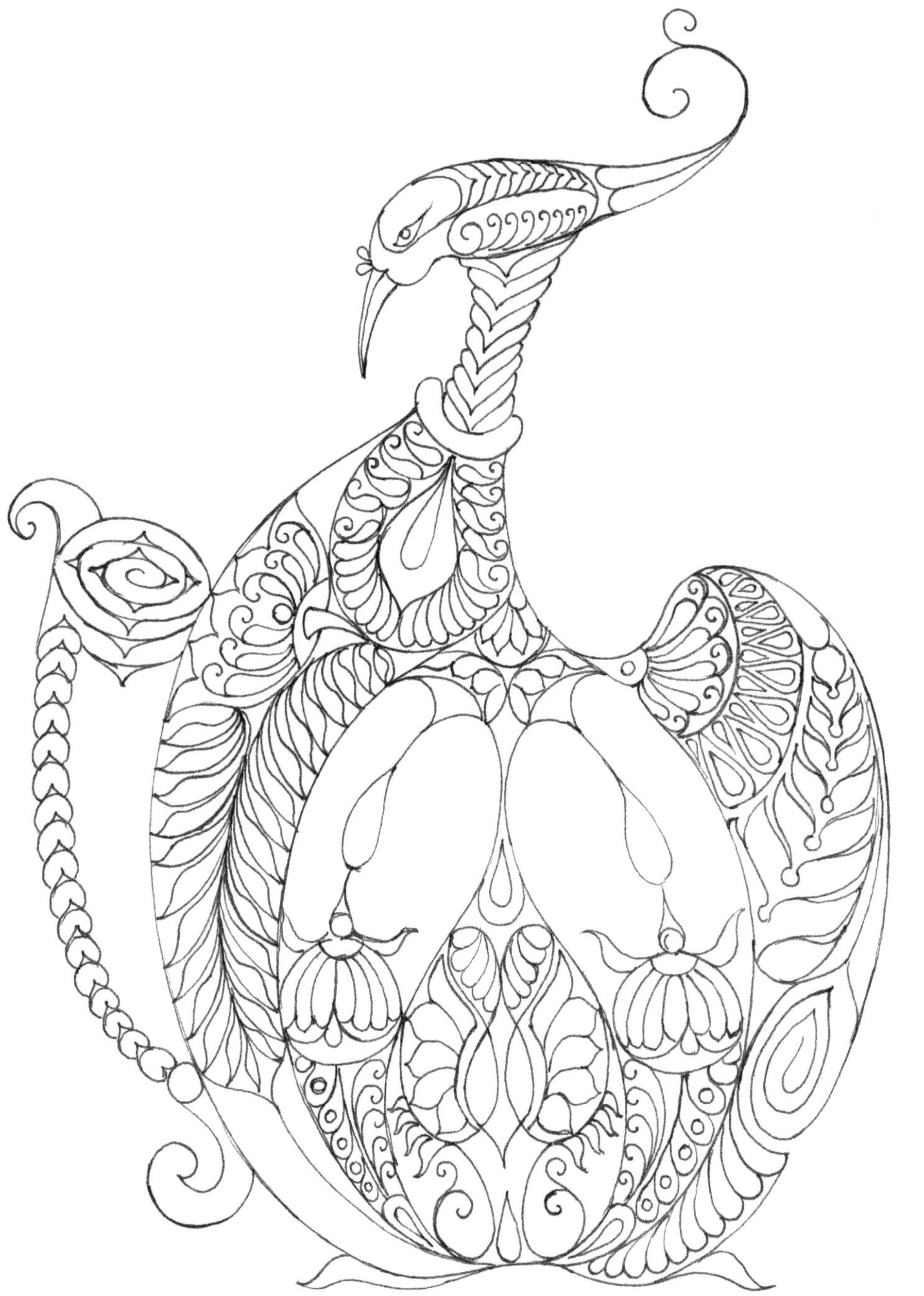

Apple Pitcher

20 March '06

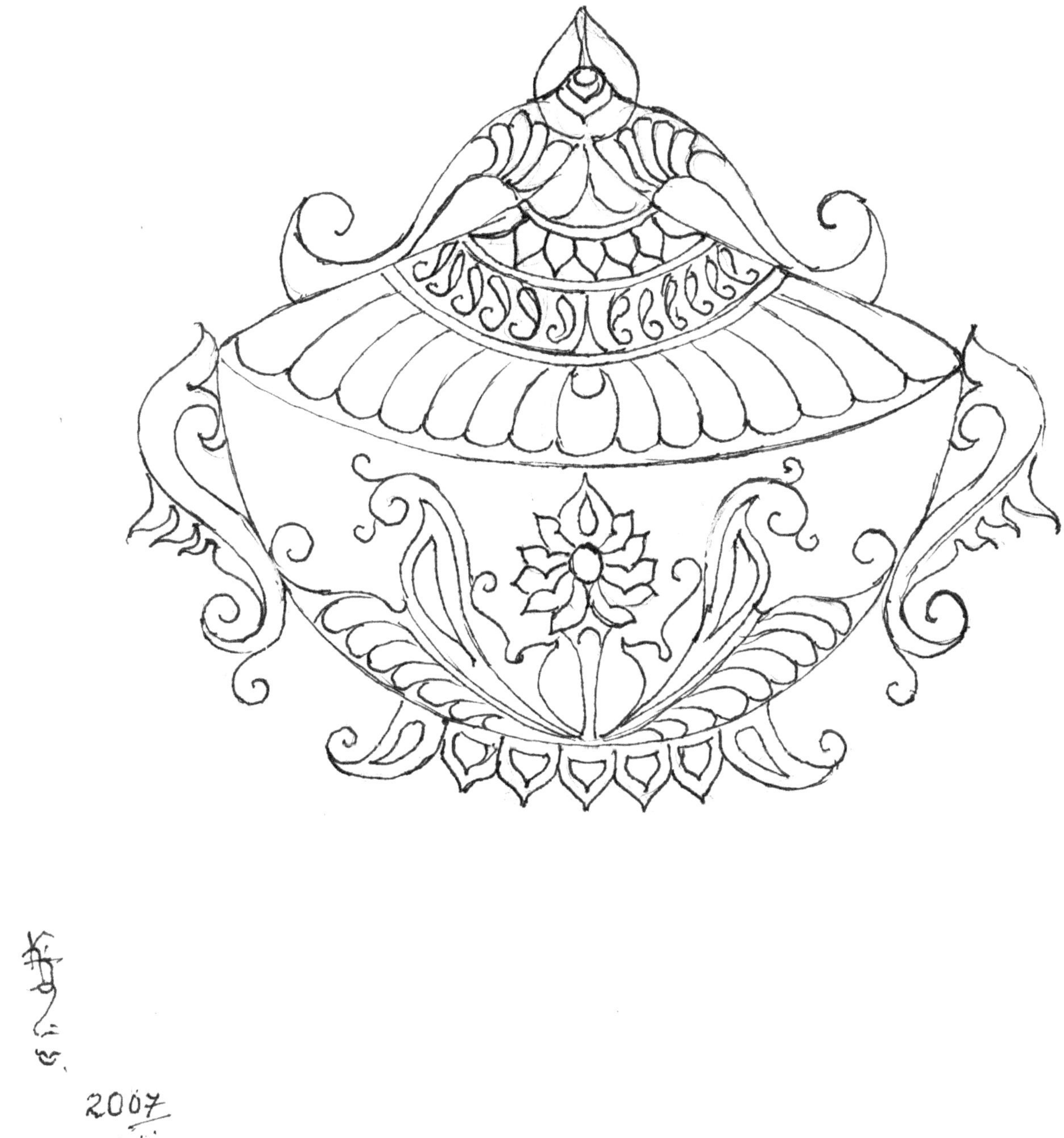
2007

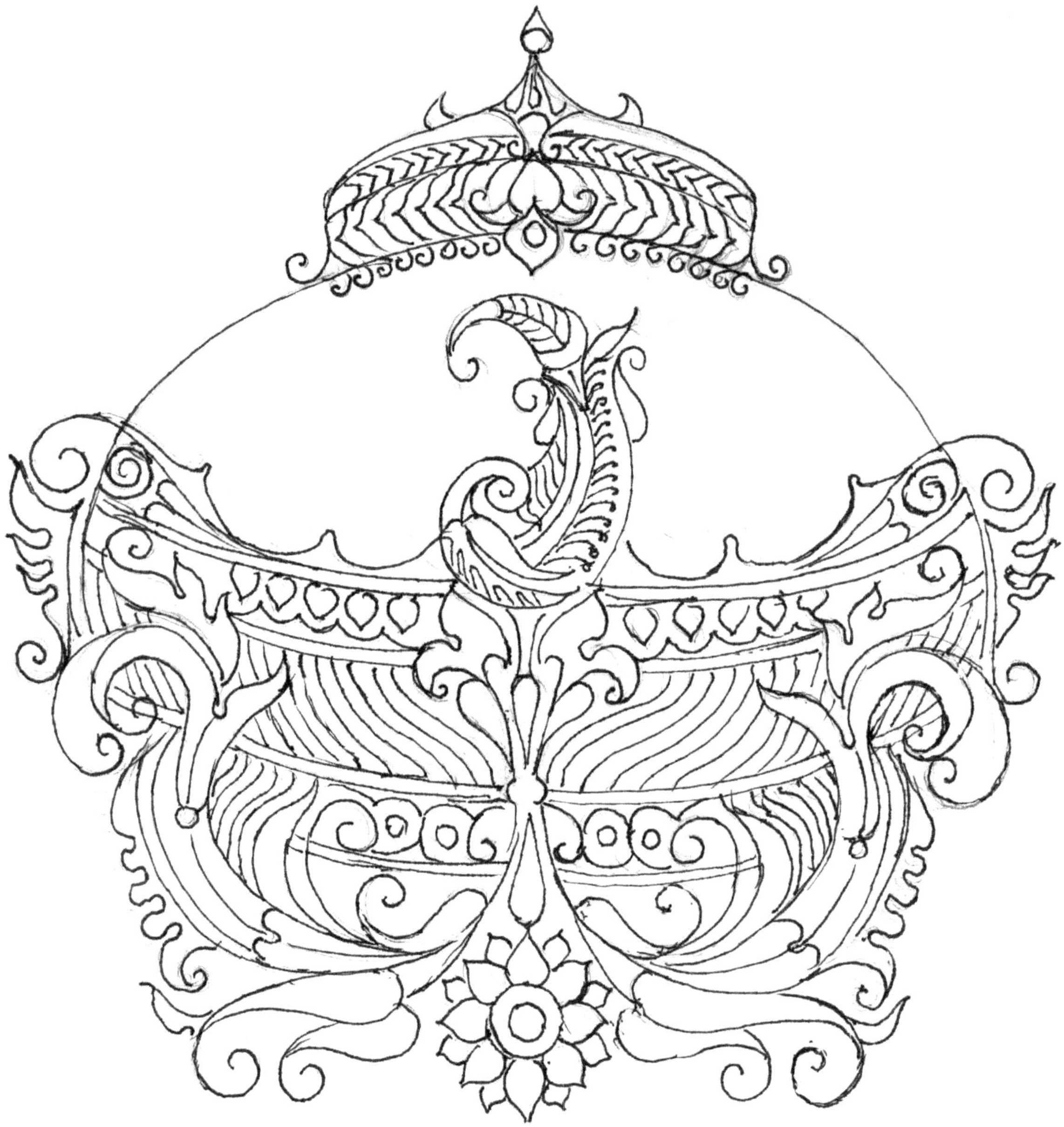

2007

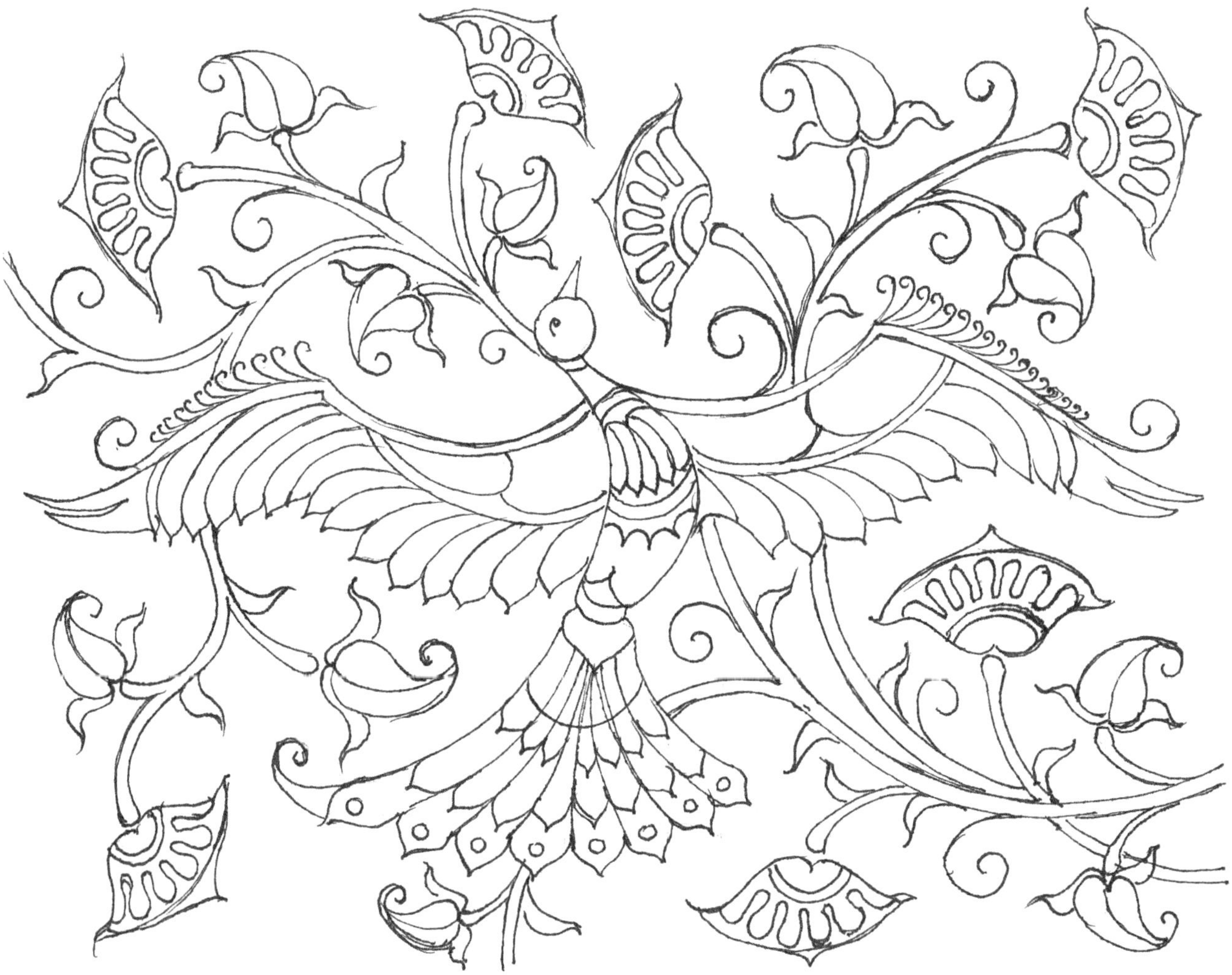

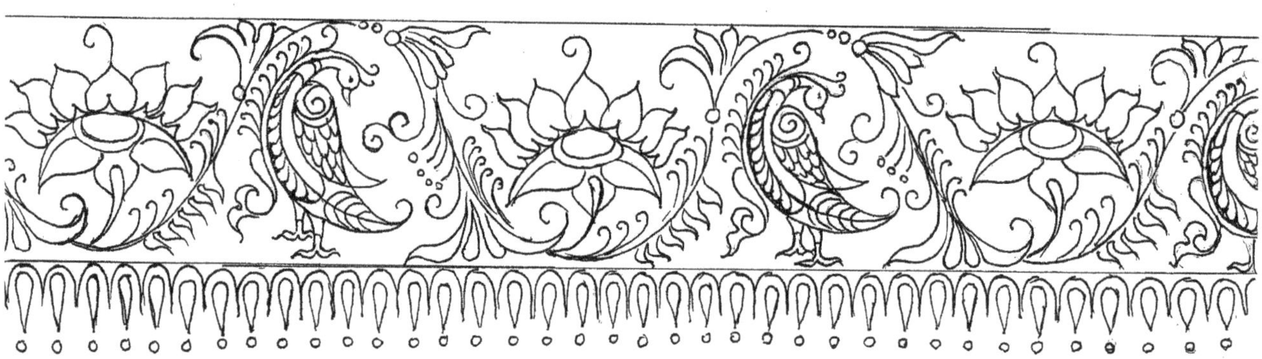

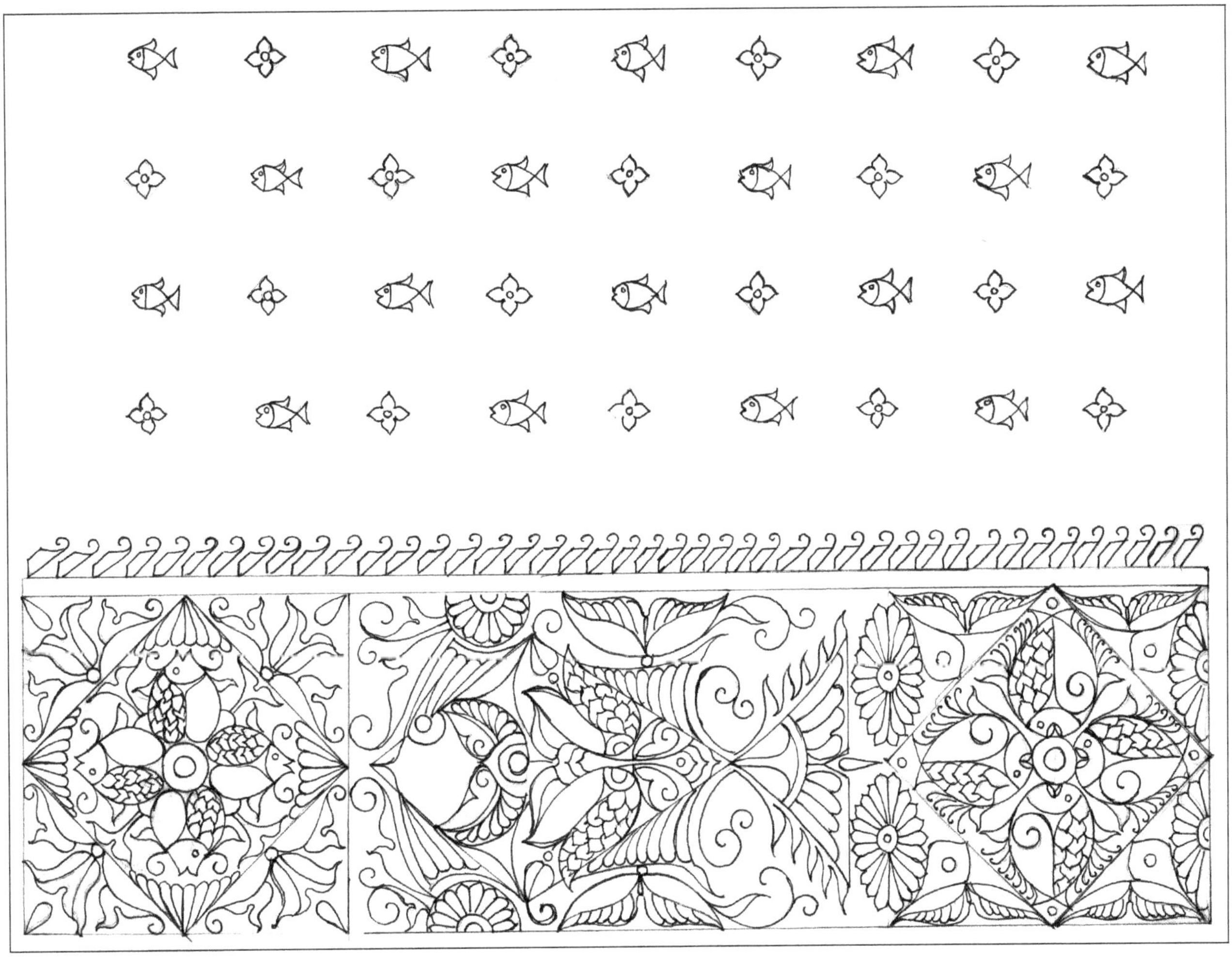

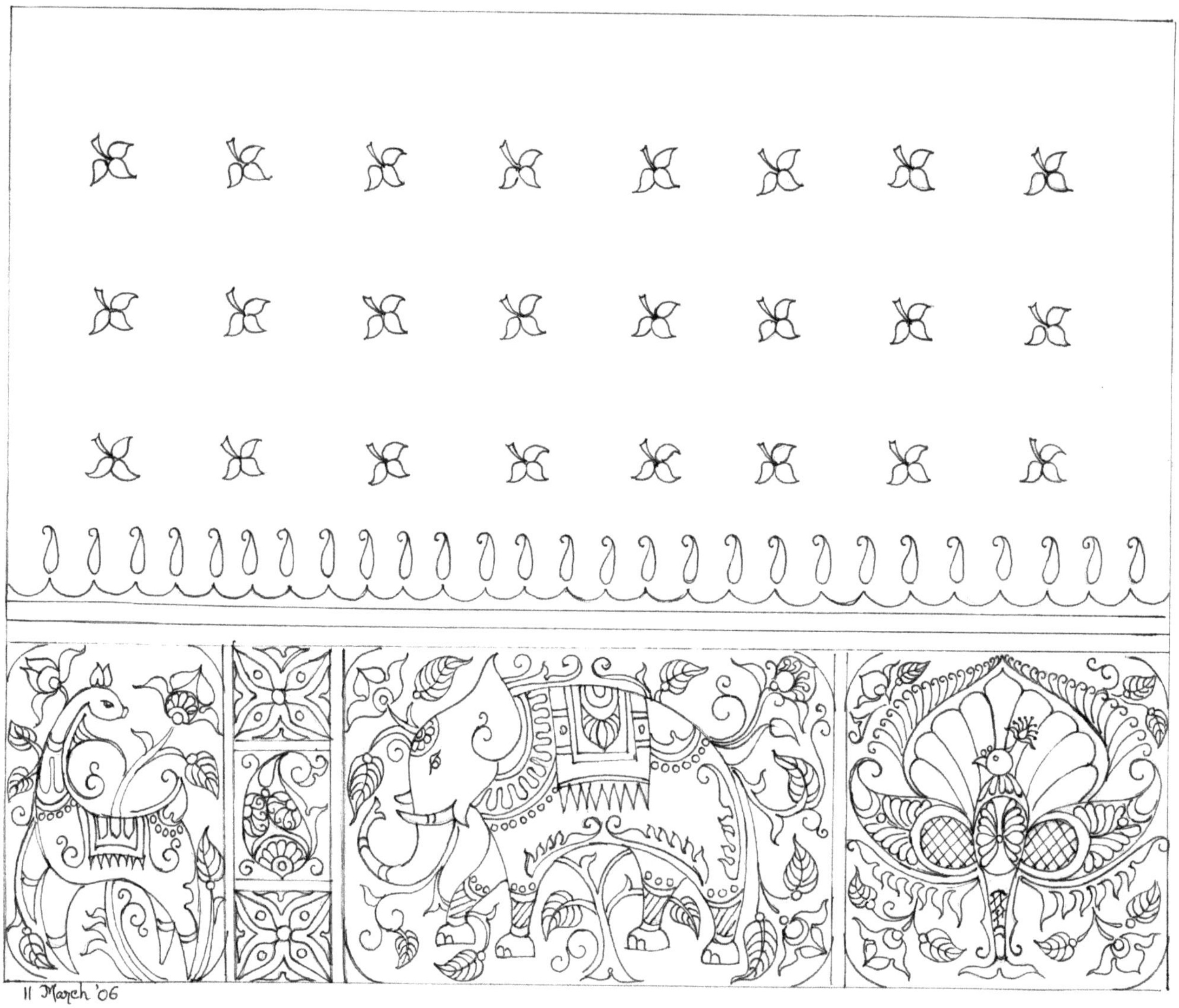
11 March '06

Part II

Color Art

Color

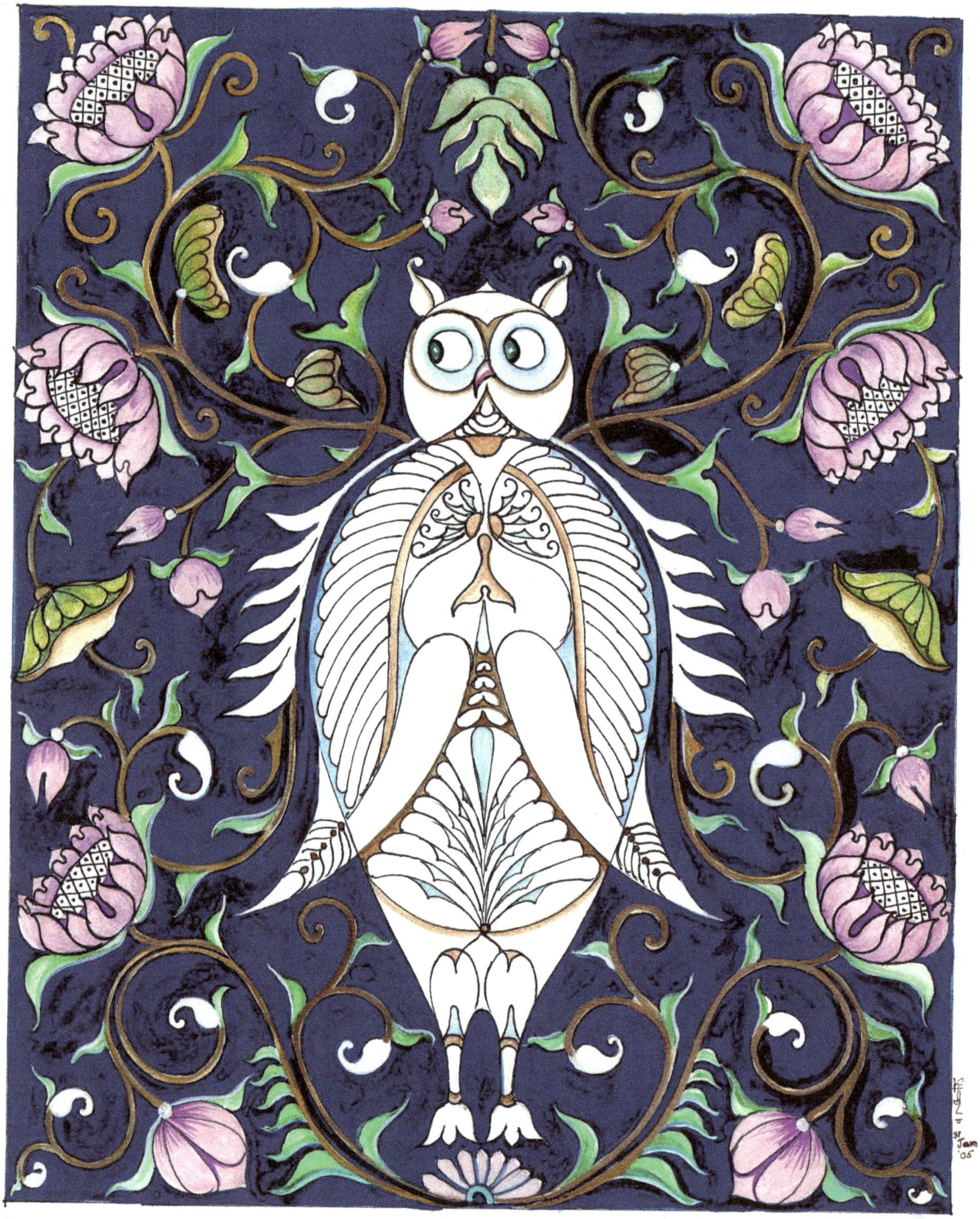

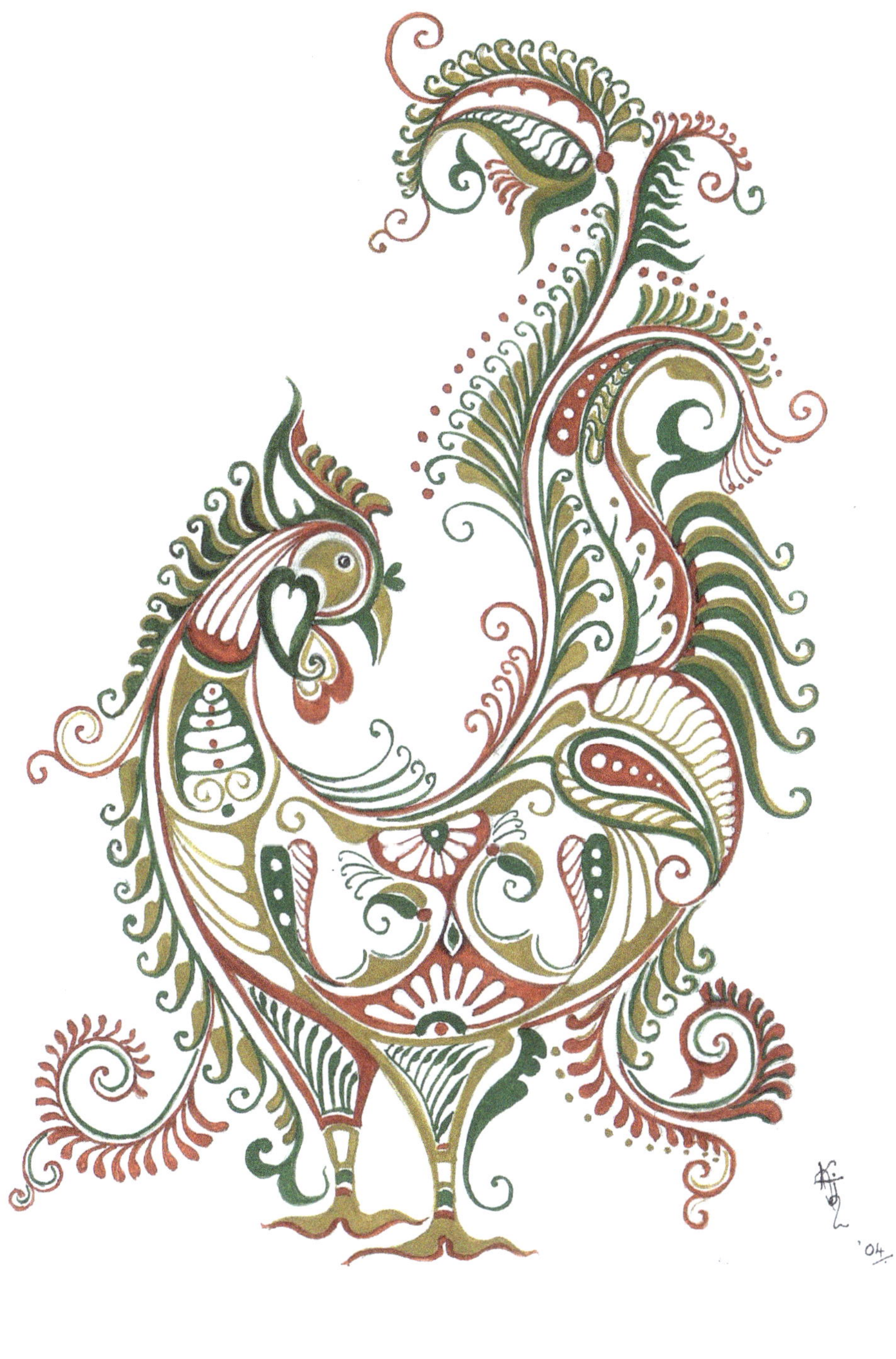

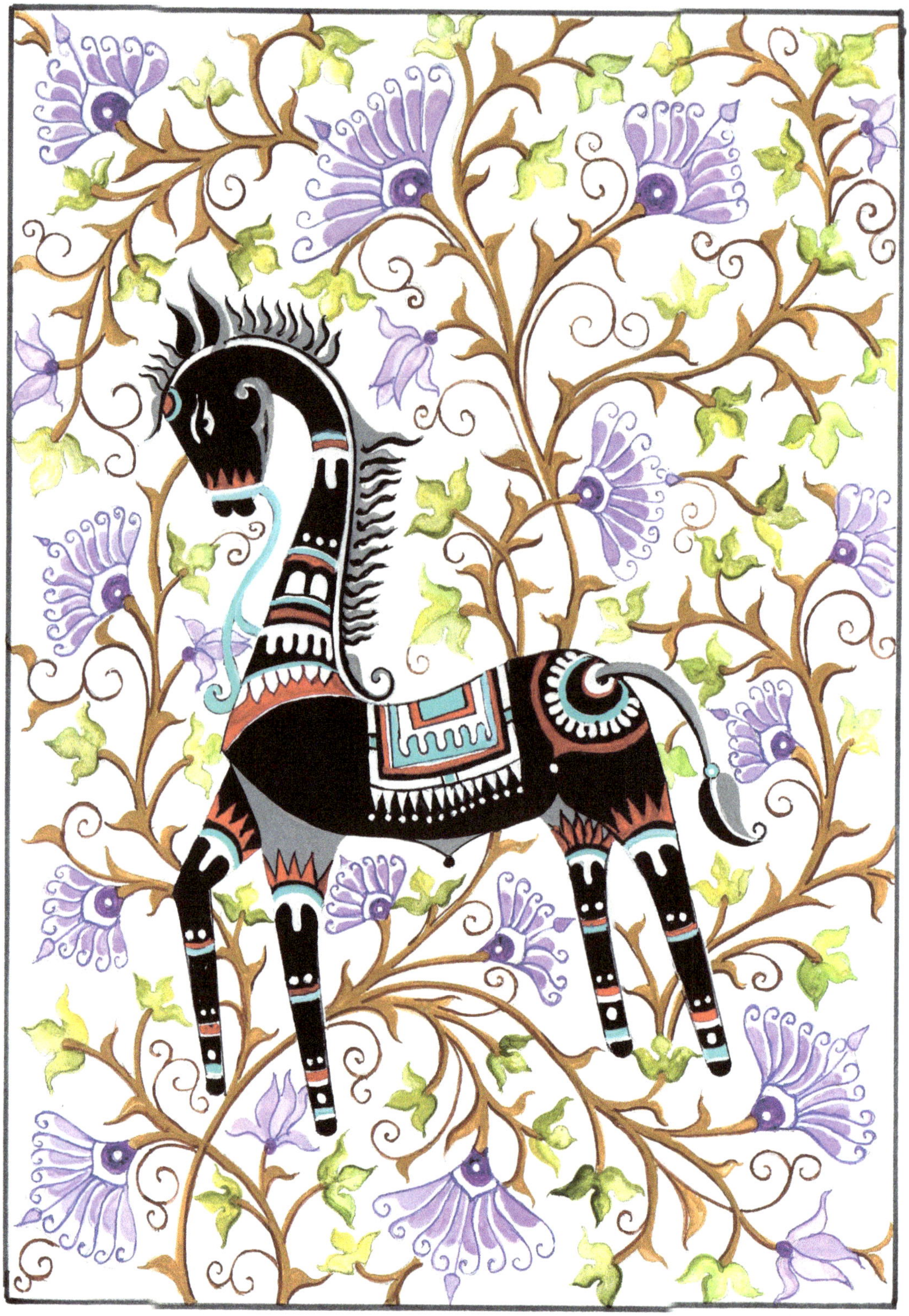

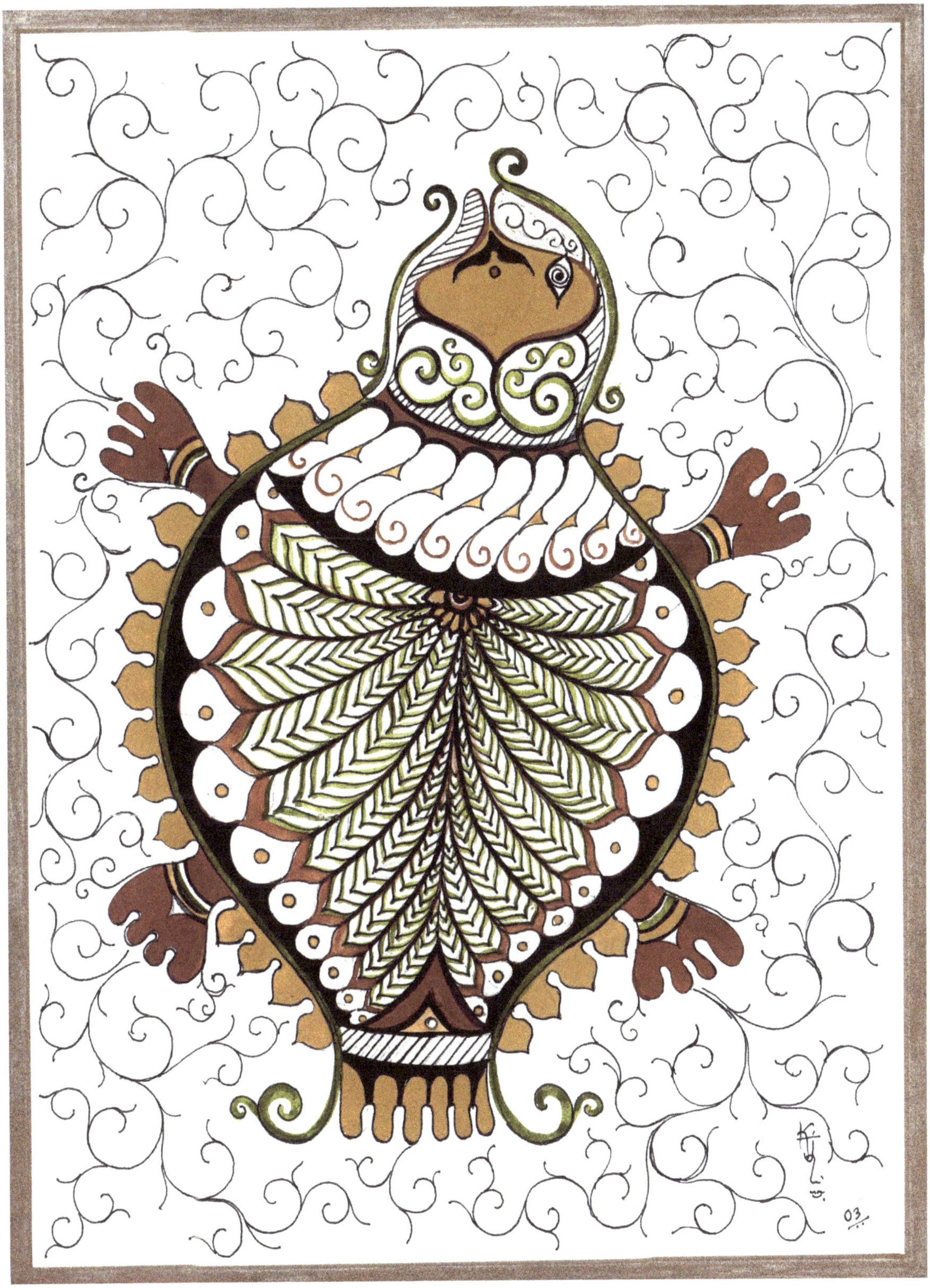

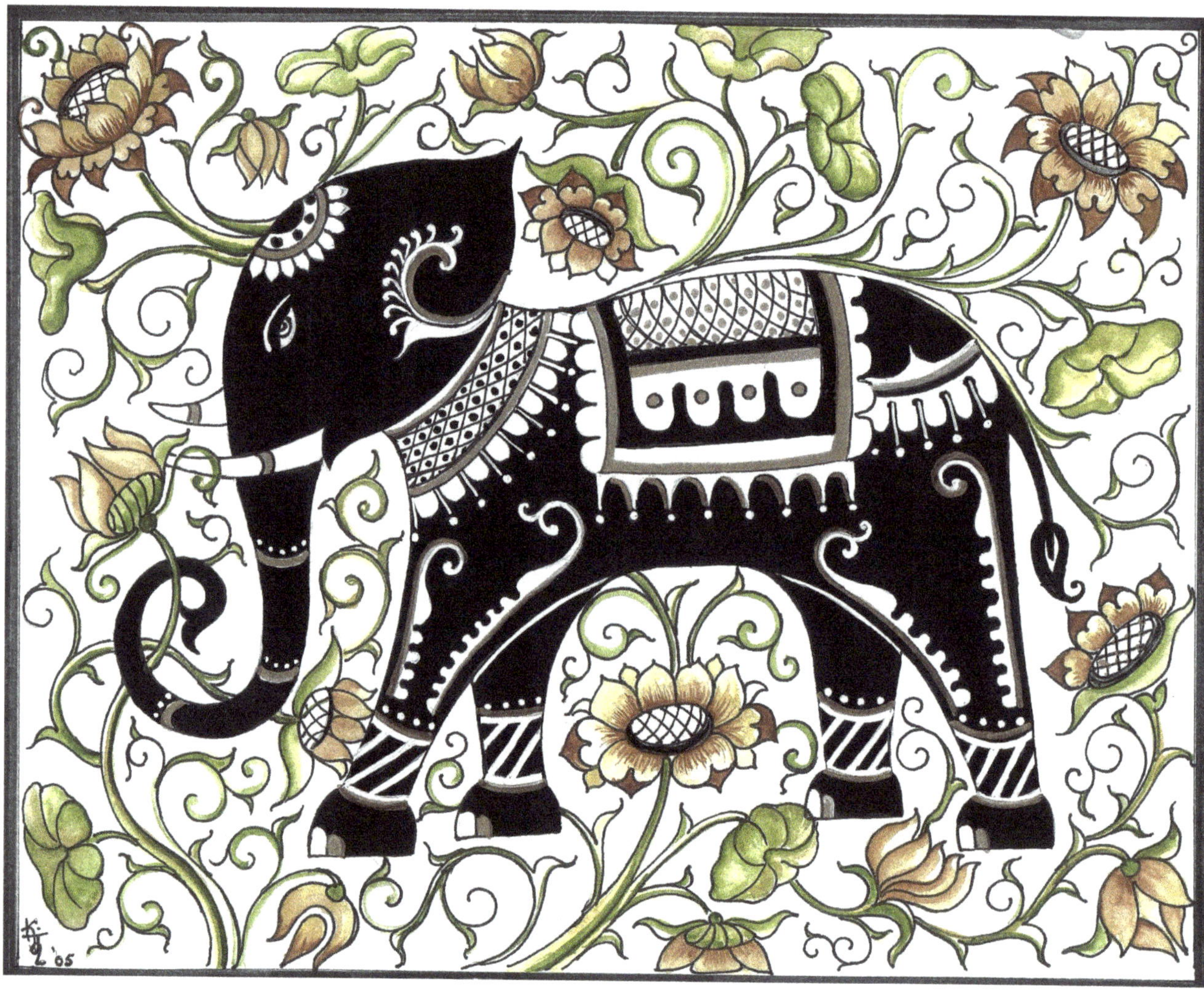

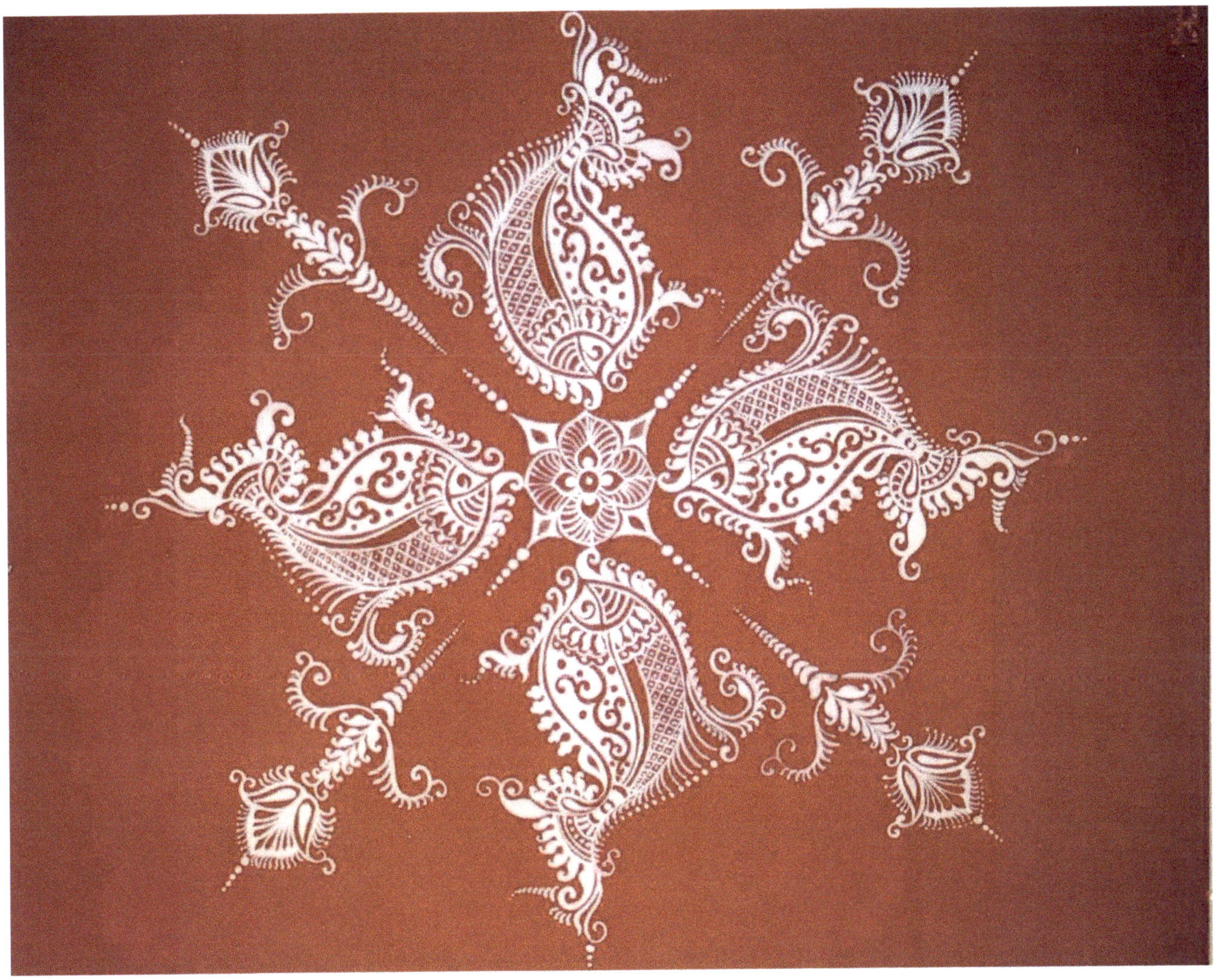

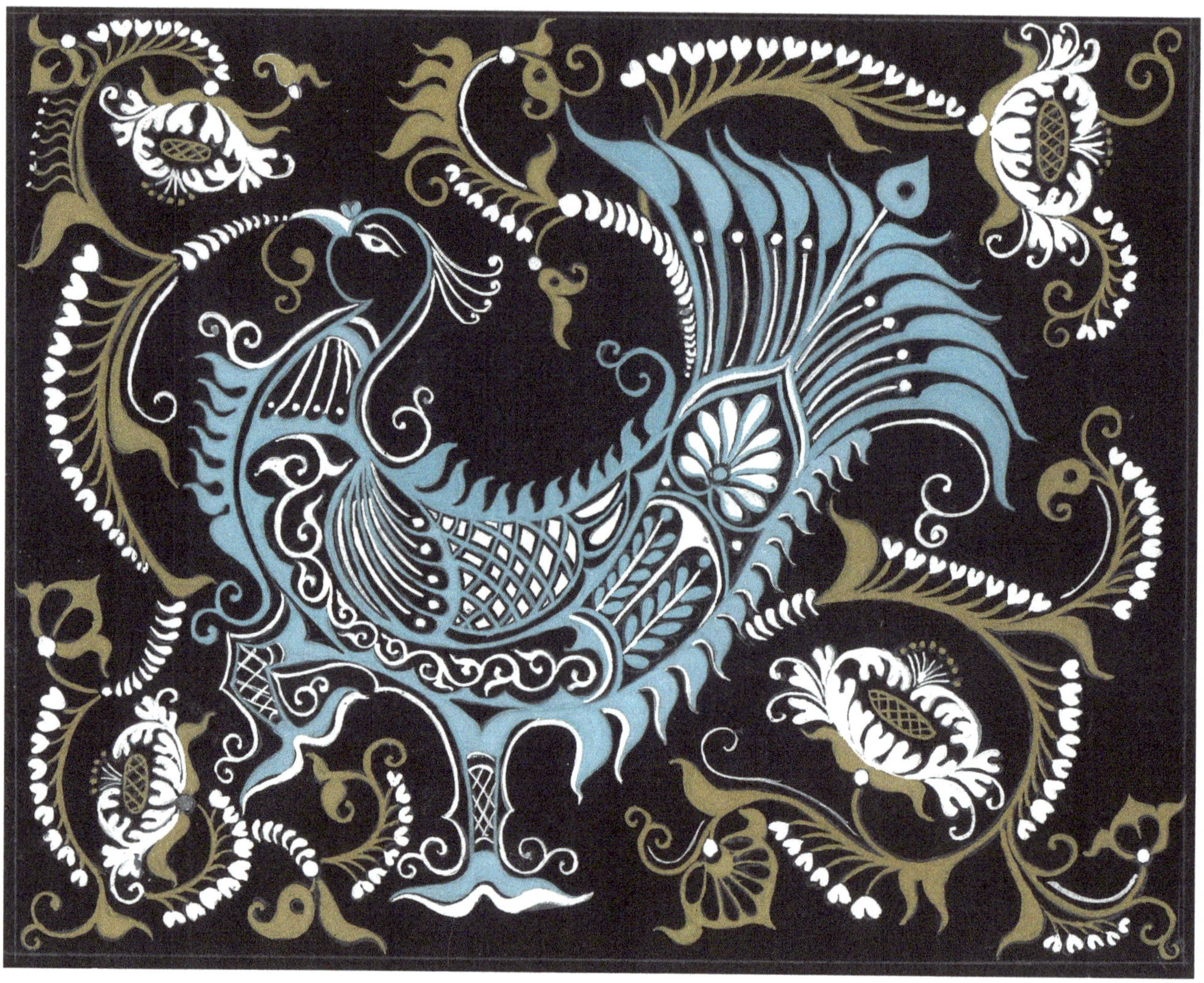

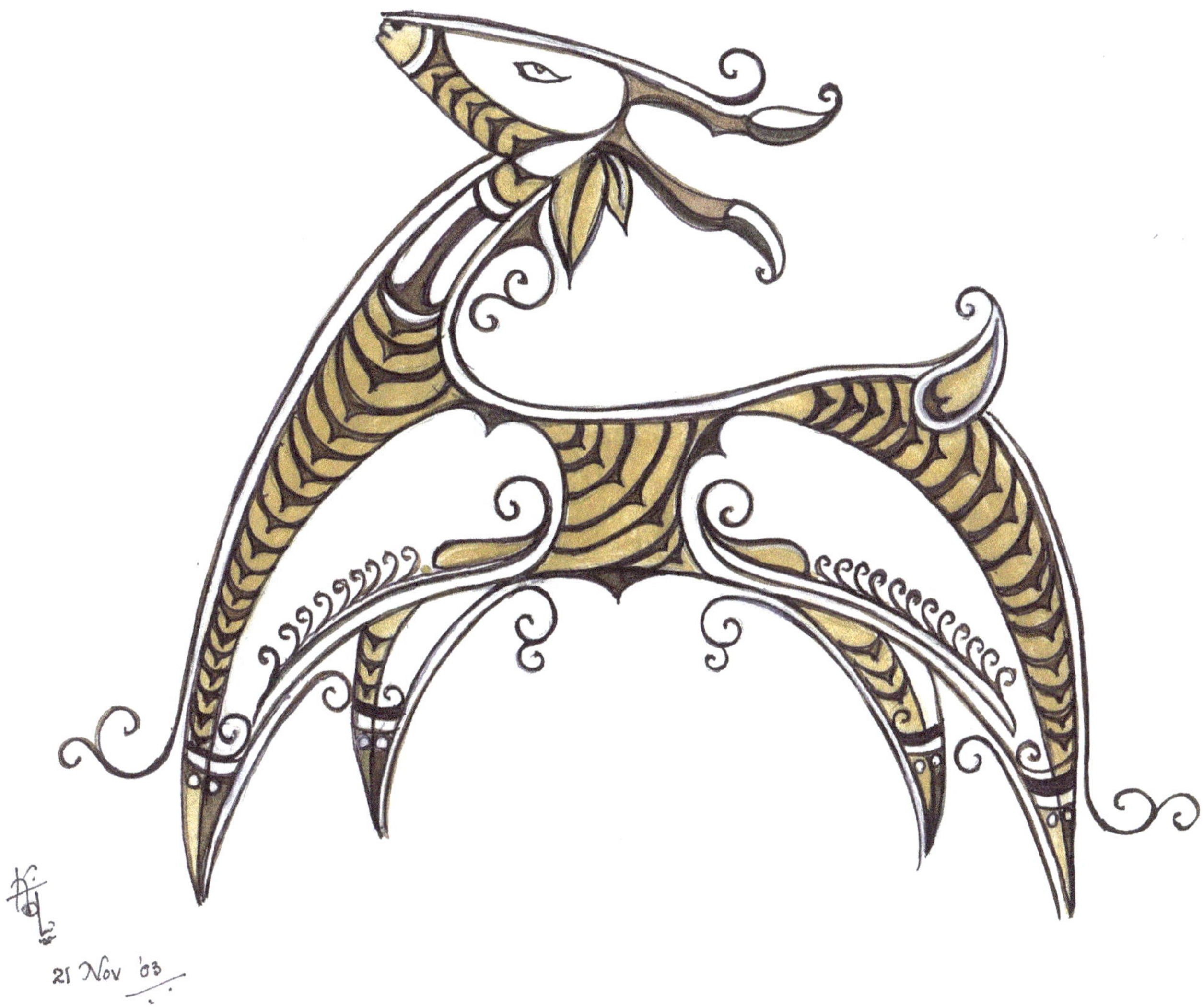
21 Nov '03

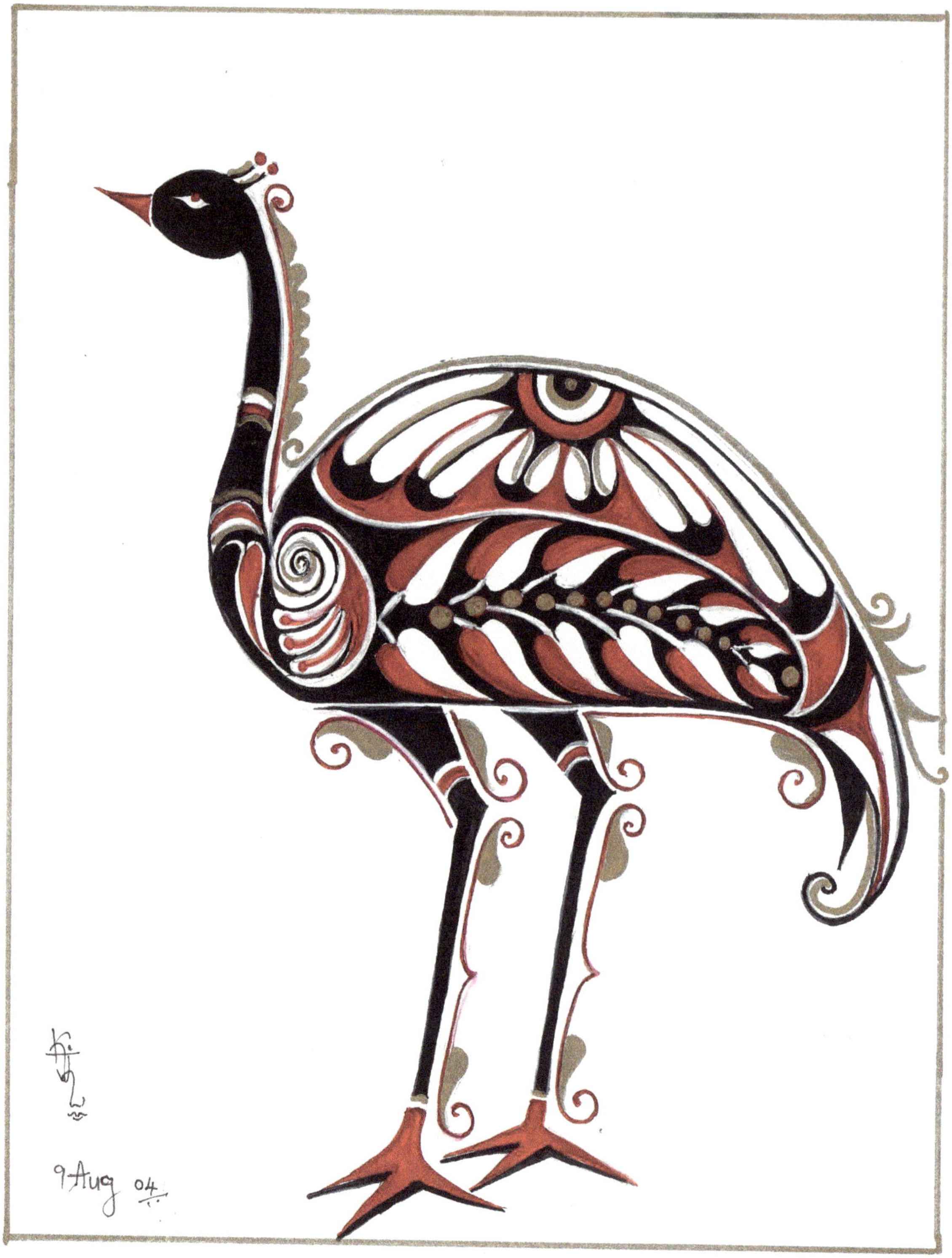
9 Aug 04

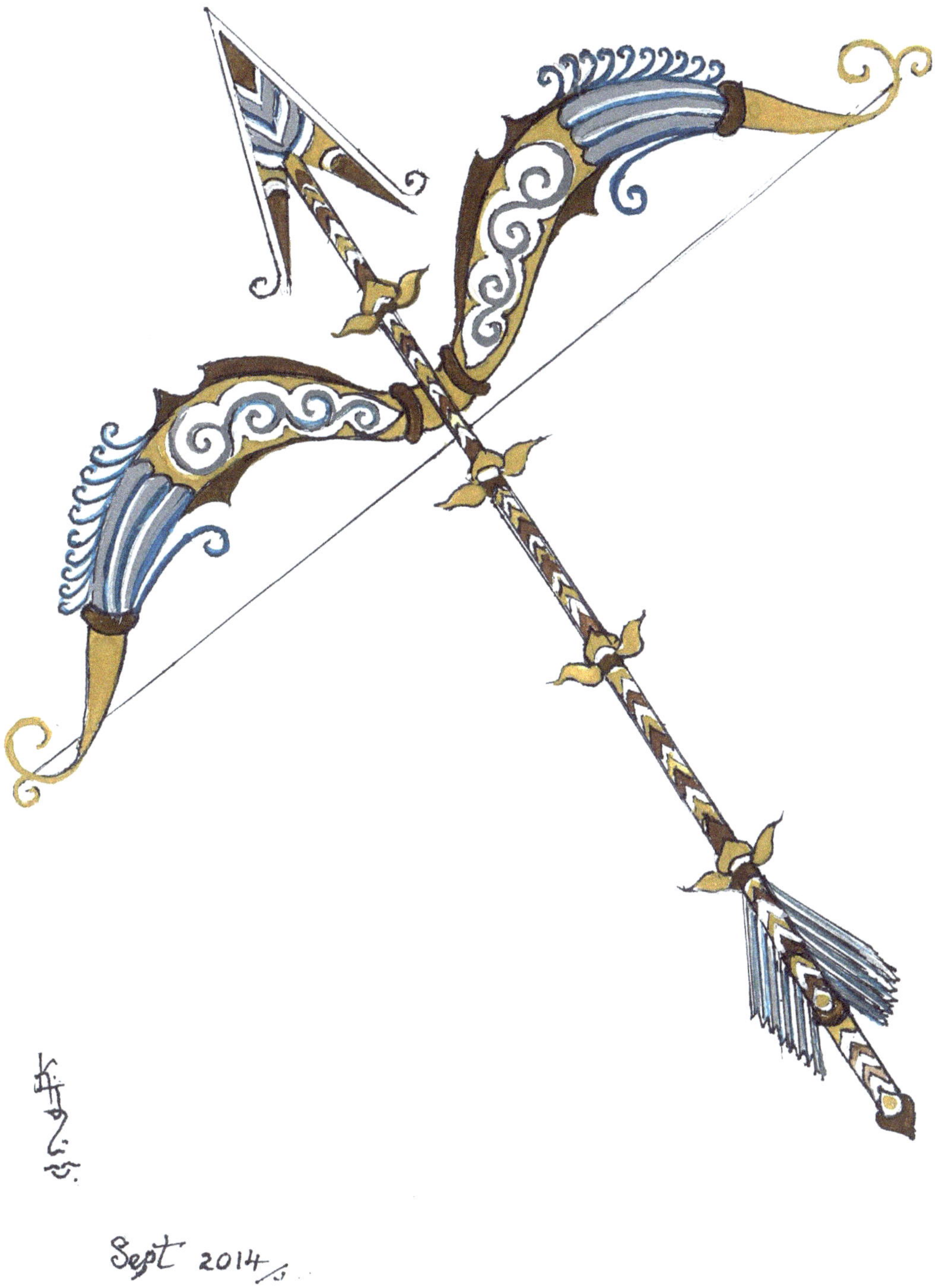
Sept 2014

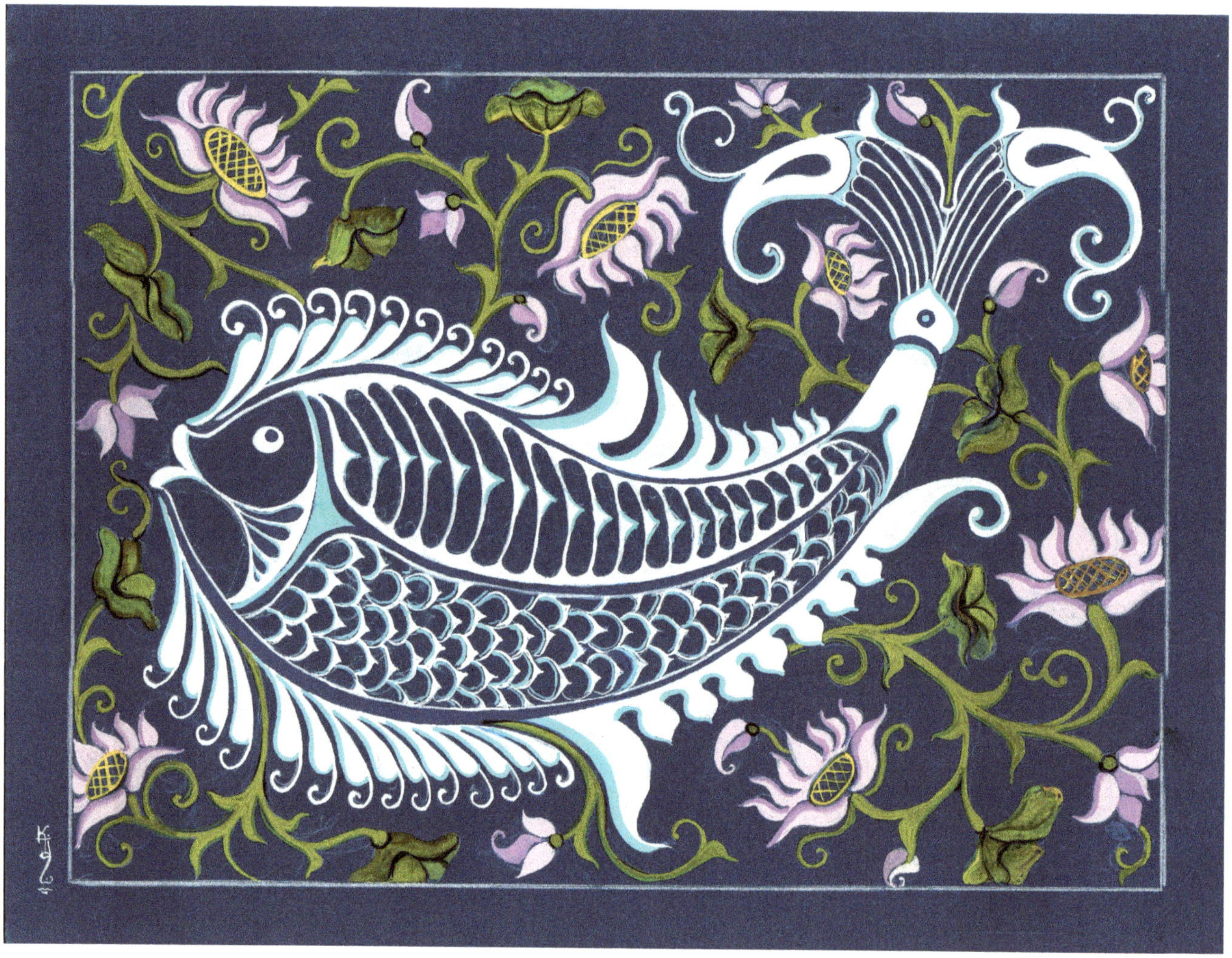

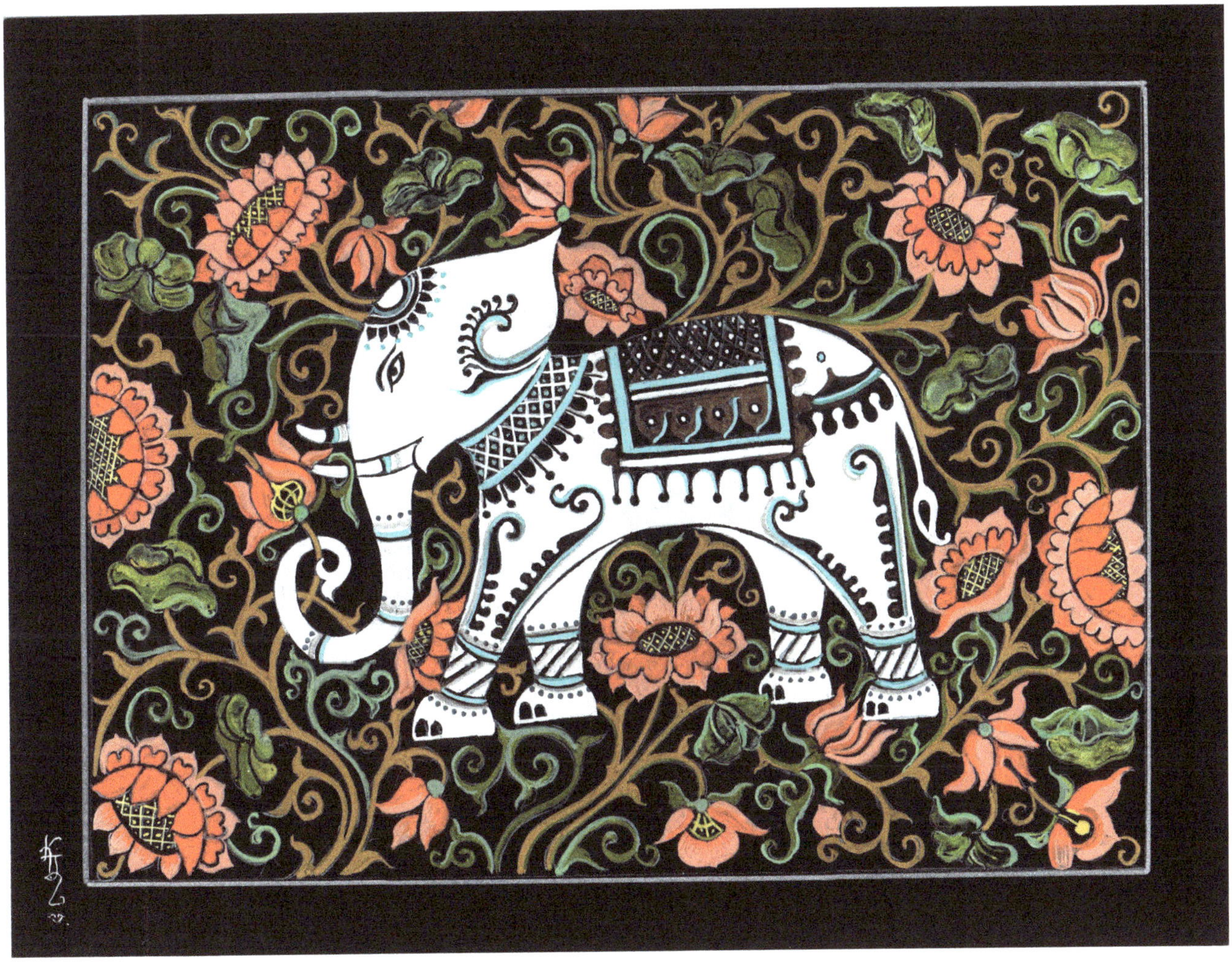

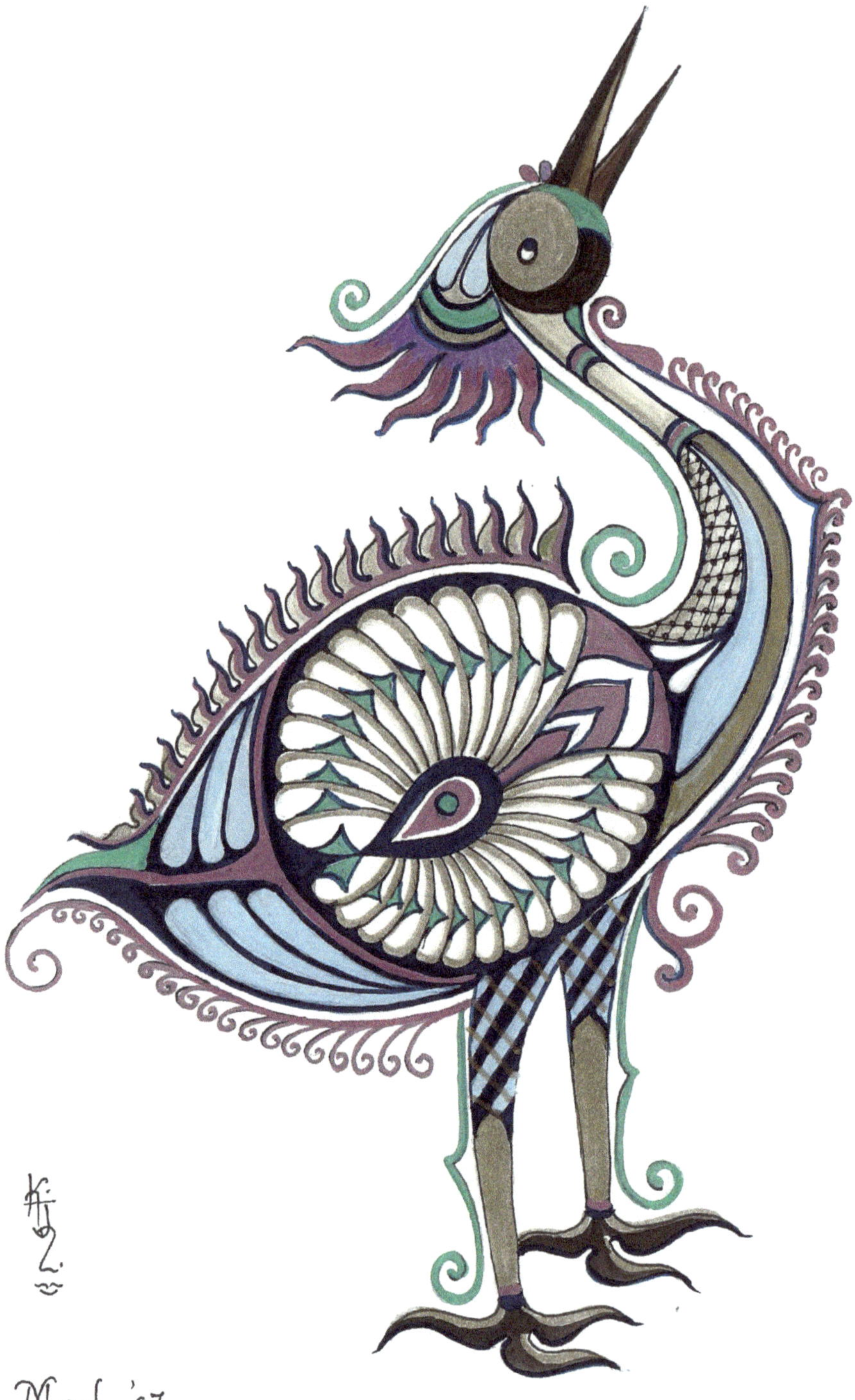
March-'07

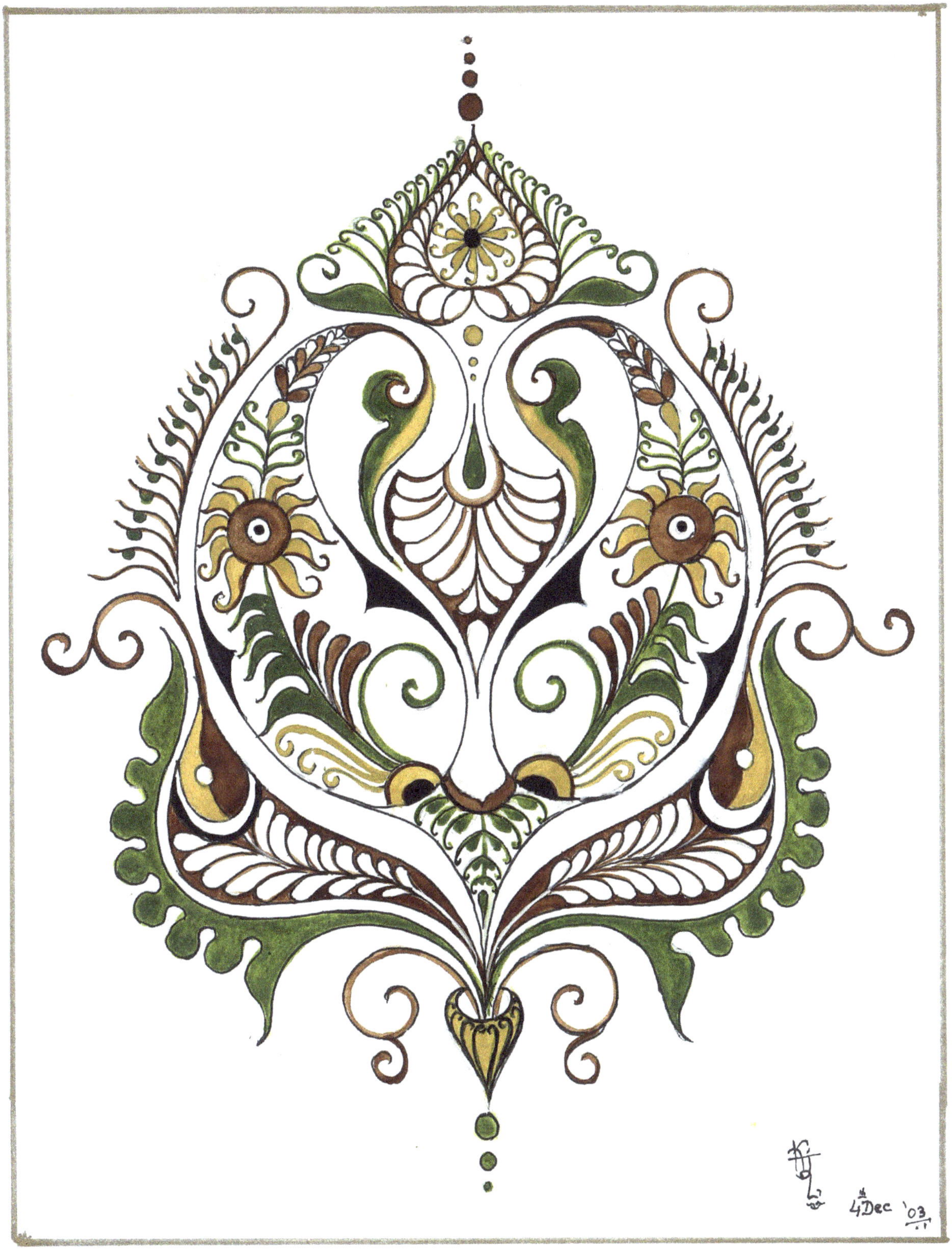
4Dec '03

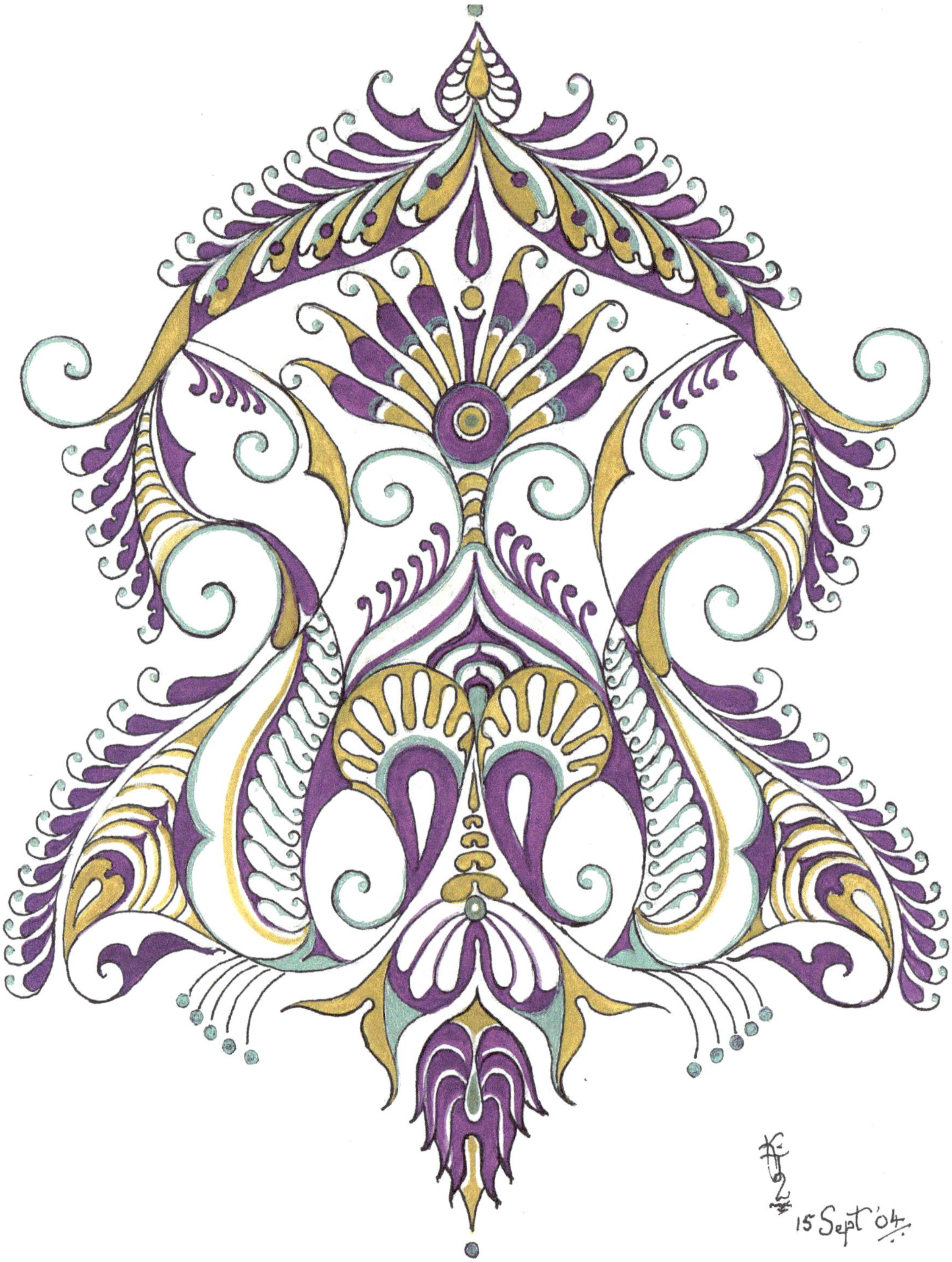
15 Sept '04

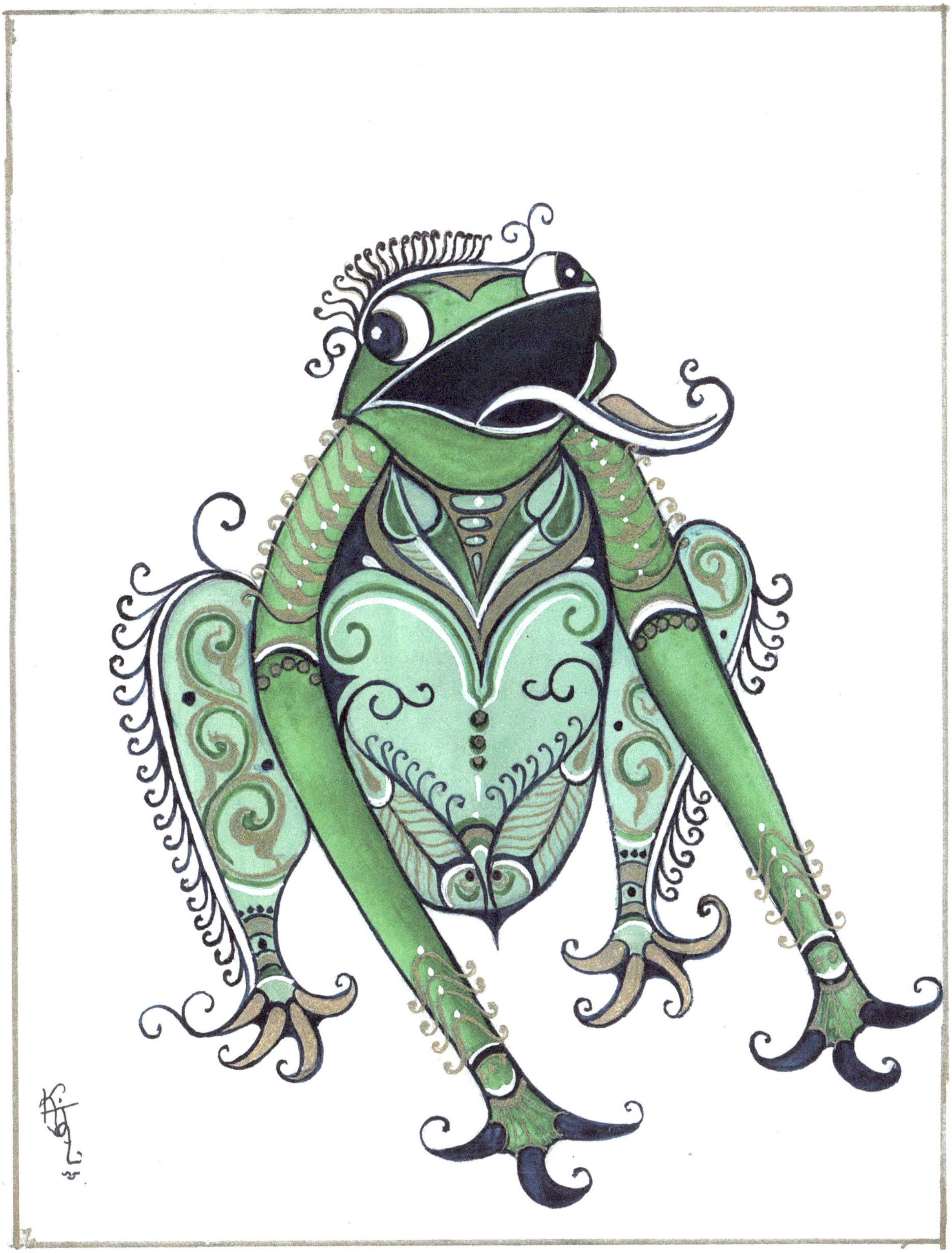

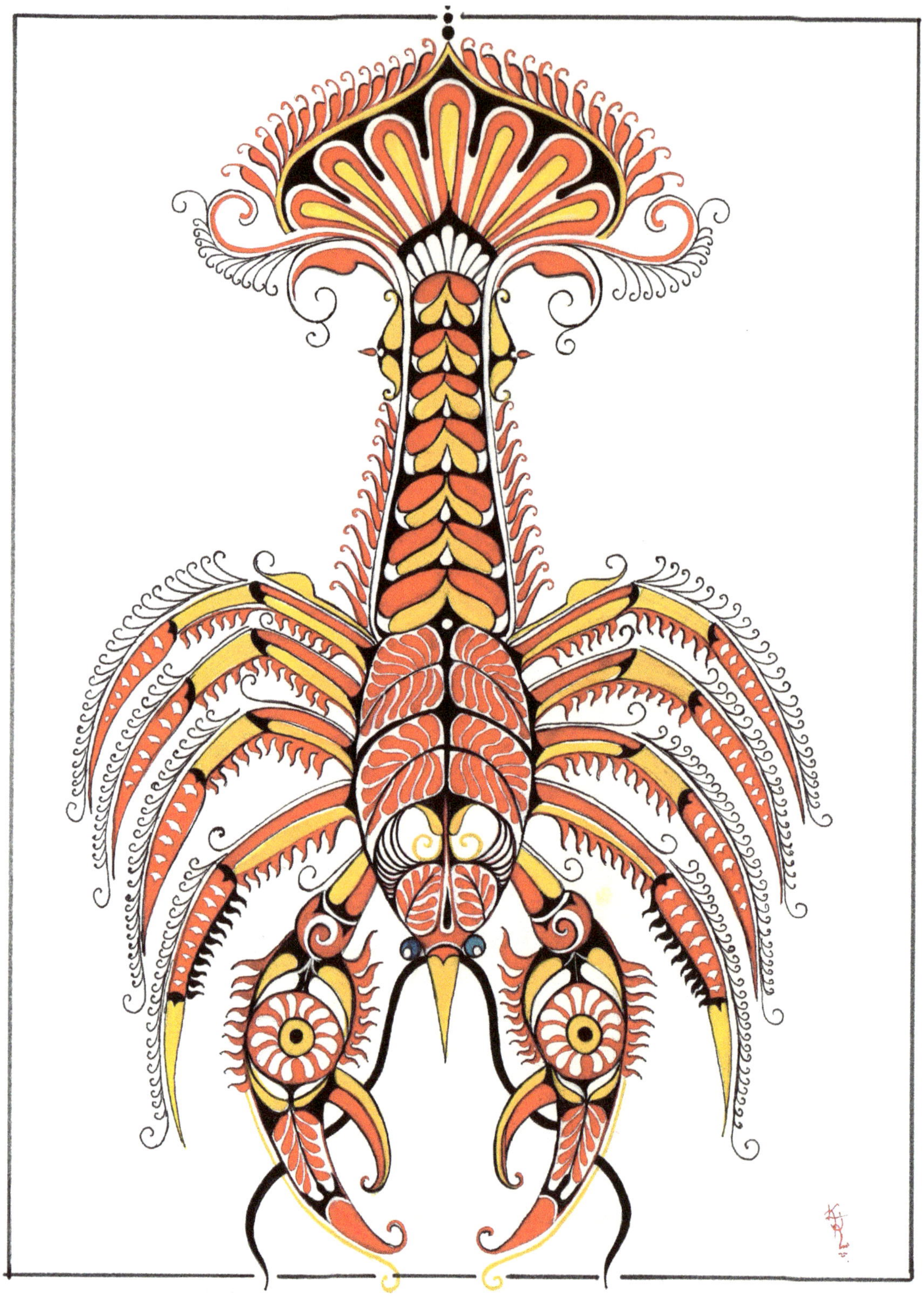

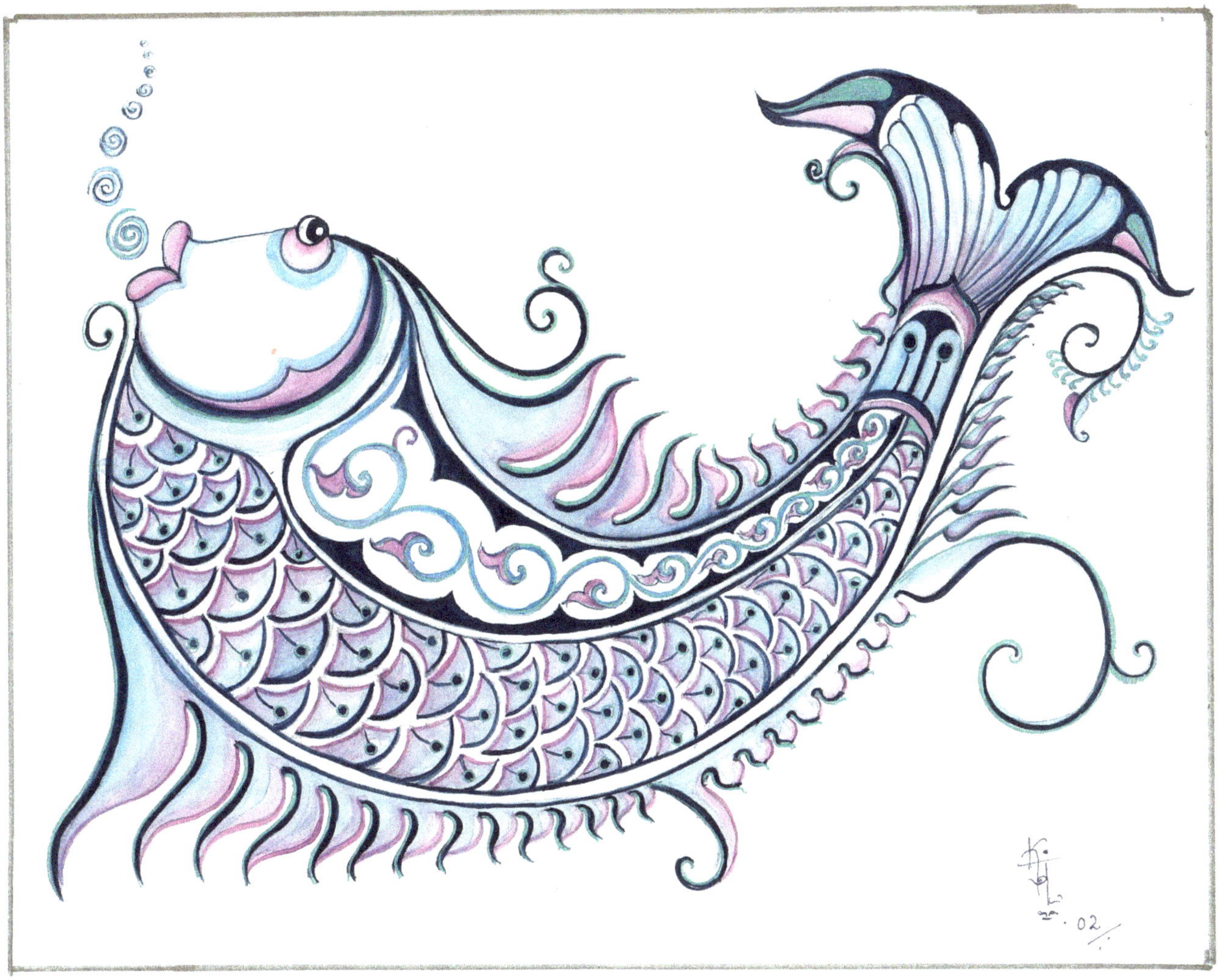

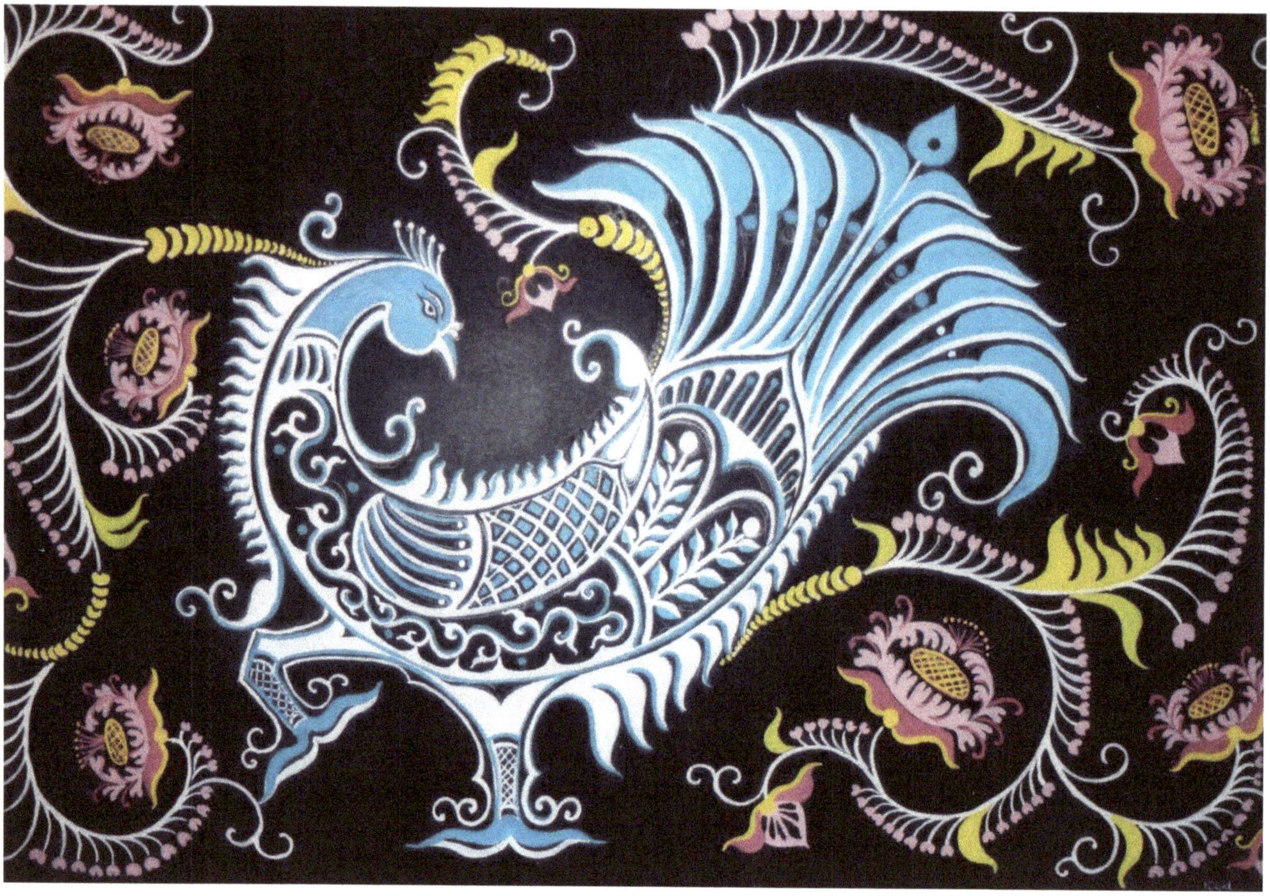

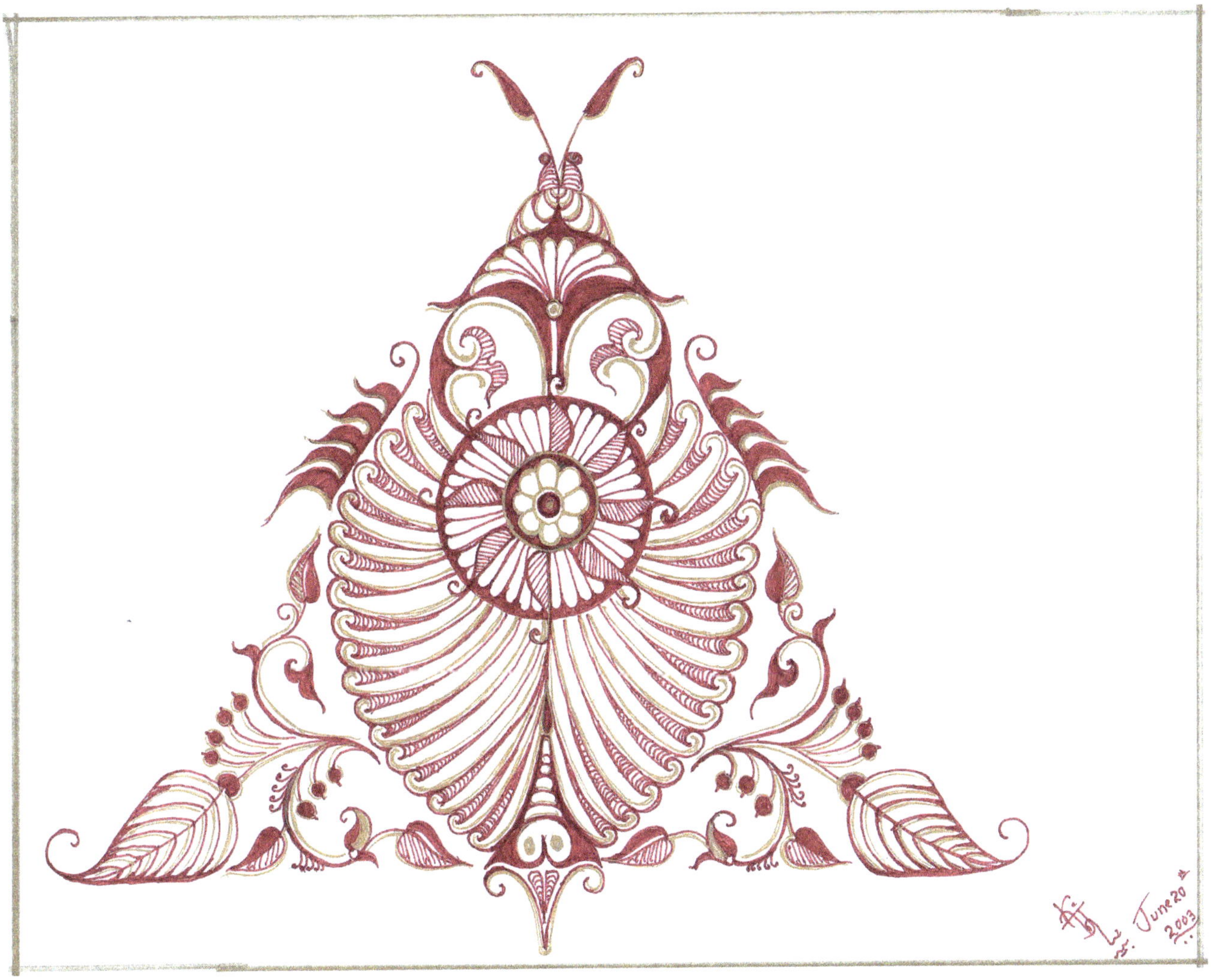
June 20
2003

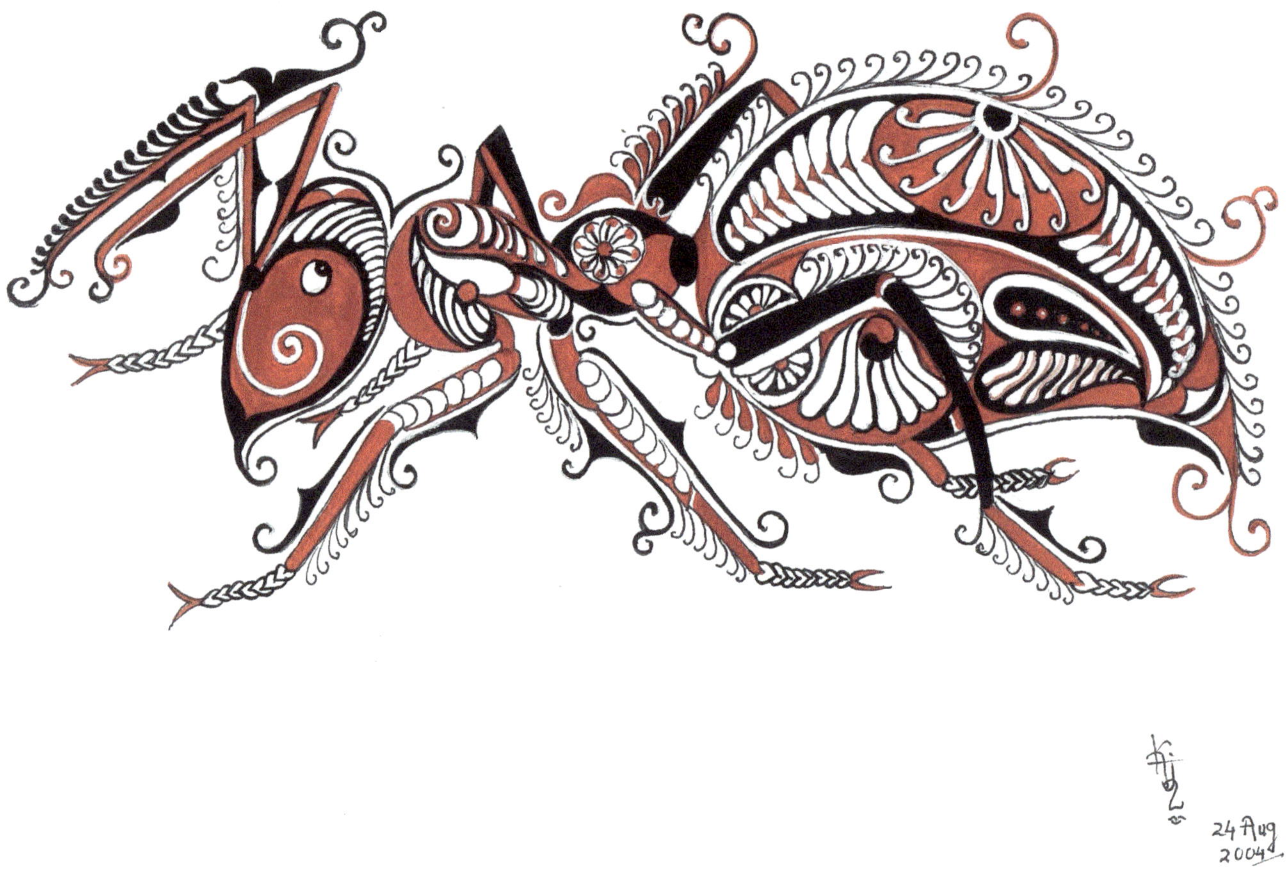

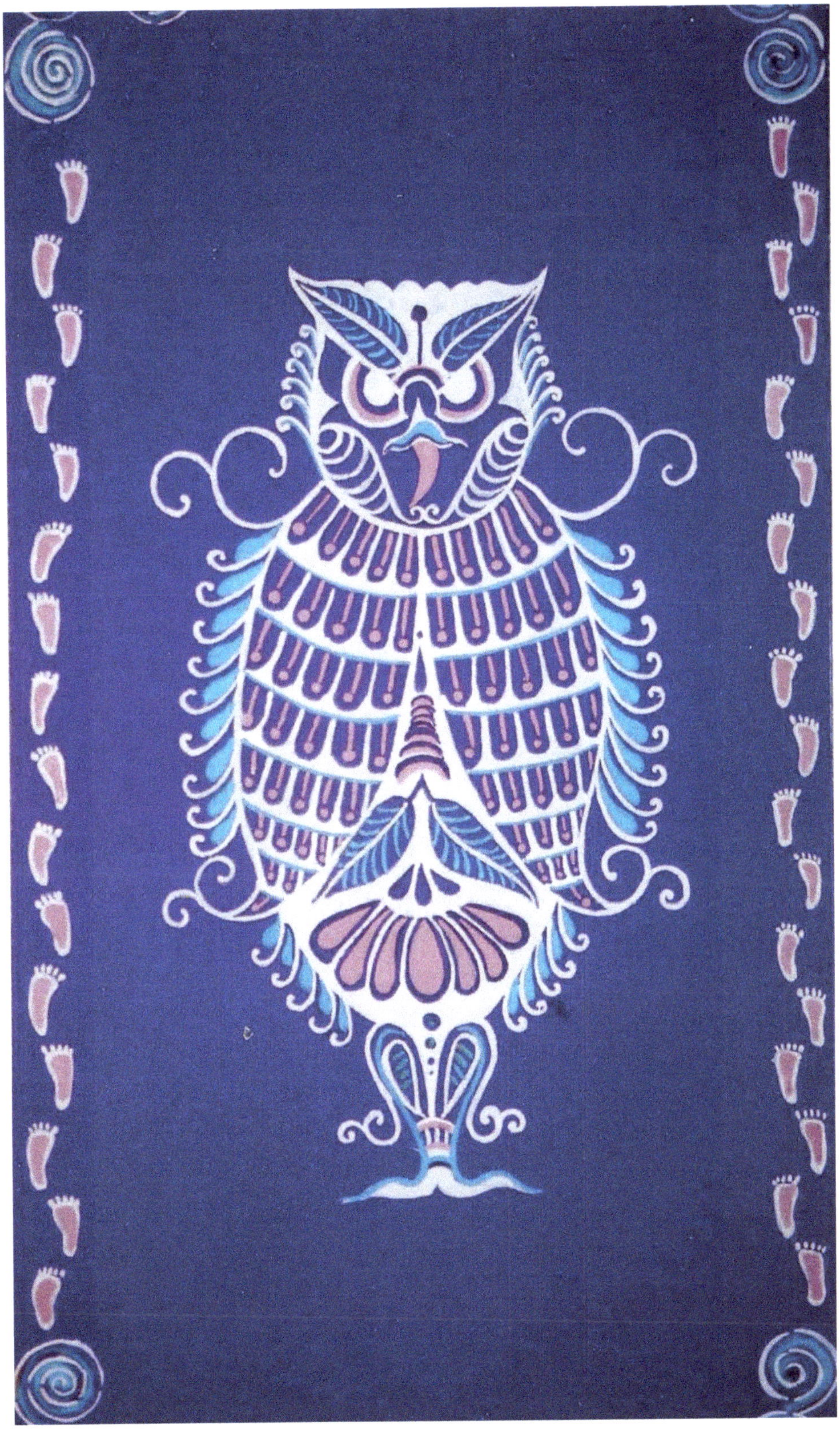

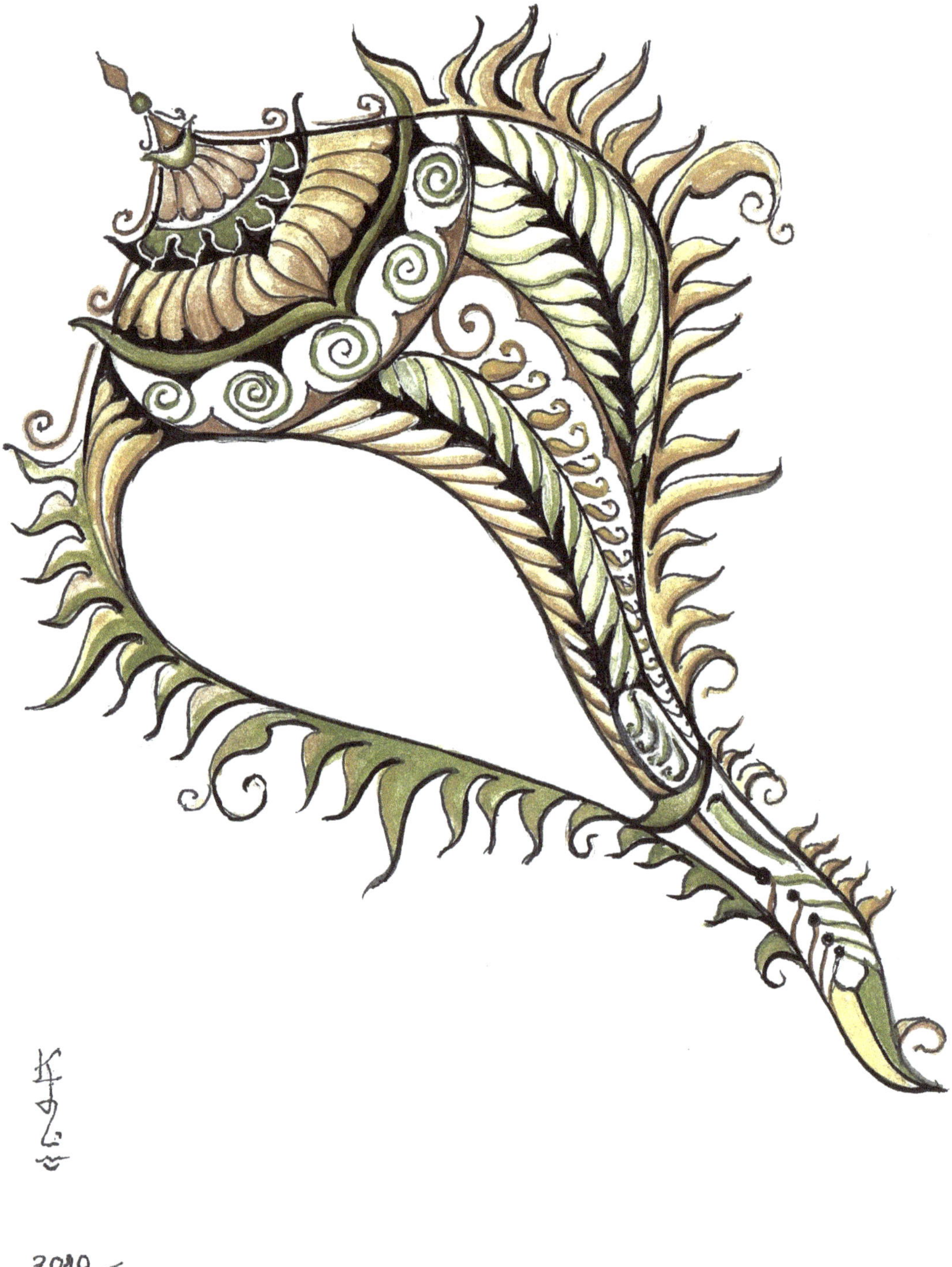

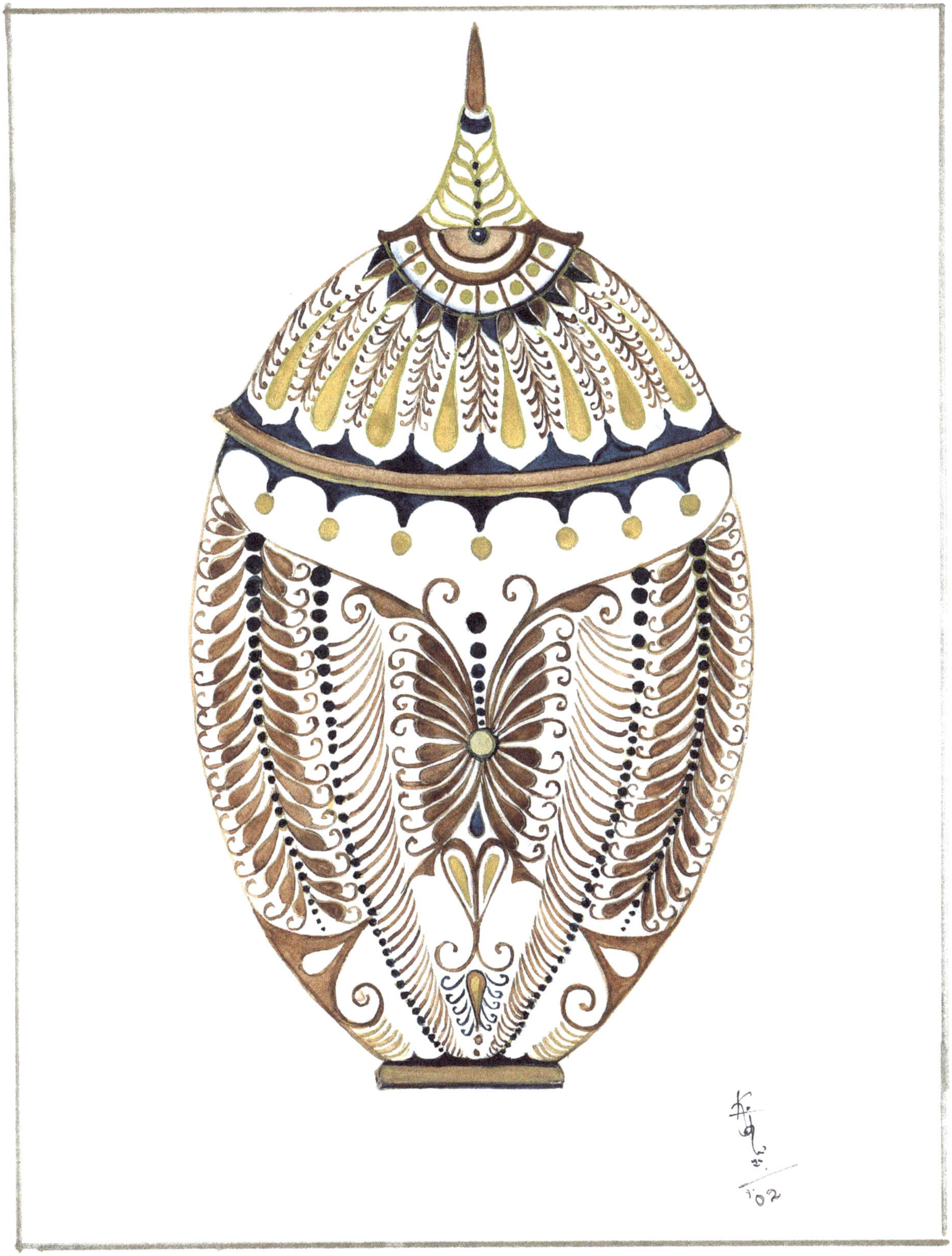

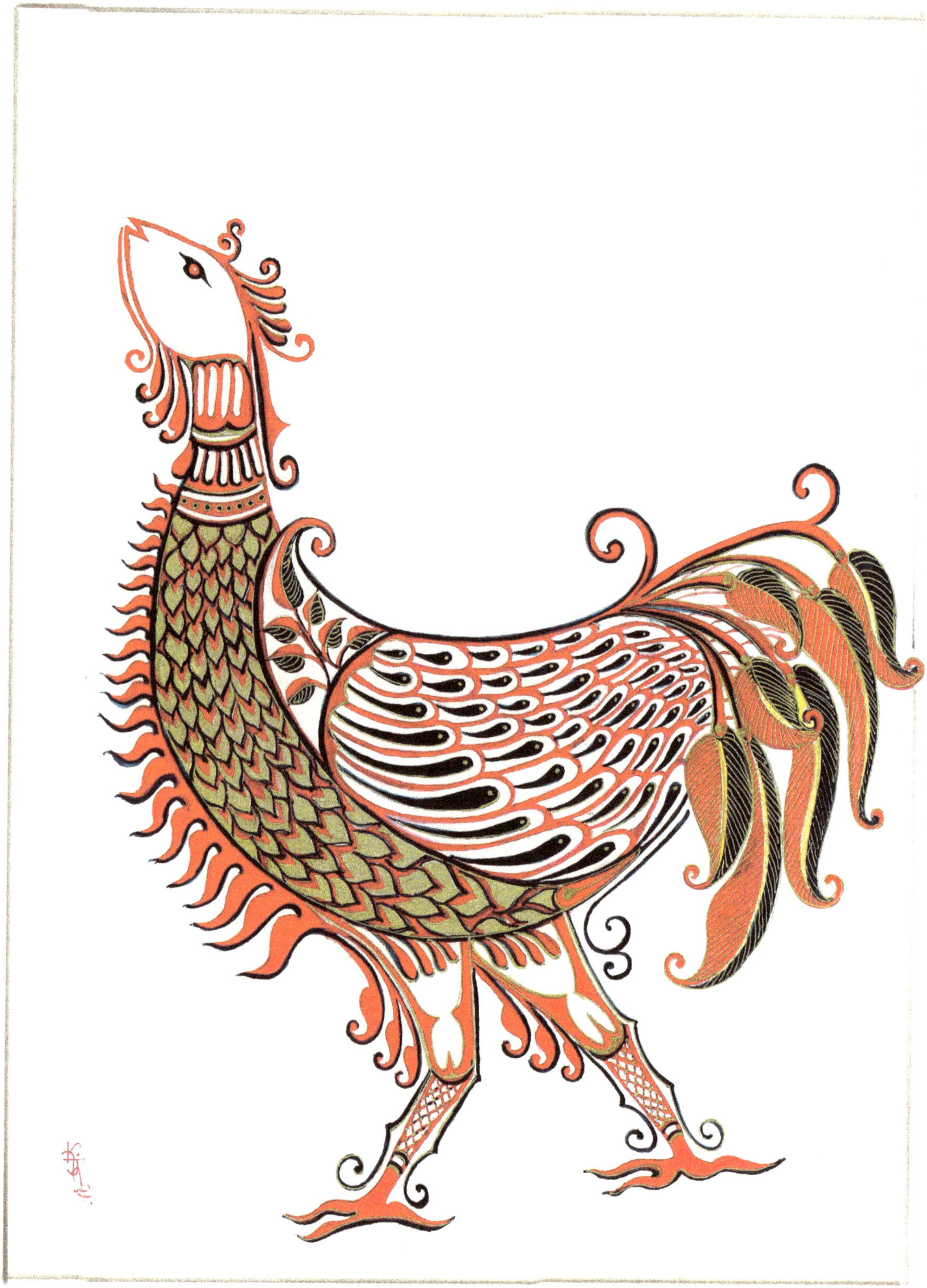

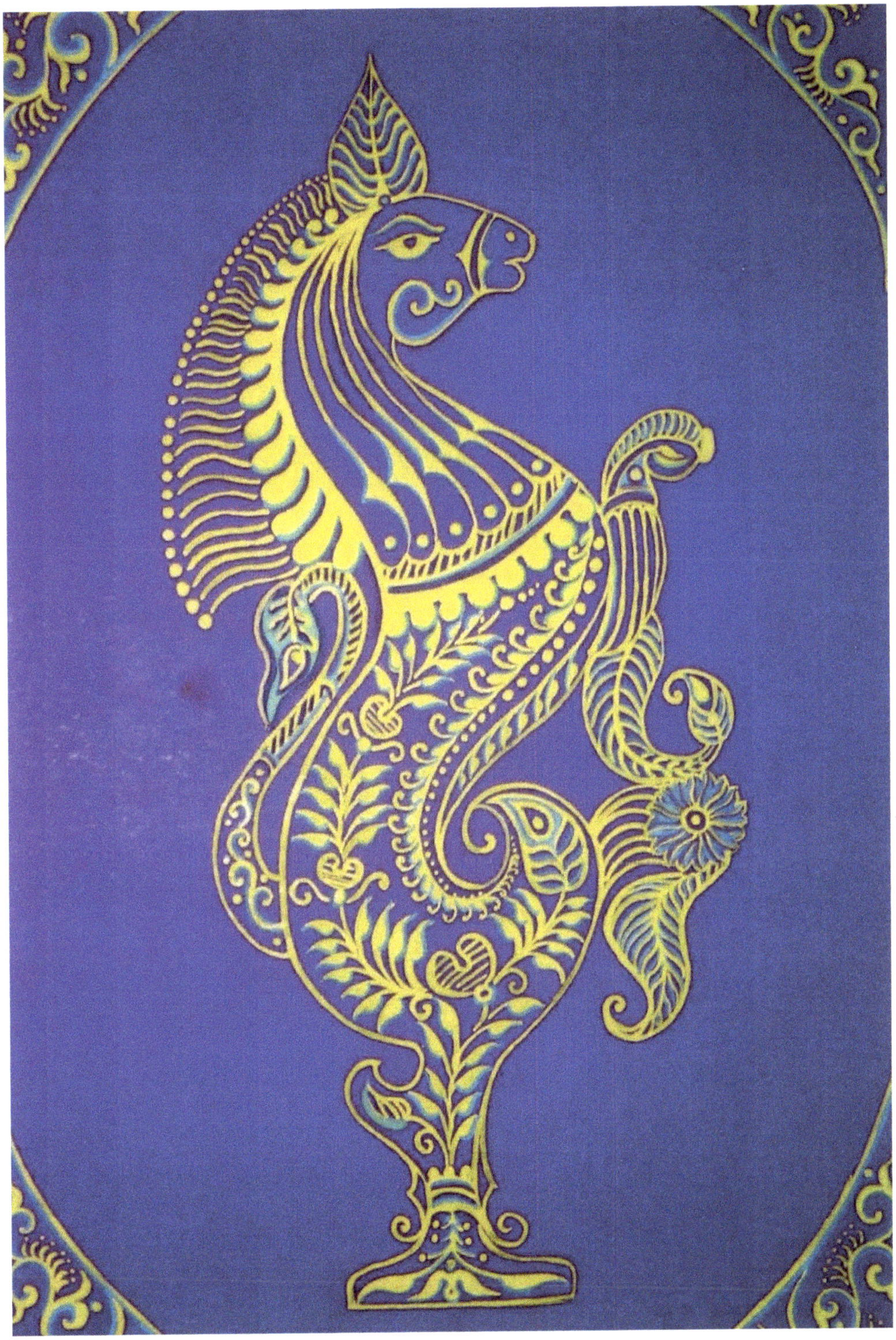

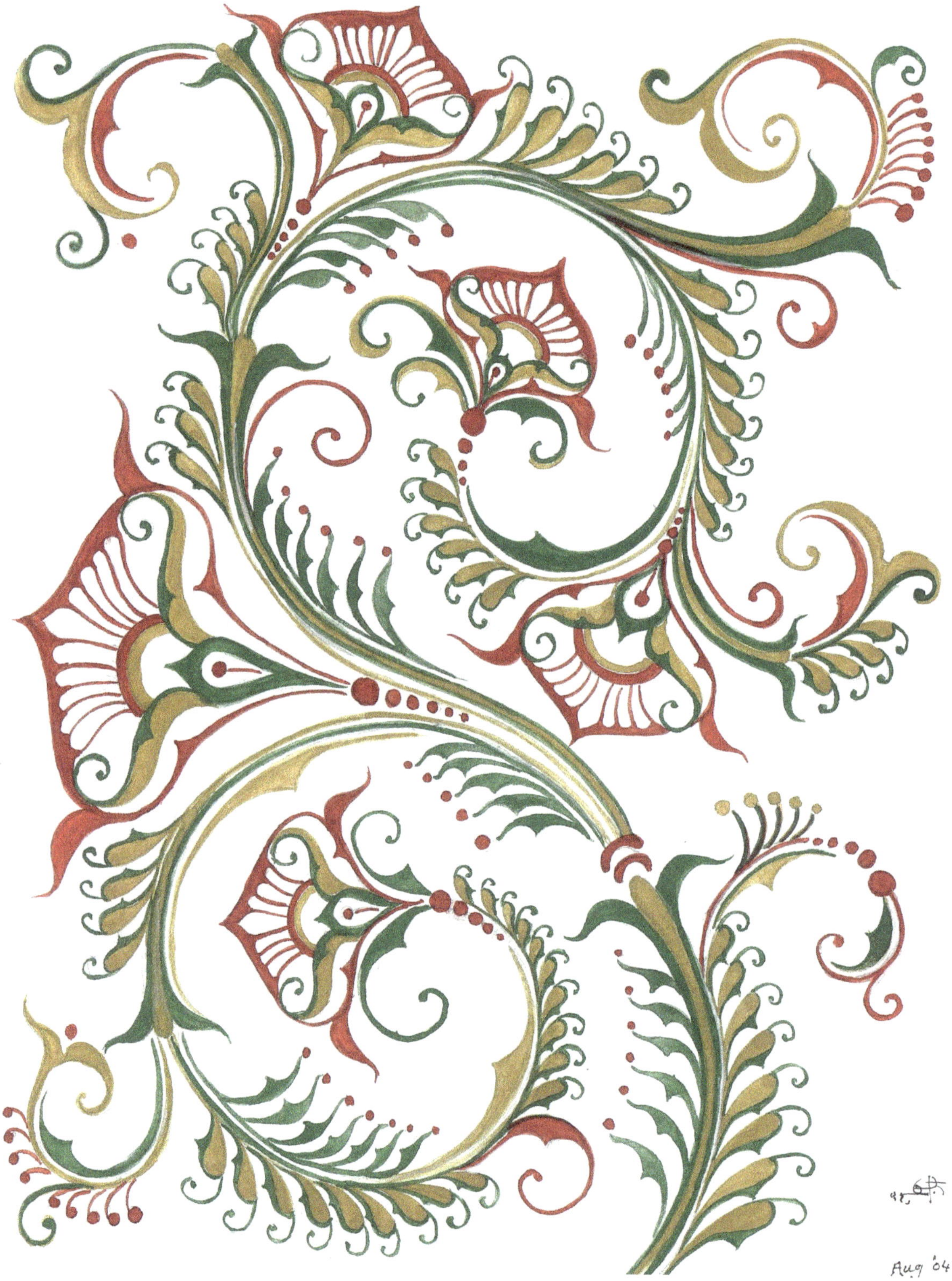
Aug '04

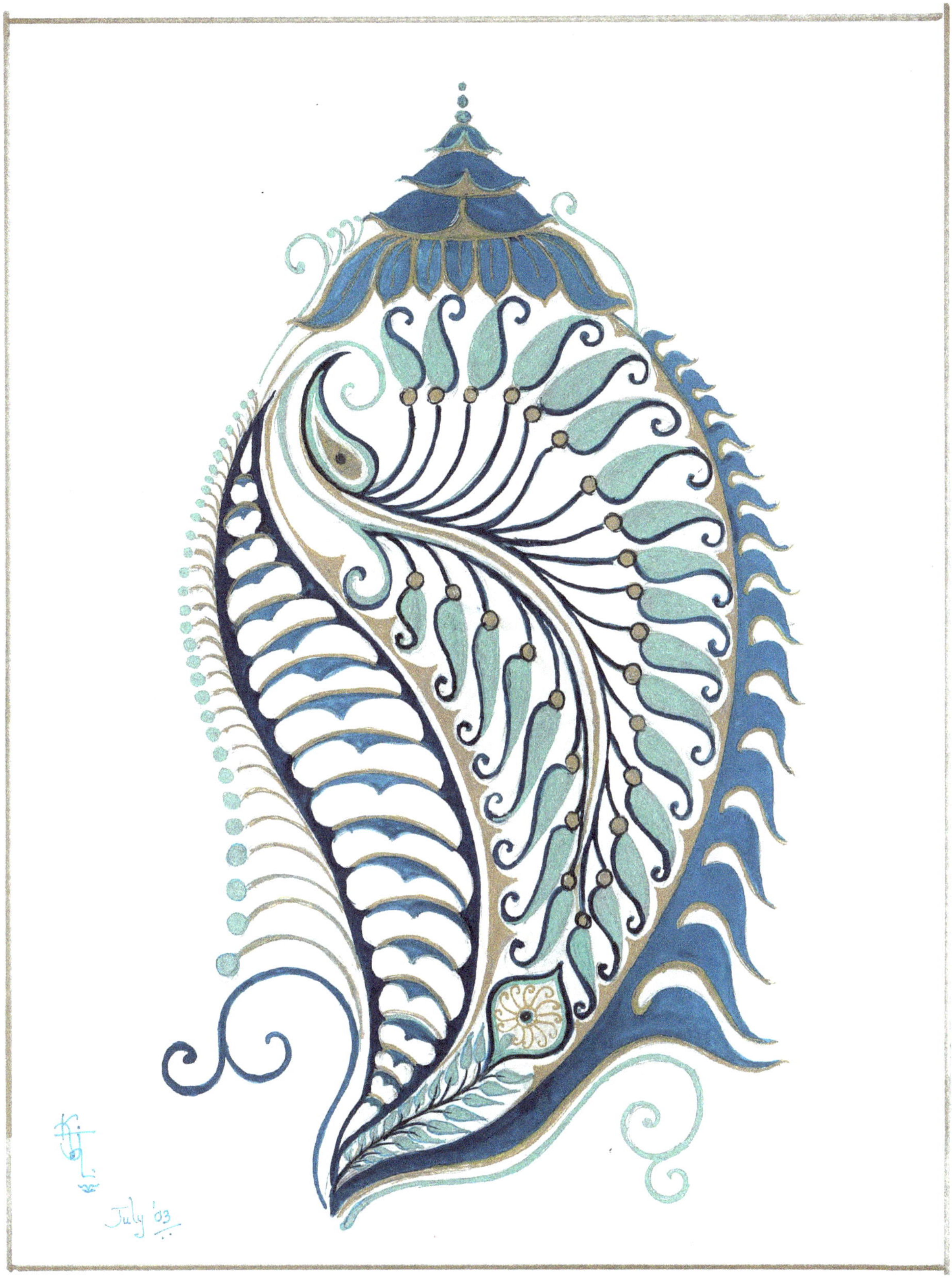
July '03

www.ingramcontent.com/pod-product-compliance
Ingram Content Group UK Ltd.
Pitfield, Milton Keynes, MK11 3LW, UK
UKHW062000290726
14090UKWH00021B/1315

9 781936 135219